SCHOLASTIC

C000212973

100 LITERACY ASSESSMENT LESSONS

TERMS AND CONDITIONS

IMPORTANT – PERMITTED USE AND WARNINGS – READ CAREFULLY BEFORE USING

Licence

YEAR 6

Scottish Primary 7

Minimum specification:
- PC or Mac with a CD-ROM drive and 512 Mb RAM (recommended)
- Windows 2000 or above/Mac OS X.4 or above
- Recommended minimum processor speed: 1 GHz

For all technical support queries, please phone Scholastic Customer Services on 0845 603 9091.

Alison Milford

CREDITS

Author
Alison Milford

Editor
Jennie Clifford and
Alex Albrighton

Series Designers
Joy Monkhouse and
Melissa Leeke

Designers
Sonja Bagley, Allison Parry and
Quadrum Ltd

Illustrations
Simon Smith (unless otherwise
credited)

CD-ROM development
CD-ROM developed in
association with Vivid
Interactive

ACKNOWLEDGEMENTS

The publishers gratefully acknowledge permission to reproduce the following copyright material: **Diana Bentley** and **Dee Reid** for the re-use of 'Fact or opinion? Children watch too much TV' by Diana Bentley and Dee Reid from *Essentials for English: Writing Non-Fiction* by Diana Bentley and Dee Reid © 1995, Diana Bentley and Dee Reid (1995, Scholastic). **Clare Bevan** for the use of the poem 'What will you do?' by Clare Bevan from *The Works 6* chosen by Pie Corbett © 2007, Clare Bevan (2007, Macmillan). **The British Deer Society** for the use of a photograph of a roaring stag © 2007, Alex Hedger. **David Higham Associates** for the use of an extract from *Movers, Shakers and Record Breakers* by Geraldine McCaughrean © 1999, Geraldine McCaughrean (1999, Dolphin); for the use of an extract from *Kensuke's Kingdom* by Michael Morpurgo © 1999, Michael Morpurgo (1999, Egmont) and for the use of 'Some Aunts and Uncles' by Mervyn Peake from *A Book of Nonsense* by Mervyn Peake © 1972, Mervyn Peake (1972, Peter Owen Books). **Graham Dean** for the use of photographs of the river Ribble © 2008, Graham Dean. **Egmont UK** for the use of an extract from 'My father is a polar bear' by Michael Morpurgo from *From Hereabout Hill* by Michael Morpurgo © 2000, Michael Morpurgo (2000, Mammoth) and for the use of illustrations from *Kensuke's Kingdom* by Michael Morpurgo, illustrated by Michael Foreman, illustrations © 1999, Michael Foreman (1999, Egmont UK). **Trevor Harvey** for the use of the poem 'The Painting Lesson' by Trevor Harvey from *The Usborne Book of Children's Poems* edited by Heather Amery © 1990, Trevor Harvey (1990, Usborne). **Wendy Helsby** for the use of 'A mixed-up myth' by Wendy Helsby from *Teacher Timesavers: Language Puzzles* by Wendy Helsby © 1993, Wendy Helsby (1993, Scholastic). **Hodder & Stoughton** for the use of an extract from *Seize the day: My autobiography* by Tanni Grey-Thompson © 2001, Tanni Grey-Thompson (2001, Hodder & Stoughton). **Nikki Hughes** for the use of 'Story Ladder' by Nikki Hughes from *100 Literacy Framework Lessons – Year 6* by Gill Matthews, Nikki Hughes and Roger Hurn © 2007, Nikki Hughes (2007, Scholastic). **Gillian Matthews** for the use of 'How to write a persuasive text' by Gillian Matthews from *100 Literacy Framework Lessons – Year 6* by Gillian Matthews, Nikki Hughes and Roger Hurn © 2007, Nikki Hughes (2007, Scholastic). **Brian Moses** for the use of the poem 'Names' by Brian Moses from *Knock down ginger and other poems* by Brian Moses © 1994, Brian Moses (1994, Cambridge University Press). **Judith Nicholls** for the use of the poem 'Orang-utan' by Judith Nicholls from *Dragonsfire* by Judith Nicholls © 1990, Judith Nicholls (1990, Faber and Faber). **Orion Publishing** for use of an extract from *Arthur: The Seeing Stone* by Kevin Crossley Holland © 2000, Kevin Crossley Holland (2000, Orion Children's Books). **Peters, Fraser and Dunlop Group Ltd** for the use of the poem 'Give and Take' by Roger McGough from *Good Enough to Eat* by Roger McGough © 2002, Roger McGough (2002, Puffin). **Piccadilly Press** for the use of an extract and illustration from *Venus Spring – Stunt Girl* by Johnny Zucker text © 2005, Johnny Zucker (2005, Piccadilly Press). **Random House Group** for the use of text and illustration from *The Last of the Sky Pirates* by Paul Stewart and Chris Riddell © 2002, Paul Stewart and Chris Riddell (2002, Corgi). **Rogers, Coleridge & White Ltd** for the use of an extract from *Arthur: The Seeing Stone* by Kevin Crossley-Holland © 2000, Kevin Crossley-Holland (2000, Orion Children's Books) and for the use of 'The River's Story' by Brian Patten from *Thawing Frozen Frogs* by Brian Patten © 1990, Brian Patten (1990, Viking). **Ian Souter** for the use of 'My dad is amazing' by Ian Souter from *The Works 6* chosen by Pie Corbett © 2007, Ian Souter (2007, Macmillan). **Roger Stevens** for the use of 'What's my name?' by Roger Stevens from *Why Otters Don't Wear Socks* by Roger Stevens © 1996, Roger Stevens (2007, Macmillan Children's Books). **Walker Books** for the use of an extract from *Pirate Diary* by Richard Platt © 2001, Richard Platt (2001, Walker Books).

Every effort has been made to trace copyright holders for the works reproduced in this book, and the publishers apologise for any inadvertent omissions.

Text © 2009, Alison Milford
© 2009, Scholastic Ltd

Designed using Adobe
InDesign

Published by Scholastic Ltd
Villiers House
Clarendon Avenue
Leamington Spa
Warwickshire CV32 5PR

Visit our website at
www.scholastic.co.uk

Printed by Bell and Bain Ltd

British Library Cataloguing-in-Publication Data
A catalogue record for this book is available from the British Library.
ISBN 978-1407-10188-0
The right of Alison Milford to be identified as the author of this work has been asserted by her in accordance with the Copyright, Designs and Patents Act 1988.

Due to the nature of the web, we cannot guarantee the content or links of any site mentioned. We strongly recommend that teachers check websites before using them in the classroom.

FSC Mixed Sources
Product group from well-managed forests and other controlled sources
www.fsc.org Cert no. TT-COC-002769
© 1996 Forest Stewardship Council

Contents

Introduction 4–7

Periodic assessment 8–9

Narrative 10
Unit 1 10–27
Unit 2 28–43
Unit 3 44–61
Unit 4 62–77

Non-fiction 78
Unit 1 78–95
Unit 2 96–111
Unit 3 112–129
Unit 4 130–145

Poetry 146
Unit 1 144–159
Unit 2 160–173

Transitional assessment 174–175

SCHOLASTIC

100 Literacy Assessment Lessons: Year 6

'Assessment' refers to all those activities undertaken by teachers, and by their students in assessing themselves, which provide information to be used as feedback to modify the teaching and learning activities in which they are engaged.'

from Black and William *Inside the Black Box*

About the series

100 Literacy Assessment Lessons is a response to the Assessment for Learning strategy (AfL) and Assessing Pupils' Progress (APP) and contains all new, stand-alone material. The lessons mirror the guidelines and viewpoints of the revised approach to assessment. The CD-ROMs provide appropriate and exciting texts and a variety of assessment activities from photocopiable pages for individual, whole-class or group work to stimulating interactive activities. Together, the books and CD-ROMs will be an invaluable resource to help you understand and implement the revised approach to assessment.

About assessment

The key points of the revised approach to assessment are as follows:
- Assessments are accurate and linked to National Curriculum levels;
- Assessments are targeted, with assessment focuses used as the guiding criteria;
- Assessments are reliable and based on a range of evidence;
- Assessments are useful and appropriate: day to day, periodic or transitional.

What are assessment focuses (AFs)?

Assessment focuses (AFs) are tools for assessment that sit between the National Curriculum programmes of study and level descriptions. The AFs provide more detailed criteria against which children's standards of attainment can be assessed and judged.

Type of assessment	Purpose	Strategies
Day to day	Ongoing and formative: encourages reflection and informs the next steps in teaching and learning.	Objectives, outcomes and success criteria are made explicit and are shared with children; observations are used to gather evidence; peer assessment and self-assessment help to develop children as responsible learners.
Periodic	Provides a periodic view of children's progress and diagnostic information linked to national standards.	Progress and attainment are reviewed regularly (half-termly or termly) against APP criteria; strengths and gaps in learning are identified to inform future planning.
Transitional	Brings together evidence, including tests, at points of transition (eg level to level or year to year); provides a formal overview of children's attainment set within the framework of national standards.	Use of formal tasks and tests; external validation and reporting.

For a complete list of strategies for day-to-day assessment and further information about periodic and transitional assessment, visit the National Strategies website (**http://nationalstrategies.standards.dcsf.gov.uk**).

About the book

Reflecting the structure of the renewed Primary Framework for Literacy (2006), the book is divided into three Blocks: Narrative, Non-fiction and Poetry. Each Block is further divided into Units, and the Units are split into Phases. The Phases are divided into a number of day-to-day assessment activities. These assessment activities, based on learning outcomes, are designed to fit easily into your existing planning.

Units

Each Unit covers a different text-type or genre and, because of this, each Unit has its own introduction containing the following:

Literacy objectives: All objectives for the Unit are listed under their strand names.

Key aspects of learning: Aspects of learning that the Unit covers are identified from the renewed Primary National Strategy (PNS) Framework.

Assessment focuses (AFs): The main assessment focuses that are addressed during the Unit are listed from APP.

Speaking and listening: Assessment areas you should look out for are linked to the Speaking and listening strand objectives.

Resources: Lists all of the resources required for the activities in each Phase.

Planning grids: There are two grids per Unit to provide an overview of the Unit and to suggest how you can build assessment opportunities into your medium-term planning. The grids show Phases, learning outcomes, a summary of lessons, assessment opportunities and potential evidence, levelled statements of the assessment focuses (AFs), and success criteria matched to the learning outcomes in the form of 'I can...' statements.

Assessment activities

Each assessment activity follows the same format:

Learning outcomes: These are relevant to individual activities or a set of activities that share objectives.

Success criteria: These are child-friendly 'I can...' statements for children or teachers to refer to during or following the activity.

Setting the context: This section provides guidance on what the task is and details the children's expected prior learning. The context for the task may also be explained: group, paired or individual work. Where adult support is required, this is also described.

Assessment opportunity: This section highlights what to assess, how to find out what children know, and what questions to ask.

Assessment evidence: This section suggests what to look for during an activity in relation to specific assessment focuses (AFs).

Next steps: This section is divided into support and extension. It provides ideas to enable children to revisit an objective or learning outcome, and gives feedback or targets to move children forward, consolidate or extend their learning.

Key aspects of learning: Key aspects of learning are linked to specific activities.

Photocopiable pages

At the end of each Unit is a selection of photocopiable activity pages. The full range of these is provided on the CD-ROM, including levelled versions where appropriate. Photocopiable pages may include self-assessment statements for ticking as well as a 'traffic light' system for colouring (see 'Self-assessment' on page 7 for more information.) Where 'I can...' statements are not included, peer assessment may be suggested within an activity.

Transitional assessment

Also included on the CD-ROM are some SATs-style formal single-level assessments. More information about these can be found on page 7, and a grid detailing their content is provided on page 174.

How to use the materials

The activities in the book provide a balance of whole-class/group/paired/ independent learning and teaching, and give the opportunity not only for day-to-day assessment but also for collection of evidence against individual assessment focuses (AFs) for periodic review. Each activity can be slotted into a lesson where appropriate and may involve discussion work, written responses, use of photocopiable pages or interactive activities.

Two periodic assessment activities are provided at the end of each Unit – one for reading and one for writing. The focus of each of these activities is usually a photocopiable page that assesses children on the learning outcomes covered during the Unit and provides further evidence against the assessment focuses. You can also use these periodic assessments to help you to make level judgements that match to the Reading and Writing Attainment Targets (ATs).

Making a level judgement

Assessment involves making a level judgement against national standards at regular intervals. The following steps will support you in adopting a strategic approach to the marking and levelling needed for assessment.

Step one: Consider evidence
- Use a range of appropriate evidence to make a level judgement, for example, written or oral;
- Remember that it is quality not quantity that matters;
- Keep examples of children's work that will provide significant evidence.

Step two: Review the evidence
- Take a broader view of a child's achievement across the whole subject and over time;
- Create a visual picture of strengths and learning gaps by highlighting criteria a child has met across a range of evidence;
- Collaborate with colleagues and agree what constitutes success for the various assessment criteria.

Step three: Make a judgement
- Consult the English Assessment Guidelines (see National Standards website: **http://nationalstrategies.standards.dcsf.gov.uk** and look at exemplar material provided in the Standards files;
- Arrive at an overall subject level judgement;
- Think about what the child demonstrates:
  - How much of the level;
  - How consistently;
  - How independently;
  - In what range of contexts.
- Finally, fine-tune your levelling to 'high', 'secure' or 'low'.

What's on the CD-ROM?

Each CD-ROM contains a wealth of resources. These include:
- **Photocopiable pages:** levelled where appropriate, including text extracts and activity sheets for day-to-day and periodic assessment.
- **Transitional assessments:** single-level tests for levels 1–5 including mark schemes and instructions.
- **Interactive activities:** for individuals or small groups, with in-built marking to assess specific learning outcomes.
- **Whiteboard tools:** a set of tools (including a pen, highlighter, eraser, notes and reward stickers) that can be used to annotate activity sheets or interactive activities. These tools will work on any interactive whiteboard or conventional screen.
- **Editable planning grids** (in Word format) are available to help teachers integrate the assessment activities into their medium-term and weekly planning.

▷ ## How to use the CD-ROM

System requirements
Minimum specification:
- PC or Mac with a CD-ROM drive and 512 Mb RAM (recommended)
- Windows 2000 or above/Mac OS X.4 or above
- Recommended minimum processor speed: 1 GHz

Getting started
The *100 Literacy Assessment Lessons* CD-ROM should auto run when inserted into your CD drive. If it does not, browse to your CD drive to view the contents of the CD-ROM and click on the *100 Literacy Assessment Lessons* icon.

From the start-up screen you will find four options: select **Credits** to view a list of acknowledgements. Click on **Register** to register the product in order to receive product updates and special offers. Click on **How to use this CD-ROM** to access support notes for using the CD-ROM. Finally, if you agree to the terms and conditions, select **Start** to move to the main menu.

For all technical support queries, contact Scholastic Customer Services help desk on 0845 6039091.

Navigating the CD-ROM
The CD-ROM allows users to search for resources by Block or Unit, or by assessment focus. Users can also search by assessment type (day to day, periodic or transitional) or by resource type (for example, worksheet, interactive resource, or text extract).

Day-to-day assessments
These should be used to support learning. They can be used during a lesson, when you judge that children are ready for an assessment activity. The materials can also be used weekly or after a unit of work has been completed.

Periodic assessments
These can be used with a group of children rather than with the whole class. This could be at the end of a unit of work (for example, at the end of a half-term or term). Decide who is ready to be assessed using the outcomes of the day-to-day assessment activities and your observations of children's performance.

NARRATIVE Unit 4 Short stories with flashbacks

Time-shift paragraphs

Self-assessment
There is a 'traffic light' system at the bottom of some photocopiable pages that children can shade to show how they feel about the activity: red for 'need help'; orange for 'having some understanding'; green for 'I found this easy!'. (Alternatively, you may wish to utilise these as a teacher marking tool for providing an at-a-glance guide to the child's progress.)

The photocopiable sheets also provide 'I can...' statements with tick boxes, to enable children to self-assess specifically in terms of the relevant learning outcomes/success criteria. A similar system is in place at the end of all the interactive activities, where the children are asked to click on a traffic light, and to type in any comments.

Transitional tests
These single-level tests provide evidence of where, in relation to national standards, children are at a given point in time. There are two Reading and Writing assessments for each level. Each reading assessment consists of a two-part reading comprehension test based on two different text types.

Each writing assessment consists of two writing tasks - shorter and longer - that focus on writing for different purposes. All the tasks and tests for levels 1–5 are included on the CD-ROM together with easy-to-follow marking schemes (see pages 174–175 for more information.)

Class PET
A whole-school version of *100 Literacy Assessment Lessons* is available with an expanded range of digital assessment activities, as well as the facility to report, record and track children's work. For further information visit the Class PET website, **www.scholastic.co.uk/classpet**.

Periodic assessment

Unit	AT	Page	Assessment focuses	Learning outcomes
Narrative 1	Reading	26	AF2, AF7	Children can identify and discuss the principal features of different genres in children's fiction. Children can analyse the language and organisational features of fiction genres.
	Writing	27	AF1, AF3	Children can plan and write an engaging short story in a particular genre using appropriate language and organisational features.
Narrative 2	Reading	42	AF4, AF5	Children extend their reading and learning skills through engagement with contemporary texts such as a non-linear adventure game. Children can identify the features and structure of a text adventure and use these as a model for writing.
	Writing	43	AF1, AF2	Children can identify the features and structure of a text adventure and use these as a model for writing. Children collaborate to develop and extend their fiction writing through the creation of a text adventure on paper or on screen.
Narrative 3	Reading	58	AF2, AF6, AF7	Children can use a range of drama and other techniques to explore characters and their conflicts and dilemmas and extend their response to stories.
	Writing	59	AF1, AF2	Children can use a range of a range of drama and other techniques to explore characters and their conflicts and dilemmas and extend their response to stories.
Narrative 4	Reading	74	AF4, AF5	Children can identify a range of techniques used by an author to indicate shifts in time between past and present. Children can use paragraphs to structure their own writing and to create pace in a short narrative.
	Writing	75	AF1, AF4, AF7	Children can use different narrative techniques to indicate the passage of time between past and present to engage a reader.
Non-fiction 1	Reading	93	AF4, AF5, AF6,	Children can recognise the structure and language, organisational and presentational features of different forms of biography and autobiography.
	Writing	94	AF1, AF2, AF7, AF8	Children can write an effective biography or autobiography selecting language, form, format and content to suit a particular purpose.

Unit	AT	Page	Assessment focuses	Learning outcomes
Non-fiction 2	Reading	110	AF2, AF4	Children can recognise the structure and language features of journalistic reports, both as written text and as scripts for oral presentation.
	Writing	111	AF1, AF3, AF5	Children can use discussion and drama techniques to explore a particular event, incident or situation, and its protagonists. Children can write an effective news article in journalistic style, selecting language, form, format and content to suit a particular audience and purpose. Children can use this as the basis for a script and present it orally in the style of a radio news item in a way which is informative and engaging.
Non-fiction 3	Reading	127	AF6	Children can identify bias when considering a controversial issue. Children can use clear language and appropriate presentational features both to present a particular case (argument) and to provide a balanced (overview) discussion.
	Writing	128	AF2	Children can write an effective argument for a particular case, selecting language, form, format and content to suit a particular audience and purpose.
Non-fiction 4	Reading	143	AF3, AF4, AF6	Children can evaluate the effectiveness of the language, organisation and presentational features of specific non-fiction texts.
	Writing	144	AF2, AF3, AF7	Children can plan and create an information leaflet using non-fiction text types.
Poetry 1	Reading	163	AF2, AF5, AF6	Children understand how poets can use powerful images to communicate with their readers.
	Writing	163	AF1, AF7	Children can write a poem that begins to use powerful imagery effectively. Children value their own poems and those of others and enjoy sharing them.
Poetry 2	Reading	172	AF2, AF5, AF6	Children understand how writers can use poetry as a powerful way of communicating their thoughts and feelings about a particular issue.
	Writing	173	AF1, AF7	Children can write a poem that begins to use language and form effectively and powerfully to communicate to a reader their thoughts and feelings about a particular issue.

NARRATIVE
UNIT 1 Fiction genres

Literacy objectives

Speak and listen for a wide range of purposes in different contexts

Strand 1 Speaking
- Use the techniques of dialogic talk to explore ideas, topics or issues.

Strand 3 Group discussion and interaction
- Understand and use a variety of ways to criticise constructively and respond to criticism.

Read and write for a range of purposes on paper and on screen

Strand 6 Word structure and spelling
- Use a range of appropriate strategies to edit, proofread and correct spelling in their own work, on paper and on screen.

Strand 7 Understanding and interpreting texts
- Understand underlying themes, causes and points of view.
- Understand how writers use different structures to create coherence and impact.

Strand 8 Engaging with and responding to texts
- Compare how writers from different times and places present experiences and use language.

Strand 9 Creating and shaping texts
- Use different narrative techniques to engage and entertain the reader.
- Select words and language drawing on their knowledge of literary features and formal and informal writing.

Strand 10 Text structure and organisation
- Use varied structures to shape and organise text coherently.
- Use paragraphs to achieve pace and emphasis.

Strand 11 Sentence structure and punctuation
- Express subtle distinctions of meaning, including hypothesis, speculation and supposition, by constructing sentences in varied ways.
- Use punctuation to clarify meaning in complex sentences.

Key aspects of learning

Information processing
- Children will identify and refine classification criteria and sort fiction examples accordingly. They will quickly appraise particular texts and look for a range of information clues to support classification of texts into different genres.

Evaluation
- Children will share responses and outcomes orally and in writing. They will apply the criteria they have identified in order to make decisions and judgements. They will give feedback to others and judge the effectiveness of their own work.

Communication
- Children will develop their ability to discuss and debate issues and personal responses in respect of both the form and the content of the stories they are reading and writing. They will often work collaboratively in pairs and groups. They will communicate outcomes orally and in writing.

Assessment focuses

Reading
AF2 *(understand, describe, select or retrieve information, events or ideas from texts and use quotation and reference to text).*
AF3 *(deduce, infer or interpret information, events or ideas from texts).*
AF6 *(identify and comment on writers' purposes and viewpoints, and the overall effect of the text on the reader).*
AF7 *(relate texts to their social, cultural and historical contexts and literary traditions).*

Writing
AF1 *(write imaginative, interesting and thoughtful texts).*
AF2 *(produce texts which are appropriate to task, reader and purpose).*
AF3 *(organise and present whole texts effectively, sequencing and structuring information, ideas and events).*
AF5 *(vary sentences for clarity, purpose and effect).*
AF7 *(select appropriate and effective vocabulary).*

Speaking and listening
Speaking (organise and use of detail).
Group discussion and interaction (support others and take turns).

Resources

Phase 1 activities
Photocopiable page, 'Fiction genres posters'
Interactive activity, 'Guess the genre'
Photocopiable page, 'Venus Spring – Stunt Girl'
Photocopiable page, 'The Last of the Sky Pirates'
Photocopiable page, 'Arthur: The Seeing Stone'
Photocopiable page, 'Genre identification sheet'
Photocopiable page, 'My book review' (versions 1 and 2)
Phase 2 activities
Photocopiable page, 'The Resurrection Men – 1829'
Photocopiable page, 'Character profiles' (versions 1 and 2)
Phase 3 activities
Photocopiable page, 'Space story ideas'
Photocopiable page, 'Story ladder: Raid of the Ice Diamonds'
Photocopiable page, 'Space story ladder'
Interactive activity, 'Space descriptions'
Interactive activity, 'Tension in space'
Photocopiable page, 'Space story evaluation sheet' (versions 1 and 2)
Periodic assessment
Photocopiable page, 'Narrative 1 Reading assessment text'
Photocopiable page, 'Narrative 1 Writing assessment'

Unit 1 ☐ Fiction genres

Learning outcomes	Assessment opportunity and evidence	Assessment focuses (AFs)		Success criteria
		Level 2	Level 3	
Phase ① activities pages 16-18				
Fiction genres posters Children can identify and discuss the principal features of different genres of children's fiction.	● Supported paired activity where children explore the features of fiction genres. ● Children's oral responses and discussion. ● Children's posters.	**Reading AF7** ● General features of a few text types identified. ● Some awareness that books are set in different times and places.	**Reading AF7** ● Some simple connections between texts identified. ● Recognition of some features of the context of texts.	● I can identify the features of different fiction genres. ● I can discuss the differences and similarities between the genres.
Guess the genre Children can identify and discuss the principal features of different genres of children's fiction.	● Paired activity where children match genres to the correct sentence extracts. ● Children's oral responses.	**Reading AF2** ● Some specific, straightforward information recalled. ● Generally clear idea of where to look for information.	**Reading AF2** ● Simple, most obvious points identified though there may also be some misunderstanding. ● Some comments include quotations from or references to text, but not always relevant.	● I can identify different fiction genres from story extracts. ● I can discuss why text belongs to a certain fiction genre.
Favourite genres Children can explain reading preferences in terms of the different genres.	● Supported group activity where children complete a book review. ● Oral responses and completed photocopiables.	**Reading AF6** ● Some awareness that writers have viewpoints and purposes. ● Simple statements about likes and dislikes in reading, sometimes with reasons.	**Reading AF6** ● Comments identify main purpose. ● Express personal response but with little awareness of writer's viewpoint or effect on reader.	● I can explain why I like reading stories from a particular genre. ● I can give examples of the features I like in my favourite genre.
Phase ② activities pages 19-20				
The Resurrection Men -1829 Children can analyse the language and organisational features of fiction genres.	● Group activity where children explore the text's genre and structure of an historical short story. ● Oral responses.	**Reading AF7** ● General features of a few text types identified. ● Some awareness that books are set in different times and places.	**Reading AF7** ● Some simple connections between texts identified. ● Recognition of some features of the context of texts.	● I can identify the structure of a short story from the past. ● I can use quotes and examples from a text to discuss a story's structure.
Burke and Hare Children can analyse the language and organisational features of fiction genres.	● Supported activity where children create profiles of two characters. ● †Notes on individuals' comments and understanding. ● Completed photocopiables.	**Reading AF3** ● Simple, plausible inference about events and information, using evidence from text. ● Comments based on textual cues, sometimes misunderstood.	**Reading AF3** ● Straightforward inference based on a single point of reference in the text. ● Responses to text show meaning established at a literal level.	● I can create character profiles by analysing and identifying language features. ● I can identify how language is used in a story set in the past.
Phase ③ activities pages 21-25				
Space story ideas Children can plan an engaging short story in a particular genre using appropriate language and organisational features.	● Group activity where children explore ideas for possible space settings, characters, situations and a plot. ● Oral and written responses.	**Writing AF2** ● Some basic purpose established. ● Some appropriate features of the given form used. ● Some attempts to adopt appropriate style.	**Writing AF2** ● Purpose established at a general level. ● Main features of selected form sometimes signalled to the reader. ● Some attempts at appropriate style, with attention to reader.	● I can use a mind map to record and choose ideas for my space story. ● I can explain and discuss my story ideas. ● I can decide on a basic plot for my space story.

Unit 1 Fiction genres

Learning outcomes	Assessment opportunity and evidence	Assessment focuses (AFs)		Success criteria
		Level 2	**Level 3**	
Space story ladder Children can plan and draft an engaging short story in a particular genre using appropriate language and organisational features.	• Group activity where children set out their space story structure on a story ladder. • Oral responses and teacher's notes. • Completed photocopiables.	**Writing AF3** • Some basic sequencing of ideas or material. • Openings and/or closings sometimes signalled.	**Writing AF3** • Some attempt to organise ideas with related points placed next to each other. • Openings and closings usually signalled. • Some attempt to sequence ideas or material logically.	• I can use a story ladder to create a structure for my space story. • I can evaluate my story structure and other structures.
Space descriptions Children can plan, draft and write an engaging short story in a particular genre using appropriate language and organisational features.	• Supported activity where children create science fiction descriptions that could be used in a space story. • Oral responses and teacher's notes. • Completed interactives.	**Writing AF7** • Simple, often speech-like vocabulary conveys relevant meanings. • Some adventurous word choices.	**Writing AF7** • Simple, generally appropriate vocabulary used, limited in range. • Some words selected for effect or occasion.	• I can identify effective descriptive language for a good science fiction story. • I can choose and use effective descriptive words to use in my space story.
Tension in space Children can plan, draft and write an engaging short story in a particular genre using appropriate language and organisational features.	• Supported paired activity where children identify simple sentences that would create tension in a good space story. • Oral responses. • Completed interactives.	**Writing AF5** • Some variation in sentence openings. • Mainly simple sentences with *and* used to connect clauses. • Past and present tense generally consistent.	**Writing AF5** • Reliance mainly on simply structured sentences, variation with support. • *and, but, so* are the most common connectives, subordination occasionally. • Some limited variation in use of tense and verb forms, not always secure.	• I can explain how tension is created in a good science fiction story. • I can use punctuation and construct sentences to create tension in my story.
Space story evaluations Children can improve an engaging short story in a particular genre using appropriate language and organisational features.	• Supported paired activity where children self-evaluate their own stories and the stories of others. • Oral responses, discussion and written work.	**Reading AF6** • Some awareness that writers have viewpoints and purposes. • Simple statements about likes and dislikes in reading, sometimes with reasons. **Writing AF2** • Some basic purpose established. • Some appropriate features of the given form used. • Some attempts to adopt appropriate style.	**Reading AF6** • Comments identify main purpose. • Express personal response but with little awareness of writer's viewpoint or effect on reader. **Writing AF2** • Purpose established at a general level. • Main features of selected form sometimes signalled to the reader. • Some attempts at appropriate style, with attention to reader.	• I can evaluate and self-evaluate the space stories. • I can revise and improve my space story.

Learning outcomes	Assessment opportunity and evidence	Assessment focuses (AFs)		Success criteria
		Level 4	**Level 5**	
Phase ① activities pages 16–18				
Fiction genres posters Children can identify and discuss the principal features of different genres of children's fiction.	• Paired activity where children give examples of features of different fiction genres. • Children's oral responses and discussion. • Children's posters.	**Reading AF7** • Features common to different texts or versions of the same text identified, with simple comment. • Simple comment on the effect that the reader's or writer's context has on the meaning of texts.	**Reading AF7** • Comments identify similarities and differences between texts, or versions, with some explanation. • Some explanation of how the contexts in which texts are written and read contribute to meaning.	• I can identify the features of different fiction genres. • I can discuss the differences and similarities between the genres.

Unit 1 ▢ Fiction genres

Learning outcomes	Assessment opportunity and evidence	Assessment focuses (AFs)		Success criteria
		Level 4	Level 5	
Guess the genre Children can identify and discuss the principal features of different genres of children's fiction.	• Paired activity where children annotate key features of three extracts to ascertain the three genres. • Discussion, highlighted extracts and worksheet.	**Reading AF2** • Some relevant points identified. • Comments supported by some generally relevant textual reference or quotation.	**Reading AF2** • Most relevant points clearly identified, including those selected from different places in the text. • Comments generally supported by relevant textual reference or quotation, even when points made are not always accurate.	• I can identify different fiction genres from story extracts. • I can discuss why text belongs to a certain fiction genre.
Favourite genres Children can explain reading preferences in terms of the different genres.	• Independent activity where children discuss their favourite genre and write down their top three stories, characters, plots, titles, settings and a short review of their favourite story. • Oral responses and completed photocopiables.	**Reading AF6** • Main purpose identified. • Simple comments show some awareness of writer's viewpoint. • Simple comment on overall effect on reader.	**Reading AF6** • Main purpose clearly identified, often through general overview. • Viewpoints in texts clearly identified, with some, often limited, explanation. • General awareness of effect on the reader, with some, often limited, explanation.	• I can explain why I like reading stories from a particular genre. • I can give examples of the features I like in my favourite genre.

Phase ② activities pages 19–20

The Resurrection Men - 1829 Children can analyse the language and organisational features of fiction genres.	• Group activity where children respond to guided questions about an historical text's genre and structure. • Oral responses.	**Reading AF7** • Features common to different texts or versions of the same text identified, with simple comment. • Simple comment on the effect that the reader's or writer's context has on the meaning of texts.	**Reading AF7** • Comments identify similarities and differences between texts, or versions, with some explanation. • Some explanation of how the contexts in which texts are written and read contribute to meaning.	• I can identify the structure of a short story from the past. • I can use quotes and examples from a text to discuss a story's structure.
Burke and Hare Children can analyse the language and organisational features of fiction genres.	• Paired activity where children create profiles of main characters. • Notes on individuals' comments and understanding. • Completed photocopiables.	**Reading AF3** • Comments make inferences based on evidence from different points in the text. • Inferences often correct, but comments are not always rooted securely in the text or repeat narrative or content.	**Reading AF3** • Comments develop explanation of inferred meanings drawing on evidence across the text. • Comments make inferences and deductions based on textual evidence.	• I can create character profiles by analysing and identifying language features. • I can identify how language is used in a story set in the past.

Phase ③ activities pages 21–25

Space story ideas Children can plan an engaging short story in a particular genre using appropriate language and organisational features.	• Independent activity where children discuss and record their ideas for possible space settings, characters, situations and ideas for a plot. • Oral and written responses.	**Writing AF2** • Main purpose of writing is clear but not always consistently maintained. • Main features of selected form are clear and appropriate to purpose. • Style generally appropriate to task, though awareness of reader not always sustained.	**Writing AF2** • Main purpose of writing is clear and consistently maintained. • Features of selected form clearly established with some adaptation to purpose. • Appropriate style clearly established to maintain reader's interest throughout.	• I can use a mind map to record and choose ideas for my space story. • I can explain and discuss my story ideas. • I can decide on a basic plot for my space story.

Unit 1 📖 Fiction genres

Learning outcomes	Assessment opportunity and evidence	Assessment focuses (AFs)		Success criteria
		Level 4	Level 5	
Space story ladder Children can plan and draft an engaging short story in a particular genre using appropriate language and organisational features.	● Independent activity where children set out their space story structure on a story ladder. ● Oral responses and teacher's notes. ● Completed photocopiables.	**Writing AF3** ● Ideas organised by clustering related points or by time sequence. ● Ideas are organised simply with a fitting opening and closing, sometimes linked. ● Ideas or material generally in logical sequence but overall direction of writing not always clearly signalled.	**Writing AF3** ● Material is structured clearly, with sentences organised into appropriate paragraphs. ● Development of material is effectively managed across text. ● Overall direction of the text supported by clear links between paragraphs.	● I can use a story ladder to create a structure for my space story. ● I can evaluate my story structure and other structures.
Space descriptions Children can plan, draft and write an engaging short story in a particular genre using appropriate language and organisational features.	● Independent activity where children select words to create science fiction descriptions that could be used in a space story. ● Oral responses and teacher's notes. ● Completed interactives.	**Writing AF7** ● Some evidence of deliberate vocabulary choices. ● Some expansion of general vocabulary to match topic.	**Writing AF7** ● Vocabulary chosen for effect. ● Reasonably wide vocabulary used, though not always appropriately.	● I can identify effective descriptive language for a good science fiction story. ● I can choose and use effective descriptive words to use in my space story.
Tension in space Children can plan, draft and write an engaging short story in a particular genre using appropriate language and organisational features.	● Paired activity where children identify simple sentences or paragraphs that would create tension in a good space story. ● Oral responses. ● Completed interactives.	**Writing AF5** ● Some variety in length, structure or subject of sentences. ● Use of some subordinating connectives. ● Some variation, generally accurate, in tense and verb forms.	**Writing AF5** ● A variety of sentence lengths, structures and subjects provides clarity and emphasis. ● Wider range of connectives used to clarify relationship between ideas. ● Some features of sentence structure used to build up detail or convey shades of meaning.	● I can explain how tension is created in a good science fiction story. ● I can use punctuation and construct sentences to create tension in my story.
Space story evaluations Children can improve an engaging short story in a particular genre using appropriate language and organisational features.	● Paired activity where children self-evaluate their own stories and the stories of others. ● Oral responses, discussion and written work.	**Reading AF6** ● Main purpose identified. ● Simple comments show some awareness of writer's viewpoint. ● Simple comment on overall effect on reader. **Writing AF2** ● Main purpose of writing is clear but not always consistently maintained. ● Main features of selected form are clear and appropriate to purpose. ● Style generally appropriate to task, though awareness of reader not always sustained.	**Reading AF6** ● Main purpose clearly identified, often through general overview. ● Viewpoints in texts clearly identified, with some, often limited, explanation. ● General awareness of effect on the reader, with some, often limited, explanation. **Writing AF2** ● Main purpose of writing is clear and consistently maintained. ● Features of selected form clearly established with some adaptation to purpose. ● Appropriate style clearly established to maintain reader's interest throughout.	● I can evaluate and self-evaluate the space stories. ● I can revise and improve my space story.

NARRATIVE

Phase ① Fiction genres posters

Learning outcome
Children can identify and discuss the principal features of different genres of children's fiction.

Success criteria
- I can identify the features of different fiction genres.
- I can discuss the differences and similarities between the genres.

Setting the context
The children should be able to understand the term 'genre'. Ask the children to think of different fiction genres and story examples. Write the genres on the board. Ask what features help readers identify the different genres, such as setting, characters, plots, language and structure. List these as bullet points and model how to write the information and examples next to them. For example, Historical genre: Setting: set in the past (such as Tudor times); Characters: from that period; Plot: can be around events or people from the past; Language: old-style words, names and descriptions of things from the past. Explain that they are going to work in their pairs to create genre posters for an imaginary book fair.

Assessment opportunity
Children at levels 2–3 work on the photocopiable page 'Fiction genres posters' with support. They cut up the descriptions and stick them by the correct features of two genres. For children working at levels 4–5 give each pair two genres, some blank paper and books of those genres. Ask them to list the features of their genres on the paper. Walk round the pairs and listen to their oral responses and ask if there are any other features they could add. Have a class discussion about all the children's ideas and choices. Record their thoughts and discussion. They can then create the posters using their notes. The children at levels 2–3 can copy the information from their photocopiables onto the computer to print off.

Assessment evidence
At levels 2–3, children should be able to identify the differences and similarities between the two texts. At levels 4–5, children should be able to discuss how genres with similar features can be categorised. Use the oral and written work as evidence against Reading AF7.

Next steps
Support: For children who struggle with examples of genre features, ask them to choose a favourite book and in a one-to-one or pair grouping, use guided questions to list the features: for fantasy – *is the setting in the real world? Is it imaginary? Is the plot an adventure or quest?*
Extension: Discuss how some genres can be mixed up. Ask children to research or read books that are a mix of genres and list their features, for example, science fiction and fantasy, crime and history.

Key aspects of learning
Information processing: Children will identify and refine classification criteria and sort fiction examples accordingly. They will quickly appraise particular texts and look for a range of information clues to support classification of texts into different genres.
Evaluation: Children will share responses and outcomes orally and in writing. They will apply the criteria they have identified in order to make decisions and judgements. They will give feedback to others and judge the effectiveness of their own work.
Communication: Children will develop their ability to discuss and debate issues and personal responses in respect of both the form and the content of the stories they are reading and writing. They will often work collaboratively in pairs and groups. They will communicate outcomes orally and in writing.

Phase ① Guess the genre

Learning outcome
Children can identify and discuss the principal features of different genres of children's fiction.

Success criteria
● I can identify different fiction genres from story extracts.
● I can discuss why text belongs to a certain fiction genre.

Setting the context
As a class, revise how each fiction genre has specific features. Ask the children to outline the main feature areas of a fiction genre and write them on the board, for example, structure, organisation or plot, characters, use of language. Children at levels 2-3 work in pairs or in a small group on the interactive activity 'Guess the genre' to match the genre to the correct sentence extracts. Put the children working at levels 4-5 into pairs. Explain that a busy children's publisher has been given three extracts of stories from three different genres and that the children need to read the extracts to work out the genres, so that they can be passed to the right editors. Display the success criteria in the classroom.

Assessment opportunity
With the children working on the interactive activity, 'Guess the genre', ask questions such as: *What type of story is this sentence from? How do you know?* Give out the three text extracts on the photocopiable pages 'Venus Spring - Stunt Girl', 'The Last of the Sky Pirates' and 'Arthur: The Seeing Stone' to children working at levels 4-5. Ask them to use highlighters to annotate the text for key features and then record the evidence on the photocopiable page 'Genre identification sheet'. Ask the children to highlight and record examples of features in the extracts and discuss why they chose them. Once the pairs have finished, ask them to share their work with another pair. Note their discussion. How have they justified their choices to each other? If possible, have a plenary class or group discussion about the extracts. What are they? What are the features of each one? How do the children know?

Assessment evidence
At levels 2-3, children will be able to answer most of the questions on the interactive activity correctly. At levels 4-5, children will be able to identify relevant parts of the texts to support their choice of genres - for example, characters' names, use of particular adjectives, sentence structure, opening sentences, layout of the text and so on. This activity will provide evidence against Reading AF2.

Next steps
Support: Write out story sentences from two genres and mix them up. Ask the children to read them out to a partner who has to decide which genre they belong to. Encourage them to make up some more to extend the game.
Extension: Have a game where groups have to identify the genre of a narrative text and then find a set number of its generic features against the clock. For example: Find and write down three language examples typical of the genre. Find and write down two characters who typify the genre. Which group is the fastest and has recorded most of the features correctly?

Key aspects of learning
Information processing: Children will identify and refine classification criteria and sort fiction examples accordingly. They will quickly appraise particular texts and look for a range of information clues to support classification of texts into different genres.
Evaluation: Children will share responses and outcomes orally and in writing. They will apply the criteria they have identified in order to make decisions and judgements. They will give feedback to others and judge the effectiveness of their own work.
Communication: Children will develop their ability to discuss and debate issues and personal responses in respect of both the form and the content of the stories they are reading and writing. They will often work collaboratively in pairs and groups. They will communicate outcomes orally and in writing.

NARRATIVE

Phase ① Favourite genres

Learning outcome
Children can explain reading preferences in terms of the different genres.

Success criteria
● I can explain why I like reading stories from a particular genre.
● I can give examples of the features I like in my favourite genre.

Setting the context
Use this activity once the children have had experience at exploring and discussing their preferences on a range of fiction genres. Discuss with the children how most readers enjoy stories from particular genres. Ask the children for their favourite fiction genres and encourage them to discuss their preferences. Children at levels 2–3 work with adult support in a group to complete version 1 of the photocopiable page 'My book review' of their favourite book. If possible, have the chosen books available for reference. Explain to the children working at levels 4–5 that they are going to write about their favourite genre, as well as reviewing their favourite book, on version 2 of the photocopiable page 'My book review'.

Assessment opportunity
Children at levels 2–3 work on their book review with adult support. As they write about the book encourage them to discuss the reasons why they like it. Ask: *Which is your favourite part of the story and why?* On version 2 of the photocopiable page 'My book review', the children at levels 4–5 are asked to think about stories they know and write down their top three stories, characters, plots, titles and settings and finally write a short review of their favourite story. Observe the children's work and ask questions such as: *What is so special about that plot? Why is that character so memorable?* At the end of the assessment, invite all the children to share their work with the class.

Assessment evidence
At levels 2–3, children should be able to give simple statements about their likes and dislikes and the reasons for their views. At levels 4–5, children should be able to choose and compare preferred features from a range of stories of the same genre as well as show some awareness of the writer's viewpoints. Use the completed photocopiables and the children's responses as evidence against Reading AF6.

Next steps
Support: If some children find it hard to explain why they like a particular genre or can't think of examples, prepare a session with a short story from a popular genre and read it to the children. Encourage them to talk about their likes and dislikes and give examples.
Extension: Encourage children to make a presentation to the class about their favourite genre using extracts from their chosen stories recorded on version 2 of the photocopiable page 'My book review'. Share ideas and reactions with the children at the end of the presentations.

Key aspects of learning
Evaluation: Children will share responses and outcomes orally and in writing. They will apply the criteria they have identified in order to make decisions and judgements. They will give feedback to others and judge the effectiveness of their own work.
Communication: Children will develop their ability to discuss and debate issues and personal responses in respect of both the form and the content of the stories they are reading and writing. They will often work collaboratively in pairs and groups. They will communicate outcomes orally and in writing.

Phase ② The Resurrection Men - 1829

Learning outcome
Children can analyse the language and organisational features of fiction genres.

Success criteria
- I can identify the structure of a short story from the past.
- I can use quotes and examples from a text to discuss a story's structure.

Setting the context
This assessment should be carried out once the children have had experience of historical stories and studied the historical genre. Put the children into their guided reading groups and work with one group at a time. Display and read out the extract from the historical short story, 'The Resurrection Men - 1829', on the photocopiable page. Before you read it, ask the children to listen carefully for clues in the text that will tell them the story's genre. After you have read the story, ask the children what the genre is. Discuss the structure of the short story by asking guided questions. Ask them to point out or quote examples and highlight the text.

Assessment opportunity
With each group ask guided questions such as: *How do we know it is set in the past? How many settings does the story have? Do you think the story is based on fact? Why? How is the end of the story connected to the beginning of the story?* (Explains what Burke and Hare are up to.) *Why are there two sections?* (To show the passage of time and to create tension and horror.) *How are the two parts of the story connected? Do you think it is a good story? Why or why not?* With lower ability groups, highlight examples in the text as the children respond to the questions. Encourage children working at levels 4-5 to quote examples or highlight the text as part of their answers.

Assessment evidence
At levels 2-3, children should be able to discuss their responses to the story and give examples of historical features, such as words like 'graverobber'. At levels 4-5, children should be able to answer guided questions by showing and discussing evidence in the text, such as language indicating it is set in the past, use of paragraphs and punctuation to create tension, and the structure of the plot. Use the children's responses and discussion as assessment towards Reading AF7.

Next steps
Support: Choose a short story from another genre, for example, a fairy tale such as 'Snow White and the Seven Dwarves', and discuss its structure. Use a story ladder to make the plot clearer for the children to understand.
Extension: Ask children to find out more about the story of Burke and Hare. *What happened to them? What happened to the surgeon?* Ask the children to write a newspaper article about their crimes and arrest.

Key aspects of learning
Information processing: Children will identify and refine classification criteria and sort fiction examples accordingly. They will quickly appraise particular texts and look for a range of information clues to support classification of texts into different genres.
Evaluation: Children will share responses and outcomes orally and in writing. They will apply the criteria they have identified in order to make decisions and judgements. They will give feedback to others and judge the effectiveness of their own work.
Communication: Children will develop their ability to discuss and debate issues and personal responses in respect of both the form and the content of the stories they are reading and writing. They will often work collaboratively in pairs and groups. They will communicate outcomes orally and in writing.

NARRATIVE

Phase ② Burke and Hare

Learning outcome
Children can analyse the language and organisational features of fiction genres.

Success criteria
● I can create character profiles by analysing and identifying language features.
● I can identify how language is used in a story set in the past.

Setting the context
Display and read the story 'The Resurrection Men – 1829' from the photocopiable page to the class. Explain that the story is based on fact. In the 19th century, graverobbers dug up bodies for medical students to dissect. However, Burke and Hare actually murdered up to 15 people, who were lured to their deaths by Burke and Hare's wives. Both were caught. Hare was freed after confessing but Burke was hanged. Explain that the story doesn't describe the characters but the readers can get an image through their actions and dialogue. Explain to the children that they are going to create profiles of the characters using clues from dialogue and language.

Assessment opportunity
Children at levels 2–3 can work with an adult to complete version 1 of the photocopiable page 'Character profiles' and then discuss their visual images of Burke and Hare. Put the children at levels 4–5 into pairs and give them a copy of the story and version 2 of the photocopiable page 'Character profiles'. Ask them to annotate the text. They will use the information to create profiles for Burke, Hare, Dr Knox and the student. As they work, ask questions, such as: *What kind of verbs are used to describe how Hare is talking? What kind of man do you think Dr Knox is?* Record their discussions and responses as children work on their profiles. Bring the class together and share the children's work. Encourage them to debate and discuss their views on the characters using quotes to support their arguments.

Assessment evidence
At levels 2–3, children will make simple inferences about Burke and Hare from the text. For example, that they live in Edinburgh, that they are both married, that they murdered a student. Children working at levels 4–5 will record examples such as 'Hare's sarcastic sentences' and explain how they conjure up an image of a ruthless character. The completed character profiles will provide evidence for Reading AF3.

Next steps
Support: Some children may find it difficult to visualise the characters from the evidence in the text. Read through the story again and encourage them to come up with a set of questions they would ask Burke and Hare if they were on the hot seat.
Extension: Encourage children to write an imagined account of Burke and Hare's last murder and how they were caught. Did the student investigate and tell the police? What happened to Dr. Knox? Remind the children to use features of a historical story. Compare the stories to the real account.

Key aspects of learning
Information processing: Children will identify and refine classification criteria and sort fiction examples accordingly. They will quickly appraise particular texts and look for a range of information clues to support classification of texts into different genres.
Evaluation: Children will share responses and outcomes orally and in writing. They will apply the criteria they have identified in order to make decisions and judgements. They will give feedback to others and judge the effectiveness of their own work.
Communication: Children will develop their ability to discuss and debate issues and personal responses in respect of both the form and the content of the stories they are reading and writing. They will often work collaboratively in pairs and groups. They will communicate outcomes orally and in writing.

Phase ③ Space story ideas

Learning outcome
Children can plan an engaging short story in a particular genre using appropriate language and organisational features.

Success criteria
● I can use a mind map to record and choose ideas for my space story.
● I can explain and discuss my story ideas.
● I can decide on a basic plot for my space story.

Setting the context
Discuss with the class the process of developing ideas for creative writing. On the board, list different methods of recording ideas, such as mind maps. Explain to the children that they are going to plan a space story. Remind them that they will need to think of ideas before they begin planning. Give out the photocopiable page 'Space story ideas' and look at its different areas: characters, settings, objects, situations. Give examples such as aliens, on a space colony, asteroids, lost in space. Stress the need to write all ideas down and then identify the ones that could be used in their story. Children at levels 2–3 work as a discussion group on one photocopiable to list their ideas, with adult support as a scribe when appropriate. At levels 4–5, children work independently on the photocopiable page.

Assessment opportunity
Walk round the class as the children work and take note of their progress. Children at levels 2–3 will create ideas for a group space story. The adult support can help them record space words and ideas under each section. Once the ideas are set down, encourage the children to discuss their basic story plot and identify ideas that could be used. Once the children who are working independently are happy with their ideas, encourage them to have a pair-share session to enable them to develop their ideas. Bring all the children together and discuss their ideas and record them on the board.

Assessment evidence
At levels 2–3, children's planning will indicate basic recognition of the science fiction genre, selecting an appropriate setting, character names and some other features. At levels 4–5, children's plans will clearly show all the main features of the genre and consistently link their ideas to the basic plot provided. This activity will provide evidence against Writing AF2.

Next steps
Support: For children needing more support, select a story title such as 'The Shape Shifter Planet'. With the children, create a mind map for ideas, for example, the setting of the shape shifter's planet, what shape shifters are like, other characters such as astronauts and a plot, such as shape shifters attack astronauts who invade their planet.
Extension: Ask children to study science fiction stories, films, TV or comics and identify the themes, the language and characters of the genre. Encourage them to take notes for ideas that will help them with their story.

Key aspects of learning
Evaluation: Children will share responses and outcomes orally and in writing. They will apply the criteria they have identified in order to make decisions and judgements. They will give feedback to others and judge the effectiveness of their own work.
Communication: Children will develop their ability to discuss and debate issues and personal responses in respect of both the form and the content of the stories they are reading and writing. They will often work collaboratively in pairs and groups. They will communicate outcomes orally and in writing.

NARRATIVE

Phase ③ Space story ladder

Learning outcome
Children can plan and draft an engaging short story in a particular genre using appropriate language and organisational features.

Success criteria
● I can use a story ladder to create a structure for my space story.
● I can evaluate my story structure and other structures.

Setting the context
Remind the children of the features of the science fiction genre. Revise the basic plot structure used in science fiction stories - opening, build-up, problem, events, resolution and end. Show the model science fiction example on the photocopiable page, 'Story ladder: Raid of the Ice Diamonds'. Show how the story's problem is resolved. Explain to the children that they are going to set out a plot for their space story using a similar story ladder. Give out the children's 'Space story ideas' photocopiables from the previous session and the photocopiable 'Space story ladder' to individual children and the supported group or groups.

Assessment opportunity
Children at levels 2-3 can work together to discuss and create a group story ladder with support, while children at levels 4-5 should complete the 'Space story ladder' photocopiable page independently. Take note of those children needing help or guidance and those who find the task within their capability. Remind them of the science fiction features. Once the ladders are completed ask the children to work with a response partner to evaluate and explain their ladder. The group ladder can be shared with another child or pair. Encourage feedback and suggestions for improvement. Allow the children time to revise their work after the discussion. Suggest all children check their work against the success criteria for self-assessment.

Assessment evidence
At levels 2-3, children should be able to distinguish the different elements of the story ladder and their effect on the story. At levels 4-5, children should be able to discuss and evaluate how the story flows, their ideas for the start and end of the story, the main problem and how it will be resolved. Use the children's story ladders and their responses as evidence against Writing AF3.

Next steps
Support: Give children a choice of three science-fiction story problems such as: stranded in space, alien invasion, and entering a time warp, and ask them to choose one. Discuss how the problem would be resolved. With the children, fill in the story ladder and go through each section being a scribe for their ideas.
Extension: Encourage children to think of suitable openings and endings for their story. How would it start? (A flashback, straight into the action, dialogue?) What kind of ending would it have? (A surprise ending, dramatic ending, humorous ending?)

Key aspects of learning
Evaluation: Children will share responses and outcomes orally and in writing. They will apply the criteria they have identified in order to make decisions and judgements. They will give feedback to others and judge the effectiveness of their own work.
Communication: Children will develop their ability to discuss and debate issues and personal responses in respect of both the form and the content of the stories they are reading and writing. They will often work collaboratively in pairs and groups. They will communicate outcomes orally and in writing.

NARRATIVE

Phase ③ Space descriptions

Success criteria
- I can identify effective descriptive language for a good science fiction story.
- I can choose and use effective descriptive words to use in my space story.

Setting the context
This activity can be used during the time the children are writing their space stories. Remind the children how science fiction stories use powerful descriptions as a main language feature. Give a few examples of words that could be used for the setting of a very hot planet, such as 'airless', 'fiery', 'volcanic', 'arid', 'barren', 'molten'. During the writing session allow one or two children at a time to work on the interactive activity 'Space descriptions'. Ask them to choose the descriptive words they think would be suitable within a good science fiction story. Children working at levels 2-3 may need adult support.

Assessment opportunity
Record the children's responses to each option of the interactive activity. Discuss why they have made their choice and the effects it would have in a story. Ask questions such as: *Why is the descriptive verb 'colliding' more effective than 'pretty' and 'many'? What image does the description conjure up?* Ask the children working at levels 4-5 if they can think of other effective words to use in the sentences. Once the children have completed the activity, encourage them to think of effective descriptive words they could use within their own stories.

Assessment evidence
At levels 2-3, children should be able to select correctly most of the descriptive words. At levels 4-5, children should correctly select all the descriptive words. They should also be able to provide their own alternative descriptive words appropriate to the science fiction genre. The completed interactive activity will provide evidence against Writing AF7.

Next steps
Support: Encourage children to choose a setting from their story and to think of as many descriptive words as they can to describe it. Invite the children to write the words. Create a descriptive word bank for their characters as well. Encourage them to use these words in their writing.
Extension: Encourage the children to create their characters' profiles using descriptive words. They could also draw their characters. Encourage them to think of powerful verbs or adjectives to describe the characters' feelings and actions.

Key aspects of learning
Evaluation: Children will share responses and outcomes orally and in writing. They will apply the criteria they have identified in order to make decisions and judgements. They will give feedback to others and judge the effectiveness of their own work.
Communication: Children will develop their ability to discuss and debate issues and personal responses in respect of both the form and the content of the stories they are reading and writing. They will often work collaboratively in pairs and groups. They will communicate outcomes orally and in writing.

NARRATIVE

Phase ③ Tension in space

Learning outcome
Children can plan, draft and write an engaging short story in a particular genre using appropriate language and organisational features.

Success criteria
● I can explain how tension is created in a good science fiction story.
● I can use punctuation and construct sentences to create tension in my story.

Setting the context
This activity can be used during the time the children are writing their space stories. Remind the children how science fiction often has situations that can be tense and full of suspense. Discuss with the children how writers can show tension in a story, for example, through use of punctuation, font size and shape, short sentences, complex sentences and use of paragraphs. During the writing session allow some children to work in pairs on the interactive activity 'Tension in space'. Children at levels 2-3 may need support.

Assessment opportunity
In pairs, the children decide which sentences from science fiction texts are effective in demonstrating tension. Encourage them to read the sentences through carefully and aloud before choosing between the options of 'Good tension' or 'No tension'. Ask the children at levels 2-3 why they have made their choices and the effects of the sentences. Identify the use of short sentences and punctuation. Encourage children at levels 4-5 to discuss the different styles of sentences and punctuation and their effects. Once the children have completed the activity, encourage them to think of ways they could add suspense or tension within their own stories.

Assessment evidence
At levels 2-3, children should be able to allocate correctly most of the sentences and recognise that punctuation and sentence length can be used to create tension. At levels 4-5, children should correctly allocate all the sentences. They should also be able to understand the use of punctuation, sentence length and language choices. The completed interactive activity will provide evidence against Writing AF5.

Next steps
Support: Look at children's writing and choose a scenario that would benefit from tension. Encourage children to read out the section or discuss what they want to achieve and together think of ways to create tension, for example, scribe dialogue as the child says it with expression and then show them how you have written it to show tension.
Extension: Encourage children to read or listen to stories that are full of suspense. Have them take notes and create a list of tension-writing features that they could use as a checklist for their own writing.

Key aspects of learning
Evaluation: Children will share responses and outcomes orally and in writing. They will apply the criteria they have identified in order to make decisions and judgements. They will give feedback to others and judge the effectiveness of their own work.
Communication: Children will develop their ability to discuss and debate issues and personal responses in respect of both the form and the content of the stories they are reading and writing. They will often work collaboratively in pairs and groups. They will communicate outcomes orally and in writing.

Phase ③ Space story evaluations

Learning outcome

Children can improve an engaging short story in a particular genre using appropriate language and organisational features.

Success criteria
- I can evaluate and self-evaluate the space stories.
- I can revise and improve my space story.

Setting the context

Use this activity once all or most of the children's space stories have been completed. Make sure they have their stories in front of them. Revise the process of evaluating stories before the final draft is written. Give out version 1 of the photocopiable page 'Space story evaluation sheet' to children at levels 2-3 and version 2 to those at levels 4-5. Explain to the children that they will use the photocopiable pages to evaluate their space stories and then pass their stories and evaluation sheets to a critical partner or critical group to be evaluated.

Assessment opportunity

As the children evaluate their own and their partner's stories, encourage them to highlight their texts for good examples and areas that need improvement, and then record them on the evaluation sheet. Encourage them to make suggestions as to how particular areas can be improved. Allow them to redraft and share the changes. Ask: *Are they happy with the changes?* Children at levels 2-3 can follow the same process and either evaluate another group or a chosen partner. Adult support may be needed as a scribe. Put the initials of the child next to their comments.

Assessment evidence

At levels 2-3, children will express their own viewpoints about the stories and what they like and dislike. At levels 4-5, children should identify examples of effective use of language and sentence structure and what the writer's intentions were. Children's comments will provide evidence against Reading AF6. At levels 2-3, children will demonstrate the use of the main features of the science fiction genre - choice of setting and characters and basic plot. They will also have made an attempt to use some suitable language features such as descriptive words. At levels 4-5, children will have developed their ideas appropriately, using short sentences and punctuation to create tension and action as well as selecting appropriate descriptive words. The completed stories will provide evidence against Writing AF2.

Next steps

Support: Give children a 10 out of 10 score sheet for different aspects of the story, such as setting, description, good plot, use of language, and so on. Highlight parts of the text they are unhappy with and work with them to think of ways to improve it.
Extension: Once children have made their improvements and redrafted their space story, let them write it up by hand or using the computer. Encourage them to create an anthology of short stories in space for the class to use and read.

Key aspects of learning

Information processing: Children will identify and refine classification criteria and sort fiction examples accordingly. They will quickly appraise particular texts and look for a range of information clues to support classification of texts into different genres.
Evaluation: Children will share responses and outcomes orally and in writing. They will apply the criteria they have identified in order to make decisions and judgements. They will give feedback to others and judge the effectiveness of their own work.
Communication: Children will develop their ability to discuss and debate issues and personal responses in respect of both the form and the content of the stories they are reading and writing. They will often work collaboratively in pairs and groups. They will communicate outcomes orally and in writing.

NARRATIVE

Periodic assessment

Reading

Learning outcomes
- Children can identify and discuss the principal features of different genres of children's fiction.
- Children can analyse the language and organisational features of fiction genres.

Success criteria
- I can identify the language features of a myth.
- I can identify the structure of a myth.

Setting the context
This assessment should be carried out once the children have had experience of identifying different fiction genres by studying the structural and language features of texts. Put the children into groups and display the extract 'The Big Flood' from the photocopiable page 'Narrative 1 Reading assessment text'. Ask them to listen carefully in order to identify the fiction genre of the story (myth). Work with one group at a time. Once you have read the story, ask the children for their thoughts. Praise those who thought it was a myth. Revise the meaning of a myth and discuss where the myth may have come from (Caribbean). Discuss the symbolic events in the story and how the same theme is used in other world myths, such as The Minator.

Assessment opportunity
In their groups, encourage the children to highlight clues in the text that identify it as a myth, such as the title, the names and actions of the characters, the plot to explain how or why something happened, rich descriptive language, symbolic imagery. Ask the children to write out a genre features list for myths on whiteboards or paper and then share them with the rest of the group. For children working at levels 2–3, discuss basic structural features, such as the main plot of the story, the characters and the use of descriptive words. Encourage them to highlight the points in the text. Work with them as a scribe to create the myth genre features list. Take observation notes of the children's responses in all the groups. At the end of the assessment, encourage the children to read through their lists and then look at the success criteria. Do they feel confident in their abilities?

Assessment evidence
Children working at levels 4–5 will identify the text as a myth by identifying a range of features, such as the specific characteristics of characters and their roles in the myth such as the cheeky monkey and the greedy gorilla. They might also discuss the main theme of the story and the symbolic ending as well as the use of effective storytelling-style language. Children working at levels 2–3 will discuss the story plot, focusing on the main events and the characters involved. They will identify the use of powerful verbs and adjectives to describe actions and dialogue, such as 'chattered', 'heaved', 'scrumptious'. Use this assessment as evidence against Reading AF2 and AF7.

Periodic assessment

Writing

Learning outcome
Children can plan and write an engaging short story in a particular genre using appropriate language and organisational features.

Success criteria
- I can reorder a plot of a well-known myth.
- I can write a myth using the same language and organisational features.
- I can evaluate my work for effective use of features of a myth genre.

Setting the context
Display the success criteria in the classroom. Remind the children about the myth, 'The Big Flood' or re-read the story. Briefly go through the features of a myth. The children are then given the photocopiable page 'Narrative 1 Writing assessment' in which they have to put the mixed-up plot of a well-known myth into the correct order. Children at levels 4–5 can work independently to complete the photocopiable and then rewrite the myth in their own words using lots of descriptive words. Children working at levels 2–3 will work in pairs or in a group with support on the photocopiable and then work independently to write out the story in a comic strip with descriptive text underneath each frame and simple cartoon dialogue in speech bubbles.

Assessment opportunity
Walk round as the children work on the photocopiable page and take note of the children's progress and understanding of the assessment. Remind the children of the myth genre features and the use of descriptive words in their own writing. Ask the children who are writing the myth in their own words questions such as: *How would you describe Narcissus? What do the gods say when they hear about Narcissus? How do you start and finish the story?* With the children working on their comic strips, encourage them to think of words that describe Narcissus such as handsome, cruel, and so on. What does Narcissus say when he sees his reflection? Encourage all the children to evaluate their work with a partner and match it to the success criteria. How would they improve their story? Has it been effective? How does it sound read aloud?

Assessment evidence
Children working at levels 4–5 should have used a wide range of descriptive vocabulary that describes how the main characters looked, behaved, moved and spoke. Their myth should include structural features of a myth with a clear progression, a catchy start and an ending that has a moral or lesson. Children working at levels 2–3 should show simple descriptive language within their text under each comic strip frame and within the speech bubbles. They should also be able to show the myth plot structure using their comic strips. This writing assessment can be used as evidence towards an understanding of Writing AF1 and AF3.

NARRATIVE
UNIT 2 Extending narrative

Literacy objectives

Speak and listen for a wide range of purposes in different contexts
Strand 1 Speaking
● Use the techniques of dialogic talk to explore ideas, topics or issues.
Strand 4 Drama
● Improvise using a range of drama strategies and conventions to explore themes such as hopes, fears and desires.

Read and write for a range of purposes on paper and on screen
Strand 6 Word structure and spelling
● Use a range of appropriate strategies to edit, proofread and correct spelling in their own work, on paper and on screen.
Strand 7 Understanding and interpreting texts
● Understand how writers use different structures to create coherence and impact.
Strand 8 Engaging with and responding to texts
● Sustain engagement with longer texts, using different techniques to make the text come alive.
● Compare how writers from different times and places present experiences and use language.
Strand 9 Creating and shaping texts
● Set their own challenges to extend achievement and experience in writing.
● Use different narrative techniques to engage and entertain the reader.
● Select words and language drawing on their knowledge of literary features and formal and informal writing.
● Integrate words, images and sounds imaginatively for different purposes.
Strand 10 Text structure and organisation
● Use varied structures to shape and organise texts coherently.
Strand 11 Sentence structure and punctuation
● Express subtle distinctions of meaning, including hypothesis, speculation and supposition, by constructing sentences in varied ways.
● Use punctuation to clarify meaning in complex sentences.

Key aspects of learning

Information processing
● Children will respond to information from a range of sources on paper and on screen and compare, combine and orchestrate this as a basis for solving or completing an adventure text.
Evaluation
● Children will share ideas, strategies and their consequences orally and in writing. They will discuss success criteria, give feedback to others and judge the effectiveness of their own and others' strategies and solutions in reading and creating an adventure text (or multimodal adventure) on paper or on screen. They will evaluate their own work and that of others against agreed criteria.

Key aspects of learning (contd)

Reasoning
- Children will construct reasoned arguments based on their views and responses to the text they read and create.

Problem solving
- Children will take decisions based on available evidence, explore their consequences and adjust future decisions accordingly.

Empathy
- In reading or playing and in writing or creating text adventures children will need to imagine themselves in another person's position. They will explore techniques that facilitate this process.

Self-awareness
- Children will discuss and reflect on their personal responses to the texts.

Communication
- Children will develop their ability to discuss and debate issues and personal responses in respect of both the form and the content of the adventures they are reading and creating. They will often work collaboratively in pairs and groups. They will communicate outcomes orally, in writing and through using other modes and media.

Assessment focuses

Reading
AF3 *(deduce, infer or interpret information, events or ideas from texts)*.
AF4 *(identify and comment on the structure and organisation of texts, including grammatical and presentational features at text level)*.
AF5 *(explain and comment on writers' use of language, including grammatical and literary features at word and sentence level)*.
AF7 *(relate texts to their social, cultural and historical contexts and literary traditions)*.

Writing
AF1 *(write imaginative, interesting and thoughtful texts)*.
AF2 *(produce texts which are appropriate to task, reader and purpose)*.

Speaking and listening
Speaking (organise and use detail).
Drama (take on different roles).

Resources

Phase 1 activities
Interactive activity, 'Fantasy features and themes'
Barrowquest story from http://nationalstrategies.standards.dcsf.gov.uk/node/113511
Photocopiable page, 'The end of a quest' (versions 1 and 2)
Phase 2 activities
Barrowquest story from http://nationalstrategies.standards.dcsf.gov.uk/node/113511
Interactive activity, 'Story map'
Periodic assessment
Barrowquest story from http://nationalstrategies.standards.dcsf.gov.uk/node/113511
Photocopiable page, 'Narrative 2 Reading assessment'
Photocopiable page, 'Narrative 2 Writing assessment'

Unit 2 ◾ Extending narrative

Learning outcomes	Assessment opportunity and evidence	Assessment focuses (AFs)		Success criteria
		Level 2	Level 3	
Phase ① activities pages 34–36				
Fantasy quiz Children extend their reading and learning skills through engagement with contemporary texts such as a non-linear adventure game.	● Independent activity where children identify common features and themes of fantasy stories and answer a multiple choice quiz. ● Children's oral responses. ● Teacher's notes.	**Reading AF7** ● General features of a few text types identified. ● Some awareness that books are set in different times and places.	**Reading AF7** ● Some simple connections between texts identified. ● Recognition of some features of the context of texts.	● I can identify the different features of fantasy stories. ● I can identify the different themes of fantasy stories.
Quest adventure endings Children extend their reading and learning skills through engagement with contemporary texts such as a non-linear adventure game.	● Supported group activity where children analyse the features and language of a quest adventure story. ● Children's oral responses. ● Teacher's notes. ● Completed photocopiables.	**Reading AF4** ● Some awareness of use of features of organisation. **Reading AF5** ● Some effective language choices noted. ● Some familiar patterns of language identified.	**Reading AF4** ● A few basic features of organisation at text level identified, with little or no linked comment. **Reading AF4** ● A few basic features of writer's use of language identified, but with little or no comment.	● I can identify and analyse the features of the endings of a quest adventure. ● I can compare and contrast language features of different quest adventure endings.
Freeze-frame descriptions Children extend their reading and learning skills through engagement with contemporary texts such as a non-linear adventure game.	● Group activity where children split an extract into freeze-frames for each action. ● Children's oral responses and discussion. ● Children's completed freeze-frames.	**Reading AF5** ● Some effective language choices noted. ● Some familiar patterns of language identified.	**Reading AF5** ● A few basic features of writer's use of language identified, but with little or no comment.	● I can identify how a writer can reveal what a character is thinking or feeling. ● I can identify a variety of language devices used to describe a character's actions and feelings.
Phase ② activities pages 37–39				
A character's qualities Children can identify the features and structure of a text adventure and use these as a model for writing.	● Supported group activity where children discuss and analyse text to complete a chart listing Lin's developing qualities and the ways these are shown. ● Children's oral responses and completed charts.	**Reading AF3** ● Simple, plausible inference about events and information, using evidence from text. ● Comments made on textual cues, sometimes misunderstood.	**Reading AF3** ● Straightforward inference based on a single point of reference in the text. ● Responses to text show meaning established at a literal.	● I can identify the different qualities of a main character within a quest adventure. ● I can understand the importance of the development of a main character.
Story maps Children can identify the features and structure of a text adventure and use these as a model for writing.	● Supported group activity where children identify and list different organisational features of a chapter. ● Children's oral responses and completed story maps.	**Reading AF4** ● Some awareness of use of features of organisation.	**Reading AF4** ● A few basic features of organisation at text level identified, with little or no linked comment.	● I can create a story map to organise chapters of a quest adventure. ● I can use my story map to discuss how individual chapters and a whole story are organised.

Unit 2 ⬛ Extending narrative

Learning outcomes	Assessment opportunity and evidence	Assessment focuses (AFs)		Success criteria
		Level 2	Level 3	
Quest adventure checklists Children can identify the features and structure of a text adventure and use these as a model for writing.	• Supported group activity where children compile a list of key questions that would help an author write a quest adventure. • Children's oral responses and discussions. • Teacher's notes. • Completed checklists.	**Writing AF2** • Some basic purpose established. • Some appropriate features of the given form used. • Some attempts to adopt appropriate style.	**Writing AF2** • Purpose established at a general level. • Main features of selected form sometimes signalled to the reader. • Some attempts at appropriate style, with attention to reader.	• I can debate and agree a list of key questions for use in writing a quest adventure. • I can list organisational and language features used in quest adventures. • I can present my quest adventure checklist attractively.

Phase ③ activities pages 40–41

Evaluating story plans Children collaborate to develop and extend their fiction writing through the creation of a text adventure on paper or on screen.	• Supported paired activity where children evaluate and revise a quest adventure story plan. • Children's oral responses and discussions. • Teacher's notes. • Completed criteria lists and story plans.	**Writing AF2** • Some basic purpose established. • Some appropriate features of the given form used. • Some attempts to adopt appropriate style.	**Writing AF2** • Purpose established at a general level. • Main features of selected form sometimes signalled to the reader. • Some attempts at appropriate style, with attention to reader.	• I can evaluate my quest adventure story plans to agreed criteria. • I can work collaboratively to explore ways to improve my plans. • I can revise my plans to make them more effective.
Revising a quest adventure Children collaborate to develop and extend their fiction writing through the creation of a text adventure on paper or on screen.	• Supported paired activity where children create evaluation criteria and evaluate and revise features within their written texts. • Children's oral responses and discussions. • Teacher's notes. • Children's amended criteria and redrafted notes.	**Writing AF1** • Mostly relevant ideas and content, sometimes repetitive or sparse. • Some apt word choices create interest. • Brief comments, questions about events or actions suggest viewpoint. **Writing AF2** • Some basic purpose established. • Some appropriate features of the given form used. • Some attempts to adopt appropriate style.	**Writing AF1** • Some appropriate ideas and content included. • Some attempt to elaborate on basic information or events. • Attempt to adopt viewpoint, though often not maintained or inconsistent. **Writing AF2** • Purpose established at a general level. • Main features of selected form sometimes signalled to the reader. • Some attempts at appropriate style, with attention to reader.	• I can use agreed criteria to evaluate sections of my story. • I can reflect on areas in my story text that need improvement. • I can work in collaboration to revise my quest adventure text.

Learning outcomes	Assessment opportunity and evidence	Assessment focuses (AFs)		Success criteria
		Level 4	Level 5	

Phase ① activities pages 34–36

Fantasy quiz Children extend their reading and learning skills through engagement with contemporary texts such as a non-linear adventure game.	• Independent activity where children identify common features and themes of fantasy stories and answer a multiple choice quiz. • Children's oral responses. • Teacher's notes.	**Reading AF7** • Features common to different texts or versions of the same text identified, with simple comment. • Simple comment on the effect that the reader's or writer's context has on the meaning of texts.	**Reading AF7** • Comments identify similarities and differences between texts, or versions, with some explanation. • Some explanation of how the contexts in which texts are written and read contribute to meaning.	• I can identify the different features of fantasy stories. • I can identify the different themes of fantasy stories.

Unit 2 ⬜ Extending narrative

Learning outcomes	Assessment opportunity and evidence	Assessment focuses (AFs)		Success criteria
		Level 4	Level 5	
Quest adventure endings Children extend their reading and learning skills through engagement with contemporary texts such as a non-linear adventure game.	• Paired activity where children analyse the features and language of a quest adventure story. • Children's oral responses. • Teacher's notes. • Completed photocopiables.	**Reading AF4** • Some structural choices identified with simple comment. • Some basic features of organisation at text level identified. **Reading AF5** • Some basic features of writer's use of language identified. • Simple comments on writer's choices.	**Reading AF4** • Comments on structural choices show some general awareness of writer's craft. • Various features relating to organisation at text level, including form, are clearly identified, with some explanation. **Reading AF5** • Various features of writer's use of language identified, with some explanation. • Comments show some awareness of the effect of writer's language choices.	• I can identify and analyse the features of the endings of a quest adventure. • I can compare and contrast language features of different quest adventure endings.
Freeze-frame descriptions Children extend their reading and learning skills through engagement with contemporary texts such as a non-linear adventure game.	• Group activity where children split an extract into freeze-frames for each action. • Children's oral responses and discussion. • Children's completed freeze-frames.	**Reading AF5** • Some basic features of writer's use of language identified. • Simple comments on writer's choices.	**Reading AF5** • Various features of writer's use of language identified, with some explanation. • Comments show some awareness of the effect of writer's language choices.	• I can identify how a writer can reveal what a character is thinking or feeling. • I can identify a variety of language devices used to describe a character's actions and feelings.

Phase ② activities pages 37–39

A character's qualities Children can identify the features and structure of a text adventure and use these as a model for writing.	• Supported group activity where children discuss and analyse text to complete a chart listing Lin's developing qualities and the different ways these are shown. • Children's oral responses and completed charts.	**Reading AF3** • Comments make inferences based on evidence from different points in the text. • Inferences often correct, but comments are not always rooted securely in the text or repeat narrative or content.	**Reading AF3** • Comments develop explanation of inferred meanings drawing on evidence across the text. • Comments make inferences and deductions based on textual evidence.	• I can identify the different qualities of a main character within a quest adventure. • I can understand the importance of the development of a main character.
Story maps Children can identify the features and structure of a text adventure and use these as a model for writing.	• Paired activity where children identify and list the different organisational features of a chapter. • Children's oral responses and completed story maps.	**Reading AF4** • Some structural choices identified with simple comment. • Some basic features of organisation at text level identified.	**Reading AF4** • Comments on structural choices show some general awareness of writer's craft. • Various features relating to organisation at text level, including form, are clearly identified, with some explanation.	• I can create a story map to organise chapters of a quest adventure. • I can use my story map to discuss how individual chapters and a whole story are organised.

Unit 2 ☐ Extending narrative

Learning outcomes	Assessment opportunity and evidence	Assessment focuses (AFs)		Success criteria
		Level 4	Level 5	
Quest adventure checklists Children can identify the features and structure of a text adventure and use these as a model for writing.	● Group activity where children compile a list of key questions that would help an author write a quest adventure. ● Children's oral responses and discussions. ● Teacher's notes. ● Completed checklists.	**Writing AF2** ● Main purpose of writing is clear but not always consistently maintained. ● Main features of selected form are clear and appropriate to purpose. ● Style generally appropriate to task, though awareness of reader not always sustained.	**Writing AF2** ● Main purpose of writing is clear and consistently maintained. ● Features of selected form clearly established with some adaptation to purpose. ● Appropriate style clearly established to maintain reader's interest throughout.	● I can debate and agree a list of key questions for use in writing a quest adventure. ● I can list organisational and language features used in quest adventures. ● I can present my quest adventure checklist attractively.

Phase ③ activities pages 40–41

Learning outcomes	Assessment opportunity and evidence	Assessment focuses (AFs)		Success criteria
		Level 4	Level 5	
Evaluating story plans Children collaborate to develop and extend their fiction writing through the creation of a text adventure on paper or on screen.	● Paired activity where children create an agreed criteria list and use it to evaluate and revise a quest adventure story plan. ● Children's oral responses and discussions. ● Teacher's notes. ● Completed criteria lists and story plans.	**Writing AF2** ● Main purpose of writing is clear but not always consistently maintained. ● Main features of selected form are clear and appropriate to purpose. ● Style generally appropriate to task, though awareness of reader not always sustained.	**Writing AF2** ● Main purpose of writing is clear and consistently maintained. ● Features of selected form clearly established with some adaptation to purpose. ● Appropriate style clearly established to maintain reader's interest throughout.	● I can evaluate my quest adventure story plans to agreed criteria. ● I can work collaboratively to explore ways to improve my plans. ● I can revise my plans to make them more effective.
Revising a quest adventure Children collaborate to develop and extend their fiction writing through the creation of a text adventure on paper or on screen.	● Independent activity where children create evaluation criteria and use it to evaluate and revise features within their written texts. ● Children's oral responses and discussions. ● Teacher's notes. ● Children's amended criteria and redrafted notes.	**Writing AF1** ● Relevant ideas and content chosen. ● Some ideas and material developed in detail. ● Straightforward viewpoint generally established and maintained. **Writing AF2** ● Main purpose of writing is clear but not always consistently maintained. ● Main features of selected form are clear and appropriate to purpose. ● Style generally appropriate to task, though awareness of reader not always sustained.	**Writing AF1** ● Relevant ideas and material developed with some imaginative detail. ● Development of ideas and material appropriately shaped for selected form. ● Clear viewpoint established, generally consistent, with some elaboration. **Writing AF2** ● Main purpose of writing is clear and consistently maintained. ● Features of selected form clearly established with some adaptation to purpose. ● Appropriate style clearly established to maintain reader's interest throughout.	● I can use agreed criteria to evaluate sections of my story. ● I can reflect on areas in my story text that need improvement. ● I can work in collaboration to revise my quest adventure text.

NARRATIVE

Phase ① Fantasy quiz

Learning outcome
Children extend their reading and learning skills through engagement with contemporary texts such as a non-linear adventure game.

Success criteria
- I can identify the different features of fantasy stories.
- I can identify the different themes of fantasy stories.

Setting the context
Use this activity once the children have had experience of stories from the fantasy genre. Introduce the activity to the class by discussing the genre of fantasy and its definition – a story not possible in the real world. With the children list the many types of fantasy such as magic fantasies, myth-based fantasies, and so on. Explain to the children that they are going to identify the common features and themes of fantasy stories.

Assessment opportunity
Display the interactive activity 'Fantasy features and themes' to the class. Read out each question and its possible answers and ask the children to identify their answer choice. Discuss their reasons. Note individual children's responses and choices. Reveal the answer and ask further questions relating to the question such as: *What types of quests can a character go on?* (Internal and external.) Continue with the other questions in the quiz.

Assessment evidence
Children at levels 2–3 should answer some or most of the questions and give simple examples such as an evil dragon versus a young knight in a quest story. Children at levels 4–5 should answer all of the questions correctly and give good examples taken from the fantasy genre. Use the assessment notes and responses as evidence against Reading AF7.

Next steps
Support: Encourage children to draw and label a set of fantasy cards, for example, six characters, six settings, six objects and six plots such as overcome evil, solve a riddle, and so on. Use them to create stories.
Extension: Explain that fantasy stories, such as Tolkien's *The Ring Trilogy,* and CS Lewis's *The Chronicles of Narnia,* have many themes with messages for the reader. Encourage the children to list some of the themes and discuss their messages.

Key aspects of learning
Reasoning: Children will construct reasoned arguments based on their views and responses to the text they read and create.
Problem solving: Children will take decisions based on available evidence, explore their consequences and adjust future decisions accordingly.
Self-awareness: Children will discuss and reflect on their personal responses to the texts.
Communication: Children will develop their ability to discuss and debate issues and personal responses in respect of both the form and the content of the adventures they are reading and creating. They will often work collaboratively in pairs and groups. They will communicate outcomes orally, in writing and through using other modes and media.

Phase ① Quest adventure endings

Learning outcome
Children extend their reading and learning skills through engagement with contemporary texts such as a non-linear adventure game.

Success criteria
● I can identify and analyse the features of the endings of a quest adventure.
● I can compare and contrast language features of different quest adventure endings.

Setting the context
Put the children in their guided reading groups. Introduce the multi-pathway quest story, *Barrowquest*, in which Lin, a young boy, is forced on a quest to find and wake a sleeping magician to save his tribe. Explain that the story has four possible endings. Discuss how quest adventures often end with a final challenge for the main character followed by a homecoming or a positive conclusion. Explain to the children that they are going to analyse the features and language of one of the endings.

Assessment opportunity
Children at levels 2–3 work as a discussion group with adult support on version 1 of the photocopiable page 'The end of a quest'. Put children working at levels 4–5 into pairs and give each pair one of the four endings and version 2 of the photocopiable page 'The end of a quest'. Ask them to read the ending and complete the photocopiable. Ask each pair to discuss their ending and its features with the rest of the group. Encourage them to compare and contrast the use of language and how it creates very different endings with pairs working on other endings. Walk around the groups and take notes of the children's discussion and responses.

Assessment evidence
Children at levels 4–5 will discuss the distinct features that appear in each ending, commenting in detail on areas such as the effect of the last sentence or paragraph, the lessons learned by the character. In their discussions with other pairs the children will notice how the same fantasy concepts can be created in different ways with different effects. As a group, children at levels 2–3 will discuss features of one ending, such as typical characters, their challenges and simple effective descriptive words. Use the photocopiables and teacher notes of the children's discussions as evidence against Reading AF4 and AF5.

Next steps
Support: Choose a range of endings from a quest adventure story with simpler texts and, with the children, compare and contrast the language and dialogue. Is there a pattern? How is language used for effect?
Extension: Encourage children to write another ending for Lin with the same positive outcome as the other four. What enemy or obstacle must he overcome? What was the magician's room like? How would they describe these images?

Key aspects of learning
Information processing: Children will respond to information from a range of sources on paper and on screen and compare, combine and orchestrate this as a basis for solving or completing an adventure text.
Evaluation: Children will share ideas, strategies and their consequences orally and in writing. They will discuss success criteria, give feedback to others and judge the effectiveness of their own and others' strategies and solutions in reading and creating an adventure text. They will evaluate their own work and that of others against agreed criteria.
Communication: Children will develop their ability to discuss and debate issues and personal responses in respect of both the form and the content of the adventures they are reading and creating. They will often work collaboratively in pairs and groups. They will communicate outcomes orally, in writing and through using other modes and media.

Phase ① Freeze-frame descriptions

Learning outcome
Children extend their reading and learning skills through engagement with contemporary texts such as a non-linear adventure game.

Success criteria
● I can identify how a writer can reveal what a character is thinking or feeling.
● I can identify a variety of language devices used to describe a character's actions and feelings.

Setting the context
Display the success criteria in the classroom. In advance of the lesson, read through the text of the class's chosen quest adventure or *Barrowquest* and choose extracts that describe a main character through action and description, such as the first paragraph of Chapter 2, 'The Well of Othene', from *Barrowquest*. Identify the different devices used to describe the action and indicate how the character feels, for example, use of adverbs, adjectives, and complex sentences.

Assessment opportunity
Put the children into mixed-ability groups and give them an extract each. Ask them to split the extract into freeze-frames for each action. Stress the need to show the character's expression and body language. Let each group demonstrate their freeze-frames to the rest of the class and ask the class to suggest descriptions to describe the frames. Record them on the board. Compare the children's suggestions to the original. Discuss with the class which devices were used to create the most effective description? Why? Make notes of the children's freeze-frames and their subsequent responses.

Assessment evidence
Record evidence of how each group successfully shows the chosen character's expression and body language compared to the text descriptions. Children at levels 2–3 should suggest effective sentences and descriptive words to describe the character's actions and feelings. Children at levels 4–5 should suggest a range of writing techniques. Evidence in this assessment can be used against Reading AF5.

Next steps
Support: Show photographs of people doing different actions. Encourage children to think of action verbs and language to describe what the person is doing, as if in a story. Write the sentences underneath each picture.
Extension: Ask children to describe a fictional character's actions and feelings as they suddenly find out they can fly.

Key aspects of learning
Evaluation: Children will share ideas, strategies and their consequences orally and in writing. They will discuss success criteria, give feedback to others and judge the effectiveness of their own and others' strategies and solutions in reading and creating an adventure text. They will evaluate their own work and that of others against agreed criteria.
Empathy: In reading, writing or creating text adventures children will need to imagine themselves in another person's position. They will explore techniques that facilitate this process.
Reasoning: Children will construct reasoned arguments based on their views and responses to the text they read and create.
Communication: Children will develop their ability to discuss and debate issues and personal responses in respect of both the form and the content of the adventures they are reading and creating. They will often work collaboratively in pairs and groups. They will communicate outcomes orally and in writing.

Phase ② A character's qualities

Learning outcome
Children can identify the features and structure of a text adventure and use these as a model for writing.

Success criteria
- I can identify the different qualities of a main character within a quest adventure.
- I can understand the importance of the development of a main character.

Setting the context
Conduct this assessment with one guided-reading group at a time. Each group will need a teacher or teaching support working with them. Display the success criteria in the classroom. Remind the group how quest adventure stories usually have a main character who develops positive qualities as they overcome challenges and achieve their quest. Discuss examples, such as the character becoming braver, wiser, and so on. Explain how other characters may give encouragement or clues about how to use qualities the main character was unaware of, such as 'listen with your heart and the message will be clear'.

Assessment opportunity
Display one of the chapters from *Barrowquest*. Discuss and analyse the text for examples of Lin's developing qualities. Draw a chart, with one column listing qualities, such as empathy and bravery, and a second column for relevant text quotes. Encourage the children to add to the chart and discuss the different ways Lin's qualities are shown, such as a simple sentence, dialogue, rhetorical question, conditional sentences, and so on. Children working at levels 2–3 may need support to read the text and act as scribe to record the examples. At the end of the session, ask the children if they think Lin has changed for the better. What will he be like in the future?

Assessment evidence
Children working at levels 4–5 will list examples of Lin's character and discuss in depth how the different devices used in the text illustrate Lin's character and how he develops. Children working at levels 2–3 should be able to identify straightforward devices and clues to Lin's character, such as the use of descriptive words, and dialogue. Use the chart and the children's responses as evidence against Reading AF3.

Next steps
Support: Children may need a simpler text to focus on a character's qualities. Choose a well-known quest, such as a myth. Let the children draw a picture of the character and, around the character, write the qualities gained with small explanation captions.
Extension: Encourage children to create rhymes that carry messages, guidance or encouragement to help a character choose the fabled Dragon's Pearl, which is mixed in with a box of normal pearls.

Key aspects of learning
Evaluation: Children will share ideas, strategies and their consequences orally and in writing. They will discuss success criteria, give feedback to others and judge the effectiveness of their own and others' strategies and solutions in reading and creating an adventure text (or multimodal adventure) on paper or on screen. They will evaluate their own work and that of others against agreed criteria.
Empathy: In reading, writing or creating text adventures children will need to imagine themselves in another person's position. They will explore techniques that facilitate this process.

Phase ② Story maps

Success criteria
● I can create a story map to organise the chapters of a quest adventure.
● I can use my story map to discuss how individual chapters and a whole story are organised.

Setting the context
Display the success criteria in the classroom. Discuss the use of story maps in outlining the structure of a story. Model a simple story map of a well-known quest adventure. Explain to the children that they are going to create story maps to outline the structure of each chapter of one of the four stories from *Barrowquest*. List criteria they would use on the maps for each chapter, such as settings, characters, main events, problems, solutions. Children at levels 2–3 can work in small groups with support. Children at levels 4–5 should work in pairs.

Assessment opportunity
Children at levels 2–3 can work with an adult to identify and list the organisational features of one chapter before completing the interactive activity 'Story map'. Give out copies of one *Barrowquest* story pathway to the children at levels 4–5. Ask them to focus on each chapter to find the features identified in the modelling and create a story map to record them. Walk round the children as they work in their pairs or groups. Note their ability to identify the structure of the story within the text and the way they use their story maps to outline each area clearly. In class feedback, go through the story maps in chapter order and discuss how they help a writer organise individual chapters and create a structure for the story.

Assessment evidence
At levels 2–3, children should be able to complete their story maps with little or no further comment. At levels 4–5, children should be able to comment on the structure and suggest reasons for the author's choices. The completed story maps and discussion will provide evidence against Reading AF4.

Next steps
Support: Allow children to create a pictorial story map. Draw the characters, setting and events with simple captions underneath. Discuss how the story map helps outline structure.
Extension: Encourage children to create one story map encompassing all the chapters and their features. How would they be able to show the natural progression of each chapter? Does it effectively enable the writer and reader to understand the way the whole story is structured?

Key aspects of learning
Evaluation: Children will share ideas, strategies and their consequences orally and in writing. They will discuss success criteria, give feedback to others and judge the effectiveness of their own and others' strategies and solutions in reading and creating an adventure text (or multimodal adventure) on paper or on screen. They will evaluate their own work and that of others against agreed criteria.
Communication: Children will develop their ability to discuss and debate issues and personal responses in respect of both the form and the content of the adventures they are reading and creating. They will often work collaboratively in pairs and groups. They will communicate outcomes orally, in writing and through using other modes and media.

Phase ② Quest adventure checklists

Learning outcome
Children can identify the features and structure of a text adventure and use these as a model for writing.

Success criteria
● I can debate and agree a list of key questions for use in writing a quest adventure.
● I can list organisational and language features used in quest adventures.
● I can present my quest adventure checklist attractively.

Setting the context
Children at levels 2–3 will work in groups with adult support as a scribe. Put the children at levels 4–5 into groups of four to six. Explain that a writer wants to write a quest adventure story but doesn't know where to begin. In their groups, the children will debate and agree a list of key questions to help the writer. Once agreed, ask all the children to individually create a checklist of the key questions that is clear and attractive to read. Display the success criteria in the classroom.

Assessment opportunity
Give the groups small whiteboards or paper for notes and ideas. Listen in to the groups' discussions. Take observation notes of children's understanding and identify those in need of more support. Encourage discussion by asking questions: *What is the goal of the quest? What language features are often used?* Once they have completed their lists, allow the children to use ICT programs or other forms to present their final lists. Display them and have a class discussion. Compliment good examples of key questions and presentation techniques.

Assessment evidence
Children at levels 2–3 should be able to form questions that cover the basic plot of a quest story, characters, the reason for the quest, and language features. Children at levels 4–5 should be able to form questions that cover both organisational features (use of sentences, paragraphs, plot outline, quest symbolism and message, character development) and language features (devices for tension, descriptive words, punctuation, and dialogue). Use the observation notes along with their checklists as evidence against Writing AF2.

Next steps
Support: For children having difficulty identifying key questions, write relevant key questions on pieces of paper mixed with non-relevant questions. Ask the children to sort them into correct piles and discuss their reasons for sorting them into the particular piles.
Extension: Encourage children to create a story map template to accompany the key questions lists. What other ideas could they add to help the writer? For example: lists of typical quest characters, story problems, moral messages, etc.

Key aspects of learning
Evaluation: Children will share ideas, strategies and their consequences orally and in writing. They will discuss success criteria, give feedback to others and judge the effectiveness of their own and others' strategies and solutions in reading and creating an adventure text (or multimodal adventure) on paper or on screen. They will evaluate their own work and that of others against agreed criteria.
Reasoning: Children will construct reasoned arguments based on their views and responses to the text they read and create.
Communication: Children will develop their ability to discuss and debate issues and personal responses in respect of both the form and the content of the adventures they are reading and creating. They will often work collaboratively in pairs and groups. They will communicate outcomes orally, in writing and through using other modes and media.

NARRATIVE

Phase ③ Evaluating story plans

Learning outcome
Children collaborate to develop and extend their fiction writing through the creation of a text adventure on paper or on screen.

Success criteria
- I can evaluate my quest adventure story plans to agreed criteria.
- I can work collaboratively to explore ways to improve my plans.
- I can revise my plans to make them more effective.

Setting the context
Display the success criteria in the classroom. Use this assessment once the children have started work to generate and explore ideas for a new adventure story or write new alternative chapters for *Barrowquest*. Encourage the children to use techniques and models from previous lessons, such as story maps and plans, key question lists, features such as character outlines, settings and imaginary maps of a place or world. Once they have completed their initial plans, the children at levels 2-3 can work in pairs with adult support to create an agreed criteria list. Children at levels 4-5 can work in pairs to create a criteria list to evaluate a quest adventure story plan.

Assessment opportunities
Once the children have completed their agreed criteria list, ask them to use it to evaluate their own plans and then the plans of their partners. Once they have finished the evaluations, ask each pair to compare and contrast their evaluations of the plans. How could they improve their plans? How does another point of view help in looking at plans? Allow the children time to use the evaluations to improve their plans. Have a class plenary to compare their evaluations. Discuss with the children which criteria were the most effective. Ask: *Why is it better to work with agreed criteria?*

Assessment evidence
Children at levels 2-3 should show words and pictures for basic characters' qualities and actions, words and phrases for settings, simple plot outline. Children at levels 4-5 should include in their planning criteria features such as: characters - names, qualities, purpose in story; main plot sequence ideas - quest, rescue, ordeal, resolution; settings, and so on. Use observation notes and the children's written criteria and plans as evidence against Writing AF2.

Next steps
Support: Work with children to complete a story planner for one segment of the story, such as the opening. Encourage the children to look at each other's work and evaluate it.
Extension: Encourage children to plan one chapter or one section in more detail, such as the opening, the conclusion, a main event or problem. Ask them to plan the work to create as much effect as possible, taking into consideration organisational and language features.

Key aspects of learning
Evaluation: Children will share ideas, strategies and their consequences orally and in writing. They will discuss success criteria, give feedback to others and judge the effectiveness of their own and others' strategies and solutions in reading and creating an adventure text (or multimodal adventure) on paper or on screen. They will evaluate their own work and that of others against agreed criteria.
Reasoning: Children will construct reasoned arguments based on their views and responses to the text they read and create.
Communication: Children will develop their ability to discuss and debate issues and personal responses in respect of both the form and the content of the adventures they are reading and creating. They will often work collaboratively in pairs and groups. They will communicate outcomes orally, in writing and through using other modes and media.

Phase ③ Revising a quest adventure

Learning outcome
Children collaborate to develop and extend their fiction writing through the creation of a text adventure on paper or on screen.

Success criteria
- I can use agreed criteria to evaluate sections of my story.
- I can reflect on areas in my story text that need improvement.
- I can work in collaboration to revise my quest adventure text.

Setting the context
Display the success criteria in the classroom. Use this assessment once the children have written their first draft of a quest adventure story and the teacher has read through them. Using one of the children's texts, display one section, such as the opening or ending to the class. Discuss the features, language and structure that would be relevant for that part of the story. Explain to the children that they are going to re-read and reflect on their own text by evaluating it using agreed criteria. Encourage the children to volunteer the different elements of the criteria and record them on the board for all the children to see.

Assessment opportunity
Children at levels 2-3 should focus on one or two criteria, for example, using more descriptive words, using different words instead of 'said' or 'then'. Ask them to find examples and then identify the areas that they think need revising. The children then work with a response partner to reflect on the areas that needed improvement on each other's texts. The children can revise their texts and discuss their changes in a class plenary. Children at levels 4-5 can re-read parts of their texts, and identify sections that may need revising. Encourage them to refer to the agreed criteria and check on features, such as the use of verbs, sentence construction and dialogue.

Assessment evidence
Children at levels 2-3 should identify words or areas that need changing. Note their responses to new word ideas. Do they need help in finding alternatives? Children at levels 4-5 should discuss why they selected those areas of the text for revision. What might they use instead? How effective would the text be after the changes? How does it match the agreed criteria? Use the children's responses along with their redrafted texts as evidence against Writing AF1 and AF2.

Next steps
Support: For children needing support, focus on one area in the text, such as the use of verbs or adjectives. Identify the ones used and think of alternatives to make the text more effective.
Extension: Children can use their agreed criteria to revise and redraft other parts of their story. Encourage them to use dictionaries, word banks and thesauruses for effective words and sentences.

Key aspects of learning
Evaluation: Children will share ideas, strategies and their consequences orally and in writing. They will discuss success criteria, give feedback to others and judge the effectiveness of their own and others' strategies and solutions in reading and creating an adventure text (or multimodal adventure) on paper or on screen. They will evaluate their own work and that of others against agreed criteria.
Reasoning: Children will construct reasoned arguments based on their views and responses to the text they read and create.
Communication: Children will develop their ability to discuss and debate issues and personal responses in respect of both the form and the content of the adventures they are reading and creating. They will often work collaboratively in pairs and groups. They will communicate outcomes orally, in writing and through using other modes and media.

Periodic assessment

Reading

Learning outcomes
• Children extend their reading and learning skills through engagement with contemporary texts such as a non-linear adventure game.
• Children can identify the features and structure of a text adventure and use these as a model for writing.

Success criteria
• I can identify different sentences that create action in a quest adventure.
• I can analyse how sentences can create impact and pace.

Setting the context
This assessment can be done during several guided reading sessions. Focus on one group at a time, working with the children. Display the success criteria in the classroom. Give each child a copy of the photocopiable page 'Narrative 2 Reading assessment'. Discuss the various features on the photocopiable page and ask for examples. Display Chapter 2, 'Green Light', from *Barrowquest*. Read the extract and ask the children to identify action features within the text and then record examples on their photocopiable page.

Assessment opportunity
Support children by asking guided questions such as: *Which powerful verbs give the effect of action? Why?* Encourage the children to create their own sentence examples for an action sequence. Once the children have completed their photocopiables, encourage them to share their findings with the rest of the group. Prompt discussion with questions about their chosen examples and their effects such as: *How does a complex sentence give the effect of pace?* (use of three verbs) *Why do none of the action sentences start with 'A' or 'The'?* Use the group discussions to enable the children to assess where they need help to develop and improve in order to meet the success criteria.

Assessment evidence
At levels 2-3, children should be able to identify some of the action features within the text. At levels 4-5, children will have more understanding about how the author has used language to create action and should be able to explain and discuss how this works. Record children's understandings and needs and use them to make level judgements against Reading AF4 and AF5.

Periodic assessment

Writing

Learning outcomes
● Children can identify the features and structure of a text adventure and use these as a model for writing.
● Children collaborate to develop and extend their fiction writing through the creation of a text adventure on paper or on screen.

Success criteria
● I can work collaboratively to create a map of a quest adventure setting.
● I can use powerful imagery to create an effective quest adventure setting.

Setting the context
Display the success criteria in the classroom. Explain to the children how settings in quest adventure stories are described using powerful imagery to create an impact. Discuss various devices used to create powerful images such as alliteration, similes, metaphors, personification and onomatopoeia. List examples on the board. Highlight the need for physical and emotional descriptions. Put the children in pairs and explain that they are going to draw a quest adventure map and then write a descriptive passage about it. Give them each a copy of the photocopiable page 'Narrative 2 Writing assessment'. On a separate piece of paper they should note down descriptions for the map using powerful imagery and then use the descriptions to write a passage to describe the setting.

Assessment opportunity
Walk around the pairs as they draw their pictures and make their notes. Encourage them to add in as much detail as possible. Ask questions such as: *What similes or alliteration could you use to describe the swamp (as slimy as a slippery snake)? How would you personify the swamp to indicate its effect on a character?* Take notes of the children's discussion and oral responses. Once the children have completed their descriptions and passages, display the pictures to the class. Ask pairs to read out their passages and ask the class to match them to the correct setting. *Which descriptions matched the setting? How effective were they in creating powerful images?* Discuss the success criteria with individual children to help them decide how to develop their skills for the future.

Assessment evidence
Record children's understandings and needs and use them to make level judgements against Writing AF1 and AF2. At levels 2-3, children should be able to include some appropriate ideas and content in their setting descriptions and make some attempt to maintain and appropriate style. At levels 4-5, children should be able to develop some ideas in detail and maintain a style that generally matches the task; this style may not be sustained throughout the piece of work.

NARRATIVE
UNIT 3 Authors and texts

Literacy objectives

Speak and listen for a wide range of purposes in different contexts

Strand 1 Speaking
- Use a range of oral techniques to present persuasive arguments and engaging narratives.
- Use the techniques of dialogic talk to explore ideas, topics or issues.

Strand 3 Group discussion and interaction
- Understand and use a variety of ways to criticise constructively and respond to criticism.

Strand 4 Drama
- Improvise using a range of drama strategies and conventions to explore themes such as hopes, fears and desires.

Read and write for a range of purposes on paper and on screen

Strand 6 Word structure and spelling
- Spell familiar words correctly and employ a range of strategies to spell difficult and unfamiliar words.
- Use a range of appropriate strategies to edit, proofread and correct spelling in their own work, on paper and on screen.

Strand 8 Engaging with and responding to texts
- Read extensively and discuss personal reading with others, including in reading groups.
- Sustain engagement with longer texts, using different techniques to make the text come alive.

Strand 9 Creating and shaping texts
- Set their own challenges to extend achievement and experience in writing.
- Use different narrative techniques to engage and entertain the reader.

Strand 10 Text structure and organisation
- Use varied structures to shape and organise text coherently.
- Use paragraphs to achieve pace and emphasis.

Strand 11 Sentence structure and punctuation
- Express subtle distinctions of meaning, including hypothesis, speculation and supposition, by constructing sentences in varied ways.
- Use punctuation to clarify meaning in complex sentences.

Key aspects of learning

Enquiry
- Children will identify their own key questions about the work of a particular writer, and then locate the evidence to answer them.

Information processing
- Children will respond to information or stimuli from a range of sources on paper and on screen and compare, combine and orchestrate this as a basis for both oral and written communication.

Evaluation
- Children will share responses orally and in writing. They will discuss success criteria, give feedback to others and judge the effectiveness of their own work.

Key aspects of learning (contd)

Empathy
- In discussing and writing about the books or stories, children will need to imagine themselves in another person's position. They will explore techniques that facilitate this process.

Communication
- Children will develop their ability to discuss and debate issues and personal responses both in respect of the form and the content of the stories they are reading and the journals they are creating. They will often work collaboratively in pairs and groups. They will communicate outcomes orally, in writing and through other modes and media.

Assessment focuses

Reading
AF2 *(understand, describe, select or retrieve information, events or ideas from texts and use quotation and reference to text).*
AF3 *(deduce, infer or interpret information, events or ideas from texts).*
AF5 *(explain and comment on writers' use of language, including grammatical and literary features at word and sentence level).*
AF6 *(identify and comment on writers' purposes and viewpoints and the overall effect of the text on the reader).*

Writing
AF2 *(produce texts which are appropriate to task, reader and purpose).*
AF3 *(organise and present whole texts effectively, sequencing and structuring information, ideas and events).*
AF7 *(select appropriate and effective vocabulary).*

Speaking and listening
Speaking (speak with clarity, intonation and pace).
Group discussion and interaction (make contributions to sustain the activity).
Drama (improvise and sustain roles; work with others in performance).

Resources

Phase 1 activities
Photocopiable page, 'Synopsis of Kensuke's Kingdom'
Photocopiable page, 'Kensuke's Kingdom (a)'
Photocopiable page, 'Kensuke's Kingdom (b)'
Phase 2 activities
Photocopiable page, 'Kensuke's Kingdom (c)'
Interactive activity, 'Kensuke's character profile'
Photocopiable page, 'Kensuke's character profile'
Phase 3 activities
Photocopiable page, 'Kensuke's Kingdom (c)'
Interactive activity, 'Feeling words' (versions 1 and 2)
Periodic assessment
Photocopiable page, 'Narrative 3 Reading assessment text'
Photocopiable page, 'Narrative 3 Reading assessment'
Photocopiable page, 'Narrative 3 Writing assessment text'
Photocopiable page, 'Narrative 3 Writing assessment'

Unit 3 ▢ Authors and texts

Learning outcomes	Assessment opportunity and evidence	Assessment focuses (AFs)		Success criteria
		Level 2	Level 3	

Phase ① activities pages 50-52

Learning outcomes	Assessment opportunity and evidence	Level 2	Level 3	Success criteria
Keeping a journal Children can use a reading journal (on paper or on screen) and can use it in a variety of ways to record, explore and extend their own reading.	• Supported group activity where children explore the uses of a writer's journal and write a synopsis of a story. • Children's oral responses. • Teacher's notes. • Children's completed synopses.	**Writing AF3** • Some basic sequencing of ideas or material. • Openings and/or closings sometimes signalled.	**Writing AF3** • Some attempt to organise ideas with related points placed next to each other. • Openings and closings usually signalled. • Some attempt to sequence ideas or material logically.	• I can summarise a story. • I can identify and sequence the main events in a story.
A character's log Children can use a reading journal (on paper or on screen) and can use it in a variety of ways to record, explore and extend their own reading.	• Group activity where children identify uses of a log. • Children's oral responses. • Teacher's notes.	**Reading AF2** • Some specific, straightforward information recalled. • Generally clear idea of where to look for information.	**Reading AF2** • Simple, most obvious points identified though there may also be some misunderstanding. • Some comments include quotations from or references to text, but not always relevant.	• I can identify the features of a log written by a story character. • I can understand why the character uses his log.
Dad's log Children can use a reading journal (on paper or on screen) and can use it in a variety of ways to record, explore and extend their own reading.	• Supported activity where children write a log. • Children's oral responses and written sentences. • Teacher's notes.	**Writing AF2** • Some basic purpose established. • Some appropriate features of the given form used. • Some attempts to adopt appropriate style.	**Writing AF2** • Purpose established at a general level. • Main features of selected form sometimes signalled to the reader. • Some attempts at appropriate style, with attention to reader.	I can write a log entry from another character's point of view.

Phase ② activities pages 53-55

Learning outcomes	Assessment opportunity and evidence	Level 2	Level 3	Success criteria
Kensuke's character profile Children can use a range of drama and other techniques to explore characters and their conflicts and dilemmas and extend their response to stories.	• Supported group activity where children choose the right descriptions of Kensuke from multiple-choice answers. • Children's oral responses and completed interactives. • Teacher's notes.	**Reading AF3** • Simple, plausible inference about events and information, using evidence from text. • Comments made on textual cues, sometimes misunderstood.	**Reading AF3** • Straightforward inference based on a single point of reference in the text. • Responses to text show meaning established at a literal level.	• I can identify and record words and phrases to describe a character. • I can discuss a character using notes from my profile sheet.
Hot spot Interviews Children can use a range of drama and other techniques to explore characters and their conflicts and dilemmas and extend their response to stories.	• Paired activity where children write interview questions for two characters and use them to interview each other. • Children's oral responses, discussions and written interviews.	**Reading AF3** • Simple, plausible inference about events and information, using evidence from text. • Comments made on textual cues, sometimes misunderstood.	**Reading AF3** • Straightforward inference based on a single point of reference in the text. • Responses to text show meaning established at a literal level.	• I can write interview questions to ask a character. • I can identify and explore a conflict between two characters. • I can understand different points of view of two characters.

Unit 3 📖 Authors and texts

Learning outcomes	Assessment opportunity and evidence	Assessment focuses (AFs)		Success criteria
		Level 2	Level 3	
Phase ③ activities pages 55–57				
Telegram sentences Children can use a range of drama and other techniques to explore characters and their conflicts and dilemmas and extend their response to stories.	● Paired activity where children explore how short sentences create an effect in dialogue. ● Children's oral responses, discussions and dialogue. ● Completed interactives.	**Reading AF2** ● Some specific, straightforward information recalled. ● Generally clear idea of where to look for information. **Reading AF5** ● Some effective language choices noted. ● Some familiar patterns of language identified.	**Reading AF2** ● Simple, most obvious points identified though there may also be some misunderstanding. ● Some comments include quotations from or references to text, but not always relevant. **Reading AF5** ● A few basic features of writer's use of language identified, but with little or no comment.	● I can identify the use of short sentences to create an effect in a story. ● I can use role play to create an effect in dialogue.
Feeling words Children can use a range of drama and other techniques to explore characters and their conflicts and dilemmas and extend their response to stories.	● Independent or paired activity where children discuss words that describe feelings and sort two sets of feeling words. ● Children's oral responses. ● Completed interactives.	**Reading AF5** ● Some effective language choices noted. ● Some familiar patterns of language identified. **Writing AF7** ● Simple, often speech-like vocabulary conveys relevant meanings. ● Some adventurous word choices.	**Reading AF5** ● A few basic features of writer's use of language identified, but with little or no comment. **Writing AF7** ● Simple, generally appropriate vocabulary used, limited in range. ● Some words selected for effect or occasion.	I can recognise words that describe different feelings.
Phase ④ activity page 57				
Evaluating reading logs Children can demonstrate how they can use a reading journal to help them reflect on a text.	● Paired activity where children evaluate each other's reading journals to agreed criteria and review their own work. ● Children's evaluations and revised work.	**Reading AF6** ● Some awareness that writers have viewpoints and purposes. ● Simple statements about likes and dislikes in reading, sometimes with reasons.	**Reading AF6** ● Comments identify main purpose. ● Express personal response but with little awareness of writer's viewpoint or effect on reader.	● I can evaluate my reading journal work and that of others. ● I can explain how my reading journal has helped me to find out more about a book. ● I can decide what needs more work in my reading journal and how to improve it.

Learning outcomes	Assessment opportunity and evidence	Assessment focuses (AFs)		Success criteria
		Level 4	Level 5	
Phase ① activities pages 50–52				
Keeping a journal Children can use a reading journal (on paper or on screen) and can use it in a variety of ways to record, explore and extend their own reading.	● Independent activity where children explore the uses of a writer's journal and write a synopsis of a story. ● Children's oral responses. ● Teacher's notes. ● Children's completed synopses.	**Writing AF3** ● Ideas organised by clustering related points or by time sequence. ● Ideas are organised simply with a fitting opening and closing, sometimes linked. ● Ideas or material generally in logical sequence but overall direction of writing not always clearly signalled.	**Writing AF3** ● Material is structured clearly, with sentences organised into appropriate paragraphs. ● Development of material is effectively managed across text. ● Overall direction of the text supported by clear links between paragraphs.	● I can summarise a story. ● I can identify and sequence the main events in a story.

Unit 3 🔲 Authors and texts

Learning outcomes	Assessment opportunity and evidence	Assessment focuses (AFs)		Success criteria
		Level 4	Level 5	
A character's log Children can use a reading journal (on paper or on screen) and can use it in a variety of ways to record, explore and extend their own reading.	• Group activity where children identify uses of a log. • Children's oral responses. • Teacher's notes.	**Reading AF2** • Some relevant points identified. • Comments supported by some generally relevant textual reference or quotation,	**Reading AF2** • Most relevant points clearly identified, including those selected from different places in the text. • Comments generally supported by relevant textual reference or quotation, even when points made are not always accurate.	• I can identify the features of a log written by a story character. • I can understand why the character uses his log.
Dad's log Children can use a reading journal (on paper or on screen) and can use it in a variety of ways to record, explore and extend their own reading.	• Independent activity where children write a log. • Children's oral responses and completed logs. • Teacher's notes.	**Writing AF2** • Main purpose of writing is clear but not always consistently maintained. • Main features of selected form are clear and appropriate to purpose. • Style generally appropriate to task, though awareness of reader not always sustained.	**Writing AF2** • Main purpose of writing is clear and consistently maintained. • Features of selected form clearly established with some adaptation to purpose. • Appropriate style clearly established to maintain reader's interest throughout.	I can write a log entry from another character's point of view.

Phase ② activities pages 53–55

Kensuke's character profile Children can use a range of drama and other techniques to explore characters and their conflicts and dilemmas and extend their response to stories.	• Independent and paired activity where children compile a character profile of Kensuke. • Children's oral responses and completed profiles. • Teacher's notes.	**Reading AF3** • Comments make inferences based on evidence from different points in the text. • Inferences often correct, but comments are not always rooted securely in the text or repeat narrative or content.	**Reading AF3** • Comments develop explanation of inferred meanings drawing on evidence across the text. • Comments make inferences and deductions based on textual evidence.	• I can identify and record words and phrases to describe a character. • I can discuss a character using notes from my profile sheet.
Hot spot Interviews Children can use a range of drama and other techniques to explore characters and their conflicts and dilemmas and extend their response to stories.	• Paired activity where children write interview questions for two characters and use them to interview each other. • Children's oral responses, discussions and written interviews.	**Reading AF3** • Comments make inferences based on evidence from different points in the text. • Inferences often correct, but comments are not always rooted securely in the text or repeat narrative or content.	**Reading AF3** • Comments develop explanation of inferred meanings drawing on evidence across the text. • Comments make inferences and deductions based on textual evidence.	• I can write interview questions to ask a character. • I can identify and explore a conflict between two characters. • I can understand different points of view of two characters.

Unit 3 📖 Authors and texts

Learning outcomes	Assessment opportunity and evidence	Assessment focuses (AFs)		Success criteria
		Level 4	Level 5	
Phase ③ activities pages 55–57				
Telegram sentences Children can use a range of drama and other techniques to explore characters and their conflicts and dilemmas and extend their response to stories.	● Paired activity where children explore how short sentences create an effect in dialogue. ● Children's oral responses, discussions and dialogue. ● Completed interactives.	**Reading AF2** ● Some relevant points identified. ● Comments supported by some generally relevant textual reference or quotation. **Reading AF5** ● Some basic features of writer's use of language identified. ● Simple comments on writer's choices.	**Reading AF2** ● Most relevant points clearly identified, including those selected from different places in the text. ● Comments generally supported by relevant textual reference or quotation, even when points made are not always accurate. **Reading AF5** ● Various features of writer's use of language identified, with some explanation. ● Comments show some awareness of the effect of writer's language.	● I can identify the use of short sentences to create an effect in a story. ● I can use role play to create an effect in dialogue.
Feeling words Children can use a range of drama and other techniques to explore characters and their conflicts and dilemmas and extend their response to stories.	● Independent or paired activity where children discuss words that describe feelings and sort two sets of feeling words. ● Children's oral responses. ● Completed interactives.	**Reading AF5** ● Some basic features of writer's use of language identified. ● Simple comments on writer's choices. **Writing AF7** ● Some evidence of deliberate vocabulary choices. ● Some expansion of general vocabulary to match topic.	**Reading AF5** ● Various features of writer's use of language identified, with some explanation. ● Comments show some awareness of the effect of writer's language choices. **Writing AF7** ● Vocabulary chosen for effect. ● Reasonably wide vocabulary used, though not always appropriately.	I can recognise words that describe different feelings.
Phase ④ activity page 57				
Evaluating reading logs Children can demonstrate how they can use a reading journal to help them reflect on a text.	● Paired activity where children evaluate each other's reading journals to agreed criteria and review their own work. ● Children's evaluations and revised work.	**Reading AF6** ● Main purpose identified.. ● Simple comments show some awareness of writer's viewpoint. ● Simple comment on overall effect on reader.	**Reading AF6** ● Main purpose clearly identified, often through general overview. ● Viewpoints in texts clearly identified, with some, often limited, explanation. ● General awareness of effect on the reader, with some, often limited, explanation.	● I can evaluate my reading journal work and that of others. ● I can explain how my reading journal has helped me to find out more about a book. ● I can decide what needs more work in my reading journal and how to improve it.

NARRATIVE

Phase ① Keeping a journal

Learning outcome
Children can use a reading journal (on paper or on screen) and can use it in a variety of ways to record, explore and extend their own reading.

Success criteria
- I can summarise a story.
- I can identify and sequence the main events in a story.

Setting the context
With the children revise the use of journals, diaries, logs, and weblogs. Explain that writers keep journals to help them with their writing. Ask: *What might writers include in their journals?* Examples should include descriptions of settings, characters, plots and ideas, dialogue, interesting words and pictures, and so on. Display the photocopiable page 'Synopsis of Kensuke's Kingdom' by Alison Milford. Highlight that it is an outline of the story, which the author might have written in a journal. Explain to the children that they are going to write a synopsis of a story they know.

Assessment opportunity
Children at levels 2-3 write simple sentences within a supported group about a story that they have recently read in their guided reading group. The children at levels 4-5 independently choose a story by Michael Morpurgo or another well-known author. Ask them to each write out an outline of the story using the synopsis example as a model. Once all the children have written their synopsis, have a class plenary where the children read out their synopsis. Discuss what other information the writer might include in the journal for that story. Take notes of individual children's responses.

Assessment evidence
At levels 2-3, children should be able to select, identify and sequence correctly the main events of the story in simple sentence format. At levels 4-5, children should write their synopses in the form of a journal. The completed synopses will provide evidence against Writing AF3.

Next steps
Support: For children who find it hard to create a synopsis, have a group discussion on one area that could be in the writer's journal such as characters. Allow them to draw and label the characters.
Extension: Encourage the children to extend the writer's story journal by adding story maps, character profiles and interesting words. Stress that the information doesn't have to be neat and organised.

Key aspects of learning
Evaluation: Children will share responses orally and in writing. They will discuss success criteria, give feedback to others and judge the effectiveness of their own work.
Empathy: In discussing and writing about the books or stories, children will need to imagine themselves in another person's position. They will explore techniques that facilitate this process.
Communication: Children will develop their ability to discuss and debate issues and personal responses both in respect of the form and the content of the stories they are reading and the journals they are creating. They will often work collaboratively in pairs and groups. They will communicate outcomes orally, in writing and through other modes and media.

Phase ① A character's log

Learning outcome
Children can use a reading journal (on paper or on screen) and can use it in a variety of ways to record, explore and extend their own reading.

Success criteria
- I can identify the features of a log written by a story character.
- I can understand why the character uses his log.

Setting the context
Introduce the use of a log. Explain how a log could be used to record basic facts or thoughts, events and feelings about a journey. Display and read out the photocopiable page 'Kensuke's Kingdom (a)'. Explain that the boy is sailing round the world on a boat with his parents and dog. Explain to the children that they are going to look closely at the text to identify why and how the boy uses his ship's log.

Assessment opportunity
Put the children into their guided reading groups and give them each a copy of the extract. Children at levels 2-3 listen as an adult reads the text slowly. The children stop the adult reading when an example of the boy's use of the log is read out. Record their findings. Ask children at levels 4-5 to highlight examples or quotes from the text that explain the boy's ideas behind his journal and how he is going to use it. Once they have completed the task, encourage the children to share their findings within their groups. Take notes of the groups' discussion.

Assessment evidence
At levels 2-3, children's findings may include responses such as 'It's short', 'He can write what he wants', 'It's personal'. At levels 4-5, children may highlight examples such as, 'This was my own version of the ship's log' and 'My own personal, private record of our voyage'. Use the children's responses and discussion as evidence against Reading AF2.

Next steps:
Support: Some children may find it hard to identify examples of why and how the boy's log is used. Discuss how they would use a ship's log if they were going on a trip round the world. Encourage them to write down their ideas.
Extension: Encourage the children to design a log. Would it have places to put sailing information such as tide times, wind directions, weather reports?

Key aspects of learning
Enquiry: Children will identify their own key questions about the work of a particular writer, and then locate the evidence to answer them.
Information processing: Children will respond to information or stimuli from a range of sources on paper and on screen and compare, combine and orchestrate this as a basis for both oral and written communication.
Empathy: In discussing and writing about the books or stories, children will need to imagine themselves in another person's position. They will explore techniques that facilitate this process.
Communication: Children will develop their ability to discuss and debate issues and personal responses both in respect of the form and the content of the stories they are reading and the journals they are creating. They will often work collaboratively in pairs and groups. They will communicate outcomes orally, in writing and through other modes and media.

NARRATIVE

Phase ① Dad's log

Learning outcome
Children can use a reading journal (on paper or on screen) and can use it in a variety of ways to record, explore and extend their own reading.

Success criteria
I can write a log entry from another character's point of view.

Setting the context
Remind the children how journals, diaries and logs can be used to record events, thoughts and information. Explain to the class that they are going to keep a reading journal about *Kensuke's Kingdom.* Display and read the photocopiable page 'Kensuke's Kingdom (b)'. Ask: *What do you think happened next?* List their ideas on the board and then tell them what happened (refer to the Synopsis). Ask: *When do you think the boy's parents realised he was missing? How did they feel? What did they think had happened? What did they do next?* Ask the children to imagine that they are the boy's dad and explain that in their reading journal they are going to write his log entry for the day after the boy fell off the boat.

Assessment opportunity
Children at levels 2-3 may need adult support in reading the extract. Children at levels 4-5 read the extract independently. Ask all the children to make a note of clues that give information, such as mum being ill, no rudder cable, possible mayday call, no harness clip for the dog. Using the clues and their imaginations the children write 'Dad's log'. Walk round the class as the children create their log and ask discussion questions. Take note of their responses. Children at levels 2-3 work with support to write simple sentences in chronological order illustrated with pictures. Encourage all the children to share their completed logs with the class and compare them to the success criteria.

Assessment evidence
Children at levels 2-3 may record simple statements in a log style with simple comments made by the character, for example: '9am. We sailed round and round but we could not see Michael or Stella.' Children at levels 4-5 may record how the father feels, his actions and the recording of log events, such as: 'It is 9am and we've been sailing round in circles for two hours. Where is he? Where is my son?' Use the children's responses about the extract and their own written work as evidence against Writing AF2.

Next Steps
Support: For children struggling to create a log for the dad, suggest they create a visual record of events based on the boy's log, adding simple sentences under the pictures.
Extension: Encourage children to create a newspaper report about the missing boy. What would the headline be? Include an interview from the parents and add diagrams and maps.

Key aspects of learning
Enquiry: Children will identify their own key questions about the work of a particular writer, and then locate the evidence to answer them.
Information processing: Children will respond to information or stimuli from a range of sources on paper and on screen and compare, combine and orchestrate this as a basis for both oral and written communication.
Empathy: In discussing and writing about the books or stories, children will need to imagine themselves in another person's position. They will explore techniques that facilitate this process.
Communication: Children will develop their ability to discuss and debate issues and personal responses both in respect of the form and the content of the stories they are reading and the journals they are creating. They will often work collaboratively in pairs and groups. They will communicate outcomes orally, in writing and through other modes and media.

Phase ② Kensuke's character profile

Learning outcome
Children can use a range of drama and other techniques to explore characters and their conflicts and dilemmas and extend their response to stories.

Success criteria
● I can identify and record words and phrases to describe a character.
● I can discuss a character using notes from my profile sheet.

Setting the context
Remind the children how a character can be described through their actions and visual descriptions. Give the children copies of the photocopiable page 'Kensuke's Kingdom (c)'. Ask: *What characters are in the extract? Which character stands out?* (Kensuke). *Why does he stand out more than the boy?* Model how the extract gives clues about Kensuke's character, such as the way he moves, how and what he says, how he behaves. Explain to the children that they are going to find and record words and phrases that describe Kensuke.

Assessment opportunity
Children at levels 2–3 work in a group with support on the interactive activity 'Kensuke's character profile'. Display the screen so that the children can see it. Ask them to choose the right description of Kensuke from multiple-choice answers. Record the children's choices and reasons. Children at levels 4–5 will individually record examples on the photocopiable page 'Kensuke's character profile'. They can discuss with a pair-share partner the descriptions they recorded. Once all the children have completed their activities, encourage them to draw a picture of how they visualise Kensuke. If time, have a class plenary for the children to discuss their profiles and pictures and their feelings about Kensuke.

Assessment evidence
Children at levels 2–3 should be able to infer simple information from the text. For example, discuss the description options of Kensuke and how they imagine him to be. They may say 'Kensuke is a very old man.' Children at levels 4–5 should be able to infer more details, for example Kensuke is described as 'moving fast, running almost' would imply that while he was old he was quite fit. Note their responses on it by listening to their discussion with their pair–share partner and in the class plenary, for example, 'I feel that he is very wary and resentful of the boy.' Use the children's responses as a class, pairs and groups and the written profiles as evidence against Reading AF3.

Next steps
Support: Some children may find it hard to extract or remember information about Kensuke or understand how certain words or phrases can describe his character. Choose one area, such as the way he looks, and ask the children to draw a picture and write a simple caption.
Extension: Encourage children to read the end of the book and produce another character profile and picture of Kensuke. Ask the children how he has changed and why?

Key aspects of learning
Enquiry: Children will identify their own key questions about the work of a particular writer, and then locate the evidence to answer them.
Evaluation: Children will share responses orally and in writing. They will discuss success criteria, give feedback to others and judge the effectiveness of their own work.
Reasoning: Children will construct reasoned arguments based on their views and responses to the books or stories read.
Communication: Children will develop their ability to discuss and debate issues and personal responses both in respect of the form and the content of the stories they are reading and the journals they are creating. They will often work collaboratively in pairs and groups. They will communicate outcomes orally, in writing and through other modes and media.

Phase ② Hot spot interviews

Learning outcome
Children can use a range of drama and other techniques to explore characters and their conflicts and dilemmas and extend their response to stories.

Success criteria
- I can write interview questions to ask a character.
- I can identify and explore a conflict between two characters.
- I can understand different points of view of two characters.

Setting the context
Remind the children how in most stories there are conflicts between two characters. Discuss how, by looking at each character's point of view, the children can make their decisions about the conflicts. Put the children into mixed ability groups of four and display the photocopiable page 'Kensuke's Kingdom (c)'. Before you read it to them, ask the children to concentrate on what the conflict or problem is between Kensuke and the boy. Explain that Kensuke and the boy have each agreed to do a hot spot interview about the conflict and the event and that they will be writing interview questions to put to the characters. Display the success criteria in the classroom.

Assessment opportunity
Read the extract. Ask: *Why do you think Kensuke was angry? Why didn't he want a fire? Why do you think he wanted the island split in half? What do you think the boy felt when he first saw Kensuke? Why did he want a fire? What did he feel about Kensuke at the end of the extract?* Split each group into two pairs and ask one pair to write a set of interview questions for Kensuke and the other pair to write a set for the boy, Michael. Once the pairs have completed their interview questions, let them take turns interviewing each other. Walk round the groups and make observational notes. Encourage the groups to feed back on their interviews to the class. Invite the children to re-enact the interviews to the class. Which character gets the most sympathy and understanding?

Assessment evidence
Children at levels 2–3 should be able to ask and answer questions that highlight the two characters' feelings about the conflict and their reasons for their actions, such as 'Why were you so angry at the boy?' 'I did not want him to light a fire.' They should be able to discuss and recognise the basic points of view of the characters. Children at levels 4–5 will be able to investigate the characters in greater depth, such as 'Why couldn't you explain peacefully why you did not want the boy to light the fire?' They should be able to debate and discuss their feelings about the characters in more depth. Use the children's responses and their written interviews as evidence against Reading AF3.

Next steps
Support: Encourage children to act out, in pairs, the event from the extract. Highlight how the characters would move and talk to convey their problems effectively to an audience. Afterwards discuss how the children felt about the conflicts.
Extension: Encourage children to film the interviews. Beforehand, discuss how the characters would move and talk to convey their case effectively. Play back the film and discuss the characters and their feelings.

Key aspects of learning
Information processing: Children will respond to information or stimuli from a range of sources on paper and on screen and compare, combine and orchestrate this as a basis for both oral and written communication.
Evaluation: Children will share responses orally and in writing. They will discuss success criteria, give feedback to others and judge the effectiveness of their own work.
Reasoning: Children will construct reasoned arguments based on their views and responses to the books or stories read.

Empathy: In discussing and writing about the books or stories, children will need to imagine themselves in another person's position. They will explore techniques that facilitate this process.

Communication: Children will develop their ability to discuss and debate issues and personal responses both in respect of the form and the content of the stories they are reading and the journals they are creating. They will often work collaboratively in pairs and groups. They will communicate outcomes orally, in writing and through other modes and media.

Phase ③ Telegram sentences

Learning outcome

Children can use a range of drama and other techniques to explore characters and their conflicts and dilemmas and extend their response to stories.

Success criteria

● I can identify the use of short sentences to create an effect in a story.
● I can use role play to create an effect in dialogue.

Setting the context

Children will need to be familiar with the story *Kensuke's Kingdom* or have read the 'Synopsis of Kensuke's Kingdom'. Remind the children how different types of sentences can have different effects on a story text - for example, to create an atmosphere, highlight thoughts, pace, impact and action. Display the photocopiable page 'Kensuke's Kingdom (c)'. Use a highlighter to show the dialogue. Emphasise the use of short sentences, single words, no conjunctions, and the lack of descriptive vocabulary. Discuss why the writer wrote the dialogue in that way - for example, to convey that the characters do not speak the same language, to communicate important messages in the simplest way. Show how the writer describes how the characters speak or act to underline their words. Explain to the children that they are going to use short sentences to create an effect in dialogue.

Assessment opportunity

Put the children in mixed ability pairs so that one child is Kensuke and the other is Michael. Kensuke tries to find out from Michael why he is on the island and Michael tries to describe what happened and how he needs help to get home. Invite the children to talk in short sentences of up to five words. Walk around and observe the use of words and actions. Encourage the children to perform their dialogue to other pairs or the class and to evaluate each other's performance. Record examples of words, sentences and actions and discuss their effect with the children. Assess the children's responses as the sentences are recorded on the board. Identify which children are able to use effective words to bring over a message. Which children understood the use of short sentences as effective dialogue?

Assessment evidence

At levels 2-3, children should be able to create short sentences that cover the basic events and reflect a few of the basic features from the text. For example, 'I fell into the water', 'Who are you?' At levels 4-5, children should be able to create short sentences that reflect the fact that the two characters do not speak the same language. The completed interactive activity will provide evidence against Reading AF2 and AF5.

Next steps

Support: Invite those who find it hard to create a conversation dialogue to write a message in a bottle sent by Michael in their reading journals. It has to be short and to the point.

Extension: Encourage children to write their dialogues in their reading journals. Did they use punctuation, such as exclamation marks, to help get the message over? How did they describe the actions and where did they place them - before the dialogue, in the middle or at the end?

Unit 3 ▢ Authors and texts

▷ **Key aspects of learning**

Information processing: Children will respond to information or stimuli from a range of sources on paper and on screen and compare, combine and orchestrate this as a basis for both oral and written communication.

Empathy: In discussing and writing about the books or stories, children will need to imagine themselves in another person's position. They will explore techniques that facilitate this process.

Communication: Children will develop their ability to discuss and debate issues and personal responses both in respect of the form and the content of the stories they are reading and the journals they are creating. They will often work collaboratively in pairs and groups. They will communicate outcomes orally, in writing and through other modes and media.

Phase ③ Feeling words

Learning outcome
Children can use a range of drama and other techniques to explore characters and their conflicts and dilemmas and extend their response to stories.

Success criteria
I can recognise words that describe different feelings.

Setting the context
This assessment can be carried out during a literacy session. The children work in pairs or individually. Children at levels 2-3 can work on version 1 of the interactive activity 'Feeling words' and children at levels 4-5 can work on version 2 of the interactive activity. Remind the children how descriptive words can be used to describe different aspects of a story. Explain that the author uses descriptive words to convey Kensuke's and the boy's mood and feelings when they first meet. Write some examples on the board, such as 'aggressive', 'agitated' versus 'relieved'.

Assessment opportunity
The children use the interactive activity to sort out two sets of words that describe the feelings of being worried or excited. As they work, discuss and record the children's selection. Once the children at levels 2-3 have completed the activity, ask them for examples of sentences that include the words and show the feelings of a character. Write them out for the children to see. For children at levels 4-5, print off their final choices and ask them to write effective sentences that include each of the descriptive feeling words. Ask all the children which sentence examples were the most effective in describing feelings? Why?

Assessment evidence
Children at levels 2-3 should be able to create simple sentences to show a character's feelings, such as 'Jodie was thrilled with the present'. Children at levels 4-5 should organise the descriptive words into the correct feeling boxes. They should identify that the words are adjectives and descriptive verbs. Sentences should be imaginative and may include dialogue such as '"Welcome!" he said, with an enthusiastic flourish of his hands'. Use the children's responses and their sentence work as evidence against Reading AF5 and Writing AF7.

Next steps
Support: Encourage children to create a wordbank of feeling words they recognise or that have simple spelling patterns, such as 'happy', 'sad', 'glad', 'jolly', 'low', 'cross'.
Extension: Encourage children to use a thesaurus to create a feeling wordbank. Suggest feeling categories such as 'happy', 'sad', 'excited', 'bored', 'angry', 'upset', 'scared', 'surprised', 'confused'.

Key aspects of learning
Information processing: Children will respond to information or stimuli from a range of sources on paper and on screen and compare, combine and orchestrate this as a basis for both oral and written communication.

Communication: Children will develop their ability to discuss and debate issues and personal responses both in respect of the form and the content of the stories they are reading and the journals they are creating. They will often work collaboratively in pairs and groups. They will communicate outcomes orally, in writing and through other modes and media.

Phase ④ Evaluating reading logs

Learning outcome
Children can demonstrate how they can use a reading journal to help them reflect on a text.

Success criteria
- I can evaluate my reading journal work and that of others.
- I can explain how my reading journal has helped me to find out more about a book.
- I can decide what needs more work in my reading journal and how to improve it.

Setting the context
Use this activity when the children have produced a range of work in their reading journals around the work of an author. Display the success criteria in the classroom. As a class, discuss the different work recorded in their reading journal. Discuss the use of the journal and how it has helped them to find out more about their chosen author and book. Explain that they are going to pass their journals to a response partner (of similar ability) who will evaluate the work to class-agreed criteria. Revise the success criteria of each item in the logs. Use these to discuss and agree evaluation criteria. Write the criteria on the board.

Assessment opportunity
Children at levels 2–3 can read their response partner's journal and identify areas that work well with a chosen icon. Use another icon to show areas that need work. The children discuss their findings with their partner and revise their own work. Using the agreed evaluation criteria, children at levels 4–5 should read their partner's journal and record the good points of each piece of work and the areas that need improvement, giving ideas on how to achieve this. They discuss each other's findings and then review their own work. Ask: *Was the evaluation helpful? What areas do you want to improve or revise? How will you do this?* Allow the children time to revise their work. In a class plenary the pairs report back, discuss and display their revised texts. How have they improved?

Assessment evidence
Children at levels 2–3 may look at use of words, simple sentences: 'You use "and" too much. Try using "however" or turn the sentence into two sentences.' Children at levels 4–5 will evaluate the journals, noting how effectively each item has achieved the success criteria, for example, 'This entry needs more descriptive vocabulary to explain a character's feelings' or 'This entry does not use typical log features. You need to cut down the sentence length'. Use the children's evaluations and revision of their work as evidence against Reading AF6.

Next steps
Support: For children needing support, have a group discussion about their own agreed criteria or a one-to-one agreed criteria, which may be on a more simplistic level, such as 'I have written five descriptive sentences showing Kensuke's feelings'.
Extension: Encourage children to produce a class anthology reading journal. Discuss its design and ways of including pictures, photos and diagrams, and so on.

Key aspects of learning
Evaluation: Children will share responses orally and in writing. They will discuss success criteria, give feedback to others and judge the effectiveness of their own work.

NARRATIVE

Periodic assessment

Reading

Learning outcome
Children can use a range of drama and other techniques to explore characters and their conflicts and dilemmas and extend their response to stories.

Success criteria
- I can identify and use information in a text to answer questions.
- I can build up a profile of a fictional character.
- I can understand the use and features of a diary.

Setting the context
Display the success criteria in the classroom. Put the children into their guided reading groups and explain that they are going to look at an extract of a fictional diary. In discussion, remind the children why people use diaries - for example, as a personal record of events and feelings. List the features of a diary, such as written in the first person, a date, conversational language, descriptions of events, dialogue and actions. Display the photocopiable page 'Narrative 3 Reading assessment text' and read it out. Explain that they will use the extract to answer the questions on the photocopiable and will then evaluate their work against the success criteria. Provide all the children with copies of the photocopiable page 'Narrative 3 Reading assessment'.

Assessment opportunity
As the children work, discuss the clues in the text that can help them answer questions such as: *How do you know the diary is set in the past? How did Jake learn to write? How do you know Jake is excited about going to sea? Why has Jake decided to start writing a diary? What is Jake's uncle like? What is Jake looking forward to doing?* Once they have finished, encourage the children in the discussion groups with support to discuss their findings within their group. Ask the children working at levels 4-5 to use a response partner to discuss what they have found out about Jake. Ask all the children to check their work against the success criteria and discuss what they have achieved and ways they could extend their understanding.

Assessment evidence
Children at levels 2-3 should find examples such as 'I think Jake likes Will because he tells stories and makes Jake laugh'. Children at levels 4-5 should record examples such as 'Jake's dad wants him to be a doctor' and then be able discuss reasons: 'I think his dad thinks Jake will be a better doctor if he experiences different situations and people'. Use the children's responses and written work to make level judgements against Reading AF2, AF6 and AF7.

Periodic assessment

Writing

Learning outcome
Children can use a range of drama and other techniques to explore characters and their conflicts and dilemmas and extend their response to stories.

Success criteria
● I can discuss an event in the text from different points of view.
● I can write a letter about an event from a different character's point of view.

Setting the context
Display the photocopiable page, 'Narrative 3 Writing assessment text'. Remind the children that the diary is written by Jake, a ten-year-old boy, nearly 300 years ago. Read the extract to the children. Ask them to imagine that they are the sailor who whipped his friend. Briefly discuss the chronology of the event. Ask: *What do you think the sailor felt or did during the day until sundown? Did he plan to choose the low card? How do you think he felt as he whipped his friend? What did he feel towards the captain? What happened after the whipping?* Explain to the children that they are going to write a letter relating what had happened and how, as the sailor, they felt. Discuss who the letter might be for – a loved one, a friend, a complaint to the ship's owner. Remind children how to set out a letter. Display the success criteria in the classroom.

Assessment opportunity
Children at levels 2-3 work in a supported group. Give out the photocopiable page 'Narrative 3 Writing assessment' and note that the letter is to the sailor's brother. Record the children's discussions about how the sailor felt about the event. The children use their ideas to independently write the letter in the frame on the photocopiable. Children at levels 4-5 work independently to make notes of the order of events and their ideas about what the sailor felt, did or said. Before writing the letters have a pair–share session where the children can discuss and compare their ideas and notes. Record their discussion and oral responses. Encourage all the children to read out their finished letters and discuss the different ways the character related the event. Invite the children to use the success criteria to evaluate their own work and that of others.

Assessment evidence
The children at levels 2-3 show a simple, logical sequence of events. They use descriptive words to describe the feelings of the sailor and the whipped man. 'I was very upset. I was shaking.' Children at levels 4-5 should show the logical sequence of events but from another point of view. They write their letters in the correct style of language relating to the recipient – for example, formal for an official complaint, informal for an emotive letter. Use the children's responses and their written work to make level judgements against Writing AF1 and AF2.

NARRATIVE

Kensuke's Kingdom (a)

It was on watch at night that I would often do my 'English'. This was my own version of the ship's log. I didn't have to show it to them, but I was encouraged to write in it every few weeks. It would be, they said, my own personal, private record of our voyage.

At school I had never been much good at writing. I could never think of what to write or how to begin. But on the *Peggy Sue* I found I could open up my log and just write. There was always so much I wanted to say. And that's the thing. I found I didn't really write it down at all. Rather, I said it. I spoke it from my head, down my arm, through my fingers and my pencil, and on to the page. And that's how it reads to me now, all these years later, like me talking.

I'm looking at my log now. The paper is a bit crinkled and the pages are yellowed with age. My scribbly writing is a little faded, but it's mostly quite legible. What follows are just a few chosen extracts from this log. The entries are quite short, but they tell the tale. This is how I recorded our great journey. This is how it was for an eleven-year-old boy as we rode the wide oceans of the world on board the *Peggy Sue*.

Text © 1999, Michael Morpurgo. Illustration © 1999, Michael Foreman (1999, Egmont UK).

Kensuke's Kingdom (b)

July 28

I look around me. It's a dark, dark night. No moon. No stars. But it's calm again, at last. I'll be twelve tomorrow, but I don't think anyone except me will remember it.

We've had a terrible time, far worse even than in the Bay of Biscay. Ever since we left Sydney, it's been just storm after storm, and each one blows us further north across the Coral Sea. The rudder cable has snapped. Dad's done what he can, but it's still not right. The self-steering doesn't work any more, so someone's got to be at the wheel all the time. And that means Dad or me, because Mum is sick. It's her stomach cramps  *again, but they're a lot worse. She doesn't want to eat at all. All she has is sugared water. She hasn't been able to look at the charts for three days. Dad wants to put out a May Day call, but Mum won't let him. She says that's giving in, and she's never giving in. Dad and I have been doing the navigation together. We've been doing our best, but I don't think we know where we are any more.*

They're both asleep down below. Dad's really wiped out. I'm at the wheel in the cockpit. I've got Eddie's football with me. It's been lucky for us so far. And now we really need it. We need Mum to get better, or we're in real trouble. I don't know if we could stand another storm.

Thank God it's calm. It'll help Mum to sleep. You can't sleep when you're being slammed about all the time.

It is so dark out there. Black. Stella's barking. She's up by the bow. She hasn't got her harness clipped on.

Those were the last words I ever wrote in my log. After that it's just empty pages.

NARRATIVE

UNIT 4 Short stories with flashbacks

Literacy objectives

Speak and listen for a wide range of purposes in different contexts

Strand 1 Speaking
● Use a range of oral techniques to present persuasive arguments and engaging narratives.

Strand 2 Listening and responding
● Make notes when listening for a sustained period and discuss how note-taking varies depending on context and purpose.

Read and write for a range of purposes on paper and on screen

Strand 6 Word structure and spelling
● Use a range of appropriate strategies to edit, proofread and correct spelling in their own work, on paper and on screen.

Strand 7 Understanding and interpreting texts
● Understand underlying themes, causes and points of views.
● Understand how writers use different structures to create coherence and impact.

Strand 9 Creating and shaping texts
● Use different narrative techniques to engage and entertain the reader.
● Integrate words, images and sounds imaginatively for different purposes.

Strand 10 Text structure and organisation
● Use varied structures to shape and organise text coherently.

Key aspects of learning

Creative thinking
● Children will generate ideas for a short narrative in response to a short story.

Reasoning
● Children will discuss a short narrative film and give their opinions about the authorial intent, drawing inferences and making deductions from the text.

Empathy
● Children will identify triggers and causes of other people's emotions.

Evaluation
● Children will make judgements and justify their views and opinions, drawing on sources to support their evaluations. Children will discuss success criteria, give feedback to others and judge the effectiveness of their own work.

Information processing
● Children will explore information communicated through different modes and use this to create their own narrative.

Assessment focuses

Reading

AF3 *(deduce, infer or interpret information, events or ideas from texts).*
AF5 *(explain and comment on writers' use of language, including grammatical and literary features at word and sentence level).*
AF6 *(identify and comment on writers' purposes and viewpoints, and the overall effect of the text on the reader).*

Writing

AF4 *(construct paragraphs and use cohesion within and between paragraphs).*
AF5 *(vary sentences for clarity, purpose and effect).*

Speaking and listening

Speaking (speak with clarity, intonation and pace).
Listening and responding (understand and recall the main points; respond appropriately).

Resources

Phase 1 activities
Short story, 'My Father is a Polar Bear' in *From Hereabout Hill: A collection of short stories* by Michael Morpurgo (ISBN 978-0749-72872-4)
Photocopiable page, 'Mood cards'
Photocopiable page, 'My Father is a Polar Bear' (versions 1 and 2)
Phase 2 activities
Short story, 'My Father is a Polar Bear' in *From Hereabout Hill: A collection of short stories* by Michael Morpurgo (ISBN 978-0749-72872-4)
Photocopiable page, 'Paragraph planner'
Photocopiable page, 'Time shift paragraphs'
Interactive activity, 'Time shift paragraphs'
Phase 3 activities
Interactive activity, 'Conditional sentences'
Interactive activity, 'Which time connective?'
Periodic assessment
Photocopiable page, 'Narrative 4 Reading assessment text'
Photocopiable page, 'Narrative 4 Writing assessment'

Unit 4 ▢ Short stories with flashbacks

Learning outcomes	Assessment opportunity and evidence	Assessment focuses (AFs)		Success criteria
		Level 2	Level 3	
Phase ① activities pages 67–69				
Emotion graph Children can express views on how an author has used a range of techniques to indicate a specific mood in a text.	• Paired activity where children sort mood cards into the right order and plot an emotion graph of a character. • Children's oral responses and completed graphs.	**Reading AF3** • Simple, plausible inference about events and information, using evidence from text. • Comments made on textual cues, sometimes misunderstood.	**Reading AF3** • Straightforward inference based on a single point of reference in the text. • Responses to text show meaning established at a literal.	• I can identify the different moods of a character in a text. • I can understand how different moods are created in a text.
A feelings chart Children can express views on how an author has used a range of techniques to indicate a specific mood in a text.	• Supported group activity where children discuss how parts of a story affected them and complete a feelings chart. • Children's oral responses and completed charts.	**Reading AF6** • Some awareness that writers have viewpoints and purposes. • Simple statements about likes and dislikes in reading, sometimes with reasons.	**Reading AF6** • Comments identify main purpose. • Express personal response but with little awareness of writer's viewpoint or effect on reader.	• I can discuss and give reasons about how I felt about the story. • I can record how I felt about the mood in different parts of the story.
Shifts in time Children can identify a range of techniques used by an author to indicate shifts in time between past and present.	• Group activity where children discuss how text indicates a time shift. • Children's oral responses and discussion.	**Reading AF5** • Some effective language choices noted. • Some familiar patterns of language identified.	**Reading AF5** • A few basic features of writer's use of language identified, but with little or no comment.	• I can identify techniques used to indicate shifts in time. • I understand the effects that time-shift techniques have on a text.
Phase ② activities pages 70–71				
A paragraph planner Children can use paragraphs to structure their own writing and to create pace in a short narrative.	• Supported paired activity where children complete a paragraph planner. • Children's oral responses and completed photocopiables.	**Writing AF4** • Ideas in sections grouped by content, some linking by simple pronouns.	**Writing AF4** • Some internal structure within sections of text. • Within some paragraphs/sections, some links between sentences. • Movement between paragraphs/sections sometimes abrupt or disjointed.	• I can use a paragraph planner to plan out a story. • I can add ideas and notes for each paragraph on my planner. • I understand how a paragraph planner helps structure a story.
Time-shift paragraphs Children can use paragraphs to structure their own writing and to create pace in a short narrative.	• Paired activity where children choose suitable words to complete paragraphs that indicate time shifts. • Children's oral responses and completed interactives.	**Writing AF4** • Ideas in sections grouped by content, some linking by simple pronouns.	**Writing AF4** • Some internal structure within sections of text. • Within some paragraphs/sections, some links between sentences. • Movement between paragraphs/sections sometimes abrupt or disjointed.	• I can write sentences that indicate shifts in time. • I can write paragraphs that indicate shifts in time.

Unit 4 📖 Short stories with flashbacks

Learning outcomes	Assessment opportunity and evidence	Assessment focuses (AFs)		Success criteria
		Level 2	Level 3	
Phase ③ activities pages 72–73				
Effective sentences Children can use different narrative techniques to indicate the passage of time between past and present to engage a reader.	● Supported paired activity where children choose sentences that need more work and explore ways to improve them for a greater effect. ● Children's oral responses and revised sentences.	**Writing AF5** ● Some variation in sentence openings. ● Mainly simple sentences with *and* used to connect clauses. ● Past and present tense generally consistent.	**Writing AF5** ● Reliance mainly on simply structured sentences, variation with support. ● *and, but, so* are the most common connectives, subordination occasionally. ● Some limited variation in use of tense and verb forms, not always secure.	● I can create more pace in my story by using more effective sentences. ● I can use different techniques to indicate the passage of time.
Time-shift sentences Children can use different narrative techniques to indicate the passage of time between past and present to engage a reader.	● Independent or paired activity where children explore the use of time connectives and how to use them in their writing. ● Children's oral responses and revised sentences.	**Reading AF5** ● Some effective language choices noted. ● Some familiar patterns of language identified. **Writing AF4** ● Ideas in sections grouped by content, some linking by simple pronouns.	**Reading AF5** ● A few basic features of writer's use of language identified, but with little or no comment. **Writing AF4** ● Some internal structure within sections of text. ● Within some paragraphs/sections, some links between sentences. ● Movement between paragraphs/sections sometimes abrupt or disjointed.	● I can understand how conditional sentences can indicate time shifts. ● I can use conditional sentences indicating the passage of time in my story.

Learning outcomes	Assessment opportunity and evidence	Assessment focuses (AFs)		Success criteria
		Level 4	Level 5	
Phase ① activities pages 67–69				
Emotion graph Children can express views on how an author has used a range of techniques to indicate a specific mood in a text.	● Paired and independent activity where children sort mood cards into the right order and plot an emotion graph of a character. ● Children's oral responses and completed graphs.	**Reading AF3** ● Comments make inferences based on evidence from different points in the text. ● Inferences often correct, but comments are not always rooted securely in the text or repeat narrative or content.	**Reading AF3** ● Comments develop explanation of inferred meanings drawing on evidence across the text. ● Comments make inferences and deductions based on textual evidence.	● I can identify the different moods of a character in a text. ● I can understand how different moods are created in a text.
A feelings chart Children can express views on how an author has used a range of techniques to indicate a specific mood in a text.	● Independent and group activity where children discuss how parts of a story affected them and complete a feelings chart. ● Children's oral responses and completed charts.	**Reading AF6** ● Main purpose identified. ● Simple comments show some awareness of writer's viewpoint. ● Simple comment on overall effect on reader.	**Reading AF6** ● Main purpose clearly identified, often through general overview. ● Viewpoints in texts clearly identified, with some, often limited, explanation. ● General awareness of effect on the reader, with some, often limited, explanation.	● I can discuss and give reasons about how I felt about the story. ● I can record how I felt about the mood in different parts of the story.
Shifts in time Children can identify a range of techniques used by an author to indicate shifts in time between past and present.	● Paired activity where children analyse how an author indicates a time shift. ● Children's oral responses and discussion.	**Reading AF5** ● Some basic features of writer's use of language identified. ● Simple comments on writer's choices.	**Reading AF5** ● Various features of writer's use of language identified, with some explanation. ● Comments show some awareness of the effect of writer's language choices.	● I can identify techniques used to indicate shifts in time. ● I understand the effects that time-shift techniques have on a text.

Unit 4 ⬛ Short stories with flashbacks

Learning outcomes	Assessment opportunity and evidence	Assessment focuses (AFs)		Success criteria
		Level 4	Level 5	
Phase ② activities pages 70-71				
A paragraph planner Children can use paragraphs to structure their own writing and to create pace in a short narrative.	● Paired activity where children create a paragraph planner of a part of a story from another character's point of view. ● Children's oral responses and completed photocopiables.	**Writing AF4** ● Paragraphs/sections help to organise content. ● Within paragraphs/sections, limited range of connections between sentences. ● Some attempts to establish simple links between paragraphs/sections not always maintained.	**Writing AF4** ● Paragraphs clearly structure main ideas across text to support purpose. ● Within paragraphs/sections, a range of devices support cohesion. ● Links between paragraphs/sections generally maintained across whole text.	● I can use a paragraph planner to plan out a story. ● I can add ideas and notes for each paragraph on my planner. ● I understand how a paragraph planner helps structure a story.
Time-shift paragraphs Children can use paragraphs to structure their own writing and to create pace in a short narrative.	● Independent activity where children write sentences used at the beginning of paragraphs and whole paragraphs that indicate time shifts. ● Children's oral responses and completed photocopiables.	**Writing AF4** ● Paragraphs/sections help to organise content. ● Within paragraphs/sections, limited range of connections between sentences. ● Some attempts to establish simple links between paragraphs/sections not always maintained.	**Writing AF4** ● Paragraphs clearly structure main ideas across text to support purpose. ● Within paragraphs/sections, a range of devices support cohesion. ● Links between paragraphs/sections generally maintained across whole text.	● I can write sentences that indicate shifts in time. ● I can write paragraphs that indicate shifts in time.
Phase ③ activities pages 72-73				
Effective sentences Children can use different narrative techniques to indicate the passage of time between past and present to engage a reader.	● Paired activity where children choose sentences that need more work and explore ways to improve them for a greater effect. ● Children's oral responses and revised sentences.	**Writing AF5** ● Some variety in length, structure or subject of sentences. ● Use of some subordinating connectives. ● Some variation, generally accurate, in tense and verb forms.	**Writing AF5** ● A variety of sentence lengths, structures and subjects provides clarity and emphasis. ● Wider range of connectives used to clarify relationship between ideas. ● Some features of sentence structure used to build up detail or convey shades of meaning.	● I can create more pace in my story by using more effective sentences. ● I can use different techniques to indicate the passage of time.
Time-shift sentences Children can use different narrative techniques to indicate the passage of time between past and present to engage a reader.	● Independent or paired activity where children explore the use of time connectives and how to use them in their writing. ● Children's oral responses and revised sentences.	**Reading AF5** ● Some basic features of writer's use of language identified. ● Simple comments on writer's choices. **Writing AF4** ● Paragraphs/sections help to organise content. ● Within paragraphs/sections, limited range of connections between sentences. ● Some attempts to establish simple links between paragraphs/sections not always maintained.	**Reading AF5** ● Various features of writer's use of language identified, with some explanation. ● Comments show some awareness of the effect of writer's language choices. **Writing AF4** ● Paragraphs clearly structure main ideas across text to support purpose. ● Within paragraphs/sections, a range of devices support cohesion. ● Links between paragraphs/sections generally maintained across whole text.	● I can understand how conditional sentences can indicate time shifts. ● I can use conditional sentences indicating the passage of time in my story.

Phase ① Emotion graph

Learning outcome
Children can express views on how an author has used a range of techniques to indicate a specific mood in a text.

Success criteria
- I can identify the different moods of a character in a text.
- I can understand how different moods are created in a text.

Setting the context
In guided reading sessions, work with one group at a time, taking notes of their responses. Remind the children how authors can show characters' feelings in different ways. Read aloud an extract from the short story 'My Father is a Polar Bear' by Michael Morpurgo, starting at the part 'Douglas went out to work a lot...' up to '...not at all easy to picture in my head as I grew up'. Discuss the main character's different moods, such as excitement at seeing his father on stage. Give out cut-up sets of the photocopiable page 'Mood cards' to pairs of children working at levels 4-5 and one set for each group of children working at levels 2-3. Read one of the extracts on the cards and discuss how the author uses language to evoke the mood. The children use the mood cards to plot an emotion graph for the story. Model an emotion graph of a character from a well-known story and highlight its features.

Assessment opportunity
With children at levels 2-3, read out the extracts on the mood cards and, as a group, debate and decide on the correct order of the mood cards. Children at levels 4-5 should read the extracts on the mood cards and, in their pairs, put them in the right story order. Once all the children have put them in order, they individually plot an emotion graph, with the mood names along the bottom and a number line of 0 to 10 along the side (10 for very happy, 0 for very sad.) Encourage them to annotate each mood, such as the boy being confused about his father being a bear. When the graphs have been completed ask: *When was Andrew excited? Which parts were sad? Why? How does the author convey Andrew's excitement? How are sentences used to convey a mood?*

Assessment evidence
At levels 2-3, children should be able to use their graphs and the extracts to understand Andrew's feelings and moods by referring to use of words such as 'confused', 'envious'. At levels 4-5, children should be able to discuss the reasons behind Andrew's changing moods and how they are conveyed in the text, for example, 'The author conveyed that Andrew was really excited when he clapped his hands, by highlighting he had sore hands in one effective sentence'. Use the children's responses along with their emotion graphs as evidence against Reading AF3.

Next steps
Support: For children requiring extra support, have a hot-seat drama session with an adult as Andrew. Encourage the children to ask questions about how he felt at different points.
Extension: Encourage children to collect words, sentences and phrases that illustrate Andrew's different moods. Invite them to use the collections along with their graphs to create a mood collage. Display them for the class to see and use as a discussion point.

Key aspects of learning
Reasoning: Children will discuss a short story and give their opinions about the authorial intent, drawing inferences and making deductions from the text.
Empathy: Children will identify triggers and causes of other people's emotions.

NARRATIVE

Phase ① A feelings chart

Success criteria
- I can discuss and give reasons about how I felt about the story.
- I can record how I felt about the mood in different parts of the story.

Setting the context
In guided reading sessions, work with one group at a time, taking notes of their responses. Within their groups, briefly revise the different ways authors can convey moods within a story. Discuss how a mood of a story can affect the reader, for example, make them sad, happy, outraged, and so on. Share reading the short story, 'My Father is a Polar Bear' by Michael Morpurgo or read it out to children working at levels 2–3. The children should explore what they felt about different parts of the story, and the mood that was created by the author.

Assessment opportunity
Break up the story into main sections and discuss the children's feelings about each part. Ask: *What is the overall mood of the section? What are the different characters feeling?* Encourage the children to quote and refer to the text for examples. Ask for words that describe how they felt about different parts of the book and discuss their reasons. Create a chart by drawing three columns with the titles 'I felt', 'When' and 'Reasons'. The children can individually complete a feelings chart. Children at levels 2–3 may need adult support as a scribe. Encourage children at levels 4–5 to include examples or quotes in their chart. Encourage all the children to discuss their charts within their group. What is their overall feeling about the story? Why?

Assessment evidence
At levels 2–3, children should be able to discuss their feelings and give clear reasons, such as 'I felt happy when Andrew and his dad met up.' At levels 4–5, children should be able to use quotes and examples to explain their feelings about the story, for example, 'I felt really sad for Andrew after the panto. His brother saw their dad but all Andrew had was "a few words and a signature on a theatre programme"'. Use the children's responses about the different emotions they feel about the story or characters and their written charts as evidence against Reading AF6.

Next steps
Support: Draw round a child on a large piece of paper and title it: 'How I feel about *My dad is a polar bear*' Add in labels for heart, head, fingers, toes, stomach, and so on. Ask the group for physical feelings that they felt during the story and write them on the board, for example, 'feel weak at the knees', 'made my hair stand on end'. Invite the children to write the words around the child shape.
Extension: Encourage the children to design eye-catching book reviews recording their thoughts about the emotion of a story, for example, a drawing of a thermometer showing very cold to hot, giving examples and reasons for parts of the text that demonstrate those emotions.

Key aspects of learning
Empathy: Children will identify triggers and causes of other people's emotions.
Evaluation: Children will make judgements and justify their views and opinions, drawing on sources to support their evaluations. Children will discuss success criteria, give feedback to others and judge the effectiveness of their own work.

NARRATIVE

Phase ① Shifts in time

Learning outcome
Children can identify a range of techniques used by an author to indicate shifts in time between past and present.

Success criteria
- I can identify techniques used to indicate shifts in time.
- I understand the effects that time-shift techniques have on a text.

Setting the context
In guided reading sessions, work with one group at a time, taking notes of their responses. The children should have listened to or read 'My Father is a Polar Bear' by Michael Morpurgo. Identify how the narrator recounts events from his past. Ask: *Who is the narrator? How old do you think he is at the beginning and end of the story?* Discuss how Andrew's recount shifts backwards and forwards in time. Discuss ways writers show the passing of time, for example, reference to date and age, details of events, use of time connectives, changes in people and things, punctuation, change in tenses, and so on. The children study an extract from the story to identify examples of the way the author shows that time has passed.

Assessment opportunity
Children working at levels 2–3 can listen to version 1 of the photocopiable page 'My Father is a Polar Bear' and work as a discussion group. Ask guided questions such as: *How many years has the story flashed forward? How do we know his treasures are not new?* Record their responses. Put the children working at levels 4–5 into pairs and give out version 2 of the photocopiable page 'My Father is a Polar Bear'. Ask them to analyse and highlight the extract for examples of how the author illustrates the passing of time. Encourage them to present their findings to the rest of their group and discuss the devices used, such as connectives. Take notes during the discussion. Encourage all the children to look at their success criteria. What have they understood? What are they still unsure of?

Assessment evidence
At levels 2–3, children should be able to discuss how the list of treasures indicates the passing of time, for example 'the four "greenish" coins from the Christmas pudding means that quite a few Christmases have gone by'. At levels 4–5, children should be able to find time-shift examples, highlight their effect on the text and identify the devices used by the author, for example, tense changes, time connectives. Record the children's responses as evidence against Reading AF5.

Next steps
Support: Create a timeline for the story. Choose passages or sentences that give information. The children make simple captions, such as 'Andrew born in 1943', and add them to the timeline.
Extension: In pairs the children read through the story and take notes of the time changes. Ask them to use the information to plot a timeline of the story. Discuss why the story shifts in time so much.

Key aspects of learning
Reasoning: Children will discuss a short story and give their opinions about the authorial intent, drawing inferences and making deductions from the text.
Evaluation: Children will make judgements and justify their views and opinions, drawing on sources to support their evaluations. Children will discuss success criteria, give feedback to others and judge the effectiveness of their own work.

NARRATIVE

Phase ② A paragraph planner

Learning outcome
Children can use paragraphs to structure their own writing and to create pace in a short narrative.

Success criteria
● I can use a paragraph planner to plan out a story.
● I can add ideas and notes for each paragraph on my planner.
● I understand how a paragraph planner helps structure a story.

Setting the context
Display the success criteria in the classroom. Discuss with the children how paragraphs can be used to show different sections of a story. Read the part of the story 'My Father is a Polar Bear' by Michael Morpurgo at the point when Andrew goes to the pantomime starting from 'So there we were a few days later…' to '… giant pixie in a bearskin'. Explain to the children that they are going to write what happened from the older brother's point of view. Discuss what happened from Terry's point of view. Ask: *How did he feel when he first saw his dad on stage? Why did Terry creep off? How did he get backstage? What happened during the time he was with his father? How did he feel on the bus home?*

Assessment opportunity
Children at levels 2–3 can work with support to complete the photocopiable page 'Paragraph planner'. Working in pairs, they should draw or write ideas within each section. Put children at levels 4–5 into pairs and ask them to list the paragraphs for their retelling, for example, 'Terry sees his father as a polar bear', 'Terry sneaks backstage'. Then ask them to draw a paragraph planner (model one if necessary), and add notes and ideas in the boxes for each paragraph. Have a class discussion to consider the different plans and how the ideas in the paragraphs give the story pace.

Assessment evidence
At levels 2–3, children should be able to draw or write their ideas in simple sentences within the planner, such as 'Terry saw a door. He crept past the guard. He ran past the stage. He saw the door for the polar bear'. At levels 4–5, children should be able to use the text to create a paragraph planner in chronological order of the brother's account. Within the planner, the children should have written notes which outline their ideas for the account, such as 'Terry burst into the changing room. He saw his dad still dressed as a polar bear. He was lost for words. His dad stared back in complete surprise.' Use the children's written notes and paragraph planners along with their discussion as evidence against Writing AF4.

Next steps
Support: For children who find it hard to use a paragraph planner to structure their story, allow them to complete a comic strip-style storyboard with simple notes and captions underneath for a given section.
Extension: Encourage the children to think of the starting and finishing sentences of each paragraph so they can develop a natural flow in their story.

Key aspects of learning
Creative thinking: Children will generate ideas for a short narrative in response to a short story.
Evaluation: Children will make judgements and justify their views and opinions, drawing on sources to support their evaluations. Children will discuss success criteria, give feedback to others and judge the effectiveness of their own work.
Information processing: Children will explore information communicated through different modes and use this to create their own narrative.

Phase ② Time-shift paragraphs

Learning outcome
Children can use paragraphs to structure their own writing and to create pace in a short narrative.

Success criteria
● I can write sentences that indicate shifts in time.
● I can write paragraphs that indicate shifts in time.

Setting the context
Briefly revise how authors use different techniques to indicate shifts in time within a story. Discuss the idea that paragraphs can be one of those techniques. Read the story 'My Father is a Polar Bear' by Michael Morpurgo and identify points in the story where the shift in time is indicated by the first few sentences of a paragraph or a whole paragraph which sets the scene and mood. Indicate the use of time connectives and phrases such as 'not long after', 'I was born', 'soon after this'.

Assessment opportunity
Children at levels 2–3 can work in pairs using the interactive activity 'Time-shift paragraphs'. They should choose suitable words to complete paragraphs that indicate time shifts. Discuss with the children why they chose the words and the effect they have on the text. Record their responses. Children at levels 4–5 can work individually on the photocopiable page 'Time-shift paragraphs'. Explain that they have to write examples of sentences used at the beginning of paragraphs and whole paragraphs that indicate time shifts. Once the children have finished, encourage them to use a response partner to feed back and discuss effective examples. Move between the pairs and take notes of their discussion.

Assessment evidence
At levels 2–3, children should be able to discuss the different effects the time-shift words have in the interactive activity. They should note the time connectives, time words such as 'lunchtime', 'minutes' and contrasting words to show changes, such as 'years', 'now', 'earlier', 'later'. At levels 4–5, children should be able to show some examples of time shifts using a range of time connectives and phrases, punctuation or use of tenses, for example, 'I looked around at the devastation. This time last week everything looked perfect when...' Use the children's responses along with written work as evidence against Writing AF4.

Next steps
Support: Choose a well-known short story, such as 'Cinderella'. Write out the main events and mix them up. Ask the children to retell the story in the role of Cinderella as an old woman using re-ordering the mixed-up cards. Review phrases and words used to indicate time.
Extension: Ask the children to write time-shift paragraph openers for a time-travelling story written within a group of four. Each child writes a time-shift opener and passes it on to another child to be completed. They share their work and develop a story around the four openers.

Key aspects of learning
Creative thinking: Children will generate ideas for a short narrative in response to a short story.
Reasoning: Children will discuss a short story and give their opinions about the authorial intent, drawing inferences and making deductions from the text.
Information processing: Children will explore information communicated through different modes and use this to create their own narrative.

Phase ③ Effective sentences

Learning outcome
Children can use different narrative techniques to indicate the passage of time between past and present to engage a reader.

Success criteria
- I can create more pace in my story by using more effective sentences.
- I can use different techniques to indicate the passage of time.

Setting the context
This activity should be done during or at the end of a writing project where the children have planned and worked on a short narrative. Show and discuss the success criteria as a class. Ask: *How do you want your story to affect your reader? How do you want to keep the reader's interest? What connectives have you used to indicate the passage of time?* Discuss how pace and flow help keep the reader's attention. Explain that they are going to practise improving sentences using different techniques to create more of an effect. Select an example and model how it can be changed, for example, by shortening compound sentences, use of connectives and conjunctions.

Assessment opportunity
Put the children into ability pairs to work as response partners. Children at levels 2-3 may need support as they work with their partners. Ask the children to read their partner's work and feed back on sentences they feel may need improving. Ask them to write out one sentence that needs improving. Encourage them to experiment with changing their sentences and share the results with their partners as part of the redrafting process. Move around and ask questions: *Why does that sentence lack pace? Why does that shorter sentence create more pace? Which connective could be used to improve the sentence?* Take notes of their responses. In a class plenary ask the children to explain how their revised sentences have improved the pace and effect of their redrafted story.

Assessment evidence
At levels 2-3, children should be able to identify sentences that make the story too slow and give suggestions to create pace, for example, 'She ran and ran all the way home' could be more effective than 'She ran as fast as she could until she reached her house'. At levels 4-5, children should be able to experiment with a range of sentences, such as 'Sam ran. He ran down the lane, round the corner and over the hill. He ran like the wind. He ran for his life!' Use the children's responses along with their sentence revision as evidence against Writing AF5.

Next steps
Support: Focus on extending simple sentences to give the reader more information using conjunctions. Show examples of conjunctions, such as 'and', 'but', 'until' and encourage the children to create sentences using them. Use the same activity to focus on connectives, such as 'also', 'next', 'later'.
Extension: Encourage the children to explore and experiment using a mix of sentence styles in one paragraph for effect, for example, a simple sentence followed by a complex sentence.

Key aspects of learning
Evaluation: Children will make judgements and justify their views and opinions, drawing on sources to support their evaluations. Children will discuss success criteria, give feedback to others and judge the effectiveness of their own work.
Information processing: Children will explore information communicated through different modes and use this to create their own narrative.

Phase ③ Time-shift sentences

Learning outcome
Children can use different narrative techniques to indicate the passage of time between past and present to engage a reader.

Success criteria
- I can understand how conditional sentences can indicate time shifts.
- I can use conditional sentences indicating the passage of time in my story.

Setting the context
Display the success criteria in the classroom. This activity should be done during or at the end of a writing project where the children have been working on stories that incorporate time shifts. As the class work on their stories, choose one child or a pair of children (at a similar level) to work on the interactive activities. Explain that they will be revising their work on creating a better time-shift effect in their stories. The children will revise the use of conditional sentences that indicate past, present or future with the interactive activity 'Conditional sentences'.

Assessment opportunity
Sit with the children as they work on the interactive activity and note their responses. Ask questions such as: *Show me a sentence which has a clause in the past and a clause in the present. Why are conditional sentences a good way of showing a change in time?* Once the children have finished the interactive activity, ask them to re-read their own stories and find ways to use or revise conditional sentences to show the passage of time. Ask the children as a class or individually how the revised or new sentences have improved the effect of their story.

Assessment evidence
At levels 2–3, children should be able to understand how basic time connectives in sentences help indicate the passing of time, for example, '"In the beginning" is the first connective as it indicates the start of the story.' At levels 4–5, children should be able to recognise that a conditional sentence explains what might happen as a result of an action, for example, 'The first clause of that sentence explains an action in the past and the second clause explains the result in the present.' Use the children's responses to the activities and their story redrafts as evidence against Reading AF5 and Writing AF4.

Next steps
Support: Ask children to write simple sentences of different events they did over the course of one week. Give the children a set of time connectives and encourage them to use them to improve the sentences. Revise the use of time connectives with the interactive activity 'Which time connectives?' Ask questions such as: *Which connectives tell the reader when the actions take place? Why are time connectives a good way of indicating when something is or has taken place?*
Extension: Encourage children to think of ways conditional sentences could be used to illustrate mood effects in a story, for example, the character, setting, and so on.

Key aspects of learning
Reasoning: Children will discuss a short story and give their opinions about the authorial intent, drawing inferences and making deductions from the text.
Evaluation: Children will make judgements and justify their views and opinions, drawing on sources to support their evaluations. Children will discuss success criteria, give feedback to others and judge the effectiveness of their own work.
Information processing: Children will explore information communicated through different modes and use this to create their own narrative.

NARRATIVE

Periodic assessment

Reading

Learning outcomes
● Children can identify a range of techniques used by an author to indicate shifts in time between past and present.
● Children can use paragraphs to structure their own writing and to create pace in a short narrative.

Success criteria
● I can identify time shifts within a story text.
● I can use paragraphs to indicate effective shifts in time.

Setting the context
Use this assessment within the children's guided reading groups. Remind the groups how authors can use a range of techniques to show time shifts. Explain that they are going to look for techniques used to show time shifts within a story called 'The Missing Necklace'. Give out copies of the photocopiable page 'Narrative 4 Reading assessment text'. Before the children read the text ask them what is unusual with the structure (there are no paragraphs and dialogue line spaces). Read through the story together and discuss the obvious time changes where the story moves from past to present. Display the success criteria in the classroom.

Assessment opportunity
Ask the children to organise the text into paragraphs to make the time shifts more effective. They can mark on their copies where the paragraphs could go to make time shifts more effective. Then ask them to highlight words or phrases used to create time shifts. Encourage the children to feed back to their group. Make notes during the discussions. Ask: *How do the paragraphs make a difference to indicating a time shift to the reader? How else could you make the time shifts more effective?* Support groups by reading through the text slowly and asking the children to stop you when you reach a word or phrase that indicates a shift in time. Discuss how the word or phrase shows a time shift and record the responses of the children in the discussion. Encourage the children to self-assess against the success criteria.

Assessment evidence
Children at levels 2-3 should identify the most obvious time-shift techniques, such as time connectives. They should explain how the main story jumps from the present to the past and then the present again. Children at levels 4-5 should identify time-shift techniques such as the change of the castle over the years, time connectives, conditional sentences and the changes of tense. Their paragraph work should show how the use of dialogue and time connectives can also indicate effective time shifts. Use the notes on the children's responses and the marked texts to make level judgements against Reading AF4 and AF5.

Periodic assessment

Writing

Learning outcome
Children can use different narrative techniques to indicate the passage of time between past and present to engage a reader.

Success criteria
● I can write a short story from the point of view of a different character.
● I can write a short story using different techniques to indicate the passage of time between past and present.
● I can write in paragraphs to indicate time shifts.

Setting the context
Put the children into levelled groups and read 'The Missing Necklace' from the photocopiable page 'Narrative 4 Reading assessment text'. Go briefly through the text to study the different time-shift techniques, focusing first of all on the time connectives. Highlight the story of Lady Jupp. Discuss her character. Ask: *How did she feel about the necklace? How did she feel once her brother died? Did she suspect Ellie? How did she feel when the children found the necklace?* Explain that they are each going to write a short story from the point of view of Lady Jupp. The groups at levels 4–5 can write their story on paper using copies of the story for reference. Display the success criteria in the classroom. If groups need support provide them with copies of the photocopiable page 'Narrative 4 Writing assessment' which has a paragraph planner and examples of time connectives they could use.

Assessment opportunity
Encourage the children to think of how their story will move from past to present. Ask: *With which time connective would you start the first paragraph of the story? What time connectives could be used to show the time changes over one day?* Encourage children to show different techniques to indicate a time shift and the use of paragraphs. *How can you describe the change of time through Lady Jupp? Who is Lady Jupp telling her story to? Is it someone in the past or the present? How would you start that paragraph to show that the story is now in the present?* Take notes of their responses. Encourage them to read their completed stories to the group and discuss their use of time-shift techniques. Ask: *What other ways could time shifts be used in the story?*

Assessment evidence
Children at levels 2–3 should write a simple short story from the point of view of Lady Jupp using time connectives and paragraphs. Children at levels 4–5 should use a wide range of techniques and explain why they wanted to use them. Use the children's written stories and their responses in the group discussion to make level judgements against Writing AF1, AF4 and AF7.

NARRATIVE

My Father is a Polar Bear (1)

Picture another Christmas Eve fourteen years later. Upstairs, still at the bottom of my cupboard, my polar bear father in the magazine in the Start-Rite shoebox; and with him all our accumulated childhood treasures: the signed programme, a battered champion conker (a sixty-fiver!), six silver ball bearings, four greenish silver threepenny bits (Christmas pudding treasure trove), a Red Devil throat pastille tin with three of my milk teeth cushioned in yellowy cotton wool, and my collection of twenty-seven cowrie shells gleaned over the many summers from the beach on Samson in the Scilly Isles. Downstairs, the whole family were gathered in the sitting room: my mother, Douglas, Terry and my two sisters (half-sisters really, but of course no one ever called them that), Aunty Betty, now married, with twin daughters, my cousins, who were truly awful – I promise you.

Text © 2000, Michael Morpurgo. Illustration © 2009, Simon Smith.

My Father is a Polar Bear (2)

Some background might be useful here. I was born, I later found out, when my father was a soldier in Baghdad during the Second World War. (You didn't know there were polar bears in Baghdad, did you?) Sometime after that my mother met and fell in love with a dashing young officer in the Royal Marines called Douglas Macleish. All this time, evacuated to the Lake District away from the bombs, blissfully unaware of the war and Douglas, I was learning to walk and talk and do my business in the right place at the right time. So my father came home from the war to discover that his place in my mother's heart had been taken. He did all he could to win her back. He took her away on a week's cycling holiday in Suffolk to see if he could rekindle the light of their love. But it was hopeless. By the end of the week they had come to an amicable arrangement. My father would simply disappear, because he didn't want to 'get in the way'. They would get divorced quickly and quietly, so that Terry and I could be brought up as a new family with Douglas as our father. Douglas would adopt us and give us Macleish as our surname. All my father insisted upon was that Terry and I should keep Van Diemen as our middle name. That's what happened. They divorced. My father disappeared, and at the age of three I became Andrew Van Diemen Macleish. It was a mouthful then and it's a mouthful now.

Text © 2000, Michael Morpurgo. Illustration © 2009, Simon Smith.

NON-FICTION
Unit 1 Biography and autobiography

Literacy objectives

Speak and listen for a wide range of purposes in different contexts
Strand 1 Speaking
- Use the techniques of dialogic talk to explore ideas, topics or issues.

Strand 2 Listening and responding
- Make notes when listening for a sustained period and discuss how note-taking varies depending on context and purpose.

Strand 4 Drama
- Devise a performance considering how to adapt the performance for a specific audience.

Read and write for a range of purposes on paper and on screen
Strand 6 Word structure and spelling
- Spell familiar words correctly and employ a range of strategies to spell difficult and unfamiliar words.
- Use a range of appropriate strategies to edit, proofread and correct spelling in their own work, on paper and on screen.

Strand 7 Understanding and interpreting texts
- Appraise a text quickly, deciding on its value, quality or usefulness.
- Understand underlying themes, causes and points of view.

Strand 8 Engaging with and responding to texts
- Sustain engagement with longer texts, using different techniques to make the text come alive.
- Compare how writers from different times and places present experiences and use language.

Strand 9 Creating and shaping texts
- Set their own challenges to extend achievement and experience in writing.
- Use different narrative techniques to engage and entertain the reader.
- Select words and language drawing on their knowledge of literary features and formal and informal writing.
- Integrate words, images and sounds imaginatively for different purposes.

Strand 10 Text structure and organisation
- Use varied structures to shape and organise text coherently.
- Use paragraphs to achieve pace and emphasis.

Strand 11 Sentence structure and punctuation
- Express subtle distinctions of meaning, including hypothesis, speculation and supposition, by constructing sentences in varied ways.

Key aspects of learning

Enquiry
- Children will identify their own key questions about a particular life, and then locate the evidence to answer it within a range of sources.

Information processing
- Children will identify relevant information from a range of sources on paper and on screen and use this as a basis for both oral presentation and writing.

Key aspects of learning (contd)

Reasoning
- Children will construct reasoned arguments based on available information and evidence.

Empathy
- Through discussing and writing simulated autobiography, children will need to imagine themselves in another person's position.

Communication
- Children will develop their ability to discuss and debate issues in respect of both the form and the content of the biographical texts they are reading and writing. They will often work collaboratively in pairs and groups. They will communicate outcomes orally, in writing and through using other modes and media.

Assessment focuses

Reading
AF2 *(understand, describe, select or retrieve information, events or ideas from texts and use quotation and reference to text).*
AF3 *(deduce, infer or interpret information, events or ideas from texts).*
AF4 *(identify and comment on the structure and organisation of texts, including grammatical and presentational features at text level).*
AF6 *(identify and comment on writers' purposes and viewpoints, and the overall effect of the text on the reader).*
AF7 *(relate texts to their social, cultural and historical contexts and literary traditions).*

Writing
AF1 *(write imaginative, interesting and thoughtful texts).*
AF2 *(produce texts which are appropriate to task, reader and purpose).*
AF5 *(vary sentences for clarity, purpose and effect).*

Speaking and listening
Speaking (organise talk and use detail).
Listening and responding (understand and recall the main points; respond appropriately).
Drama (support others and take turns).

Resources

Phase 1 activities
Interactive activity, 'Tanni Grey-Thompson'
Photocopiable page, 'Tanni Grey-Thompson'
Access to Tanni Grey-Thompson's website: www.tanni.co.uk
Photocopiable page, 'Reliable accounts.'

Phase 3 activities
Access to Tanni Grey-Thompson's website: www.tanni.co.uk
Interactive activity, 'Chronological order' (versions 1 and 2)
Photocopiable page 'Marie Curie'

Phase 4 activities
Photocopiable page, 'Biography checklist' (versions 1 and 2)
Photocopiable page, 'Marie Curie – my life'

Periodic assessment
Photocopiable page, 'Non-fiction 1 Reading assessment text'
Photocopiable page, 'Non-fiction 1 Writing assessment'

Unit 1 📖 Biography and autobiography

Learning outcomes	Assessment opportunity and evidence	Assessment focuses (AFs)		Success criteria
		Level 2	Level 3	
Phase ① activities pages 84–86				
Biography or autobiography? Children can understand the terms 'biography' and 'autobiography' and can use them appropriately.	• Group activity where children decide if texts are biographical or autobiographical. • Children's oral responses and discussion. • Teacher's notes.	**Reading AF7** • General features of a few text types identified. • Some awareness that books are set in different times and places.	**Reading AF7** • Some simple connections between texts identified. • Recognition of some features of the context of texts.	• I can identify the features of a biography. • I can identify the features of an autobiography.
Tanni Grey-Thompson's timeline Children can extract and interpret information effectively from biographical and autobiographical sources.	• Supported group activity where children create a timeline of Tanni Grey-Thompson. • Children's oral responses and observational notes. • Written timelines.	**Reading AF2** • Some specific, straightforward information recalled. • Generally clear idea of where to look for information.	**Reading AF2** • Simple, most obvious points identified though there may also be some misunderstanding. • Some comments include quotations from or references to text, but not always relevant.	• I can extract information from a range of sources. • I can select relevant information to create a timeline of a person's life.
Reliable accounts Children can evaluate the reliability and usefulness of biographical information from different sources.	• Supported group activity where children rank accounts from least to most reliable. • Children's oral responses. • Completed photocopiables.	**Reading AF6** • Some awareness that writers have viewpoints and purposes. • Simple statements about likes and dislikes in reading, sometimes with reasons.	**Reading AF6** • Comments identify main purpose. • Express personal response but with little awareness of writer's viewpoint or effect on reader.	• I can evaluate information for its reliability, bias and usefulness. • I can give information a score out of 10 for reliability and justify my reasons.
Phase ② activities pages 87–88				
Key question checklists Children can research, prepare and present orally a reasoned account of a particular life.	• Group activity where children agree a set of key questions that could be used to help a writer research the life of a person. • Children's oral responses and discussion. • Feedback and written checklists. • Teacher's notes.	**Reading AF2** • Some specific, straightforward information recalled. • Generally clear idea of where to look for information. **Writing AF2** • Some basic purpose established. • Some appropriate features of the given form used. • Some attempts to adopt appropriate style.	**Reading AF2** • Simple, most obvious points identified though there may also be some misunderstanding. • Some comments include quotations from or references to text, but not always relevant. **Writing AF2** • Purpose established at a general level. • Main features of selected form sometimes signalled to the reader. • Some attempts at appropriate style, with attention to reader.	• I can debate and agree to a set of key questions for researching a person's life. • I can use a list of key questions to help me research a person's life. • I can evaluate how well a set of key questions helped me to research a person.
Presentations Children can research, prepare and present orally a reasoned account of a particular life.	• Group activity where children use researched information to prepare and present a short oral presentation. • Children's oral responses and discussion. • Feedback and written notes.	**Writing AF1** • Mostly relevant ideas and content, sometimes repetitive or sparse. • Some apt word choices create interest. • Brief comments, questions about events or actions suggest viewpoint.	**Writing AF1** • Some appropriate ideas and content included. • Some attempt to elaborate on basic information or events, eg nouns expanded by simple adjectives. • Attempt to adopt viewpoint, though often not maintained or inconsistent.	• I can debate and agree to the resources and materials needed for a presentation. • I can present orally an account of a life of a chosen person. • I can evaluate a presentation about a chosen person.

Unit 1 📖 Biography and autobiography

Learning outcomes	Assessment opportunity and evidence	Assessment focuses (AFs)		Success criteria
		Level 2	Level 3	
Phase ③ activities pages 89–90				
Chronological order Children can recognise the structure and language, organisational and presentational features of different forms of biography and autobiography.	• Independent or paired activity where children put extracts in chronological order. • Children's oral responses and discussion. • Completed interactives.	**Reading AF4** • Some awareness of use of features of organisation.	**Reading AF4** • A few basic features of organisation at text level identified, with little or no linked comment.	• I can understand how important events in a biography are often ordered chronologically. • I can put biographical sentences in chronological order.
Marie Curie's account Children can recognise the structure and language, organisational and presentational features of different forms of biography and autobiography.	• Supported activity where children re-write a part of Marie Curie's biography into an autobiography. • Children's oral responses and discussion. • Children's written accounts.	**Writing AF1** • Mostly relevant ideas and content, sometimes repetitive or sparse. • Some apt word choices create interest. • Brief comments, questions about events or actions suggest viewpoint.	**Writing AF1** • Some appropriate ideas and content included. • Some attempt to elaborate on basic information or events. • Attempt to adopt viewpoint, though often not maintained or inconsistent.	• I can rewrite a biography as an autobiography. • I can use autobiographical features in a text.
Phase ④ activities pages 91–92				
Biography checklist Children can write an effective biography or autobiography selecting language, form, format and content to suit a particular audience and purpose.	• Group activity where children evaluate each other's biographies. • Children's oral responses and discussion. • Children's written biographies and checklists. • Teacher's notes.	**Reading AF2** • Some specific, straightforward information recalled. • Generally clear idea of where to look for information.	**Reading AF2** • Simple, most obvious points identified though there may also be some misunderstanding. • Some comments include quotations from or references to text, but not always relevant.	• I can identify biographical features in a text. • I can evaluate my partner's biographical text.
Autobiographical sentences Children can write an effective biography or autobiography selecting language, form, format and content to suit a particular audience and purpose.	• Supported group activity where children look at how they can write more personal and expressive sentences. • Children's oral responses. • Children's revised written autobiographies. • Teacher's notes.	**Writing AF5** • Some variation in sentence openings. • Mainly simple sentences with *and* used to connect clauses. • Past and present tense generally consistent.	**Writing AF5** • Reliance mainly on simply structured sentences, variation with support. • *and, but, so* are the most common connectives, subordination occasionally. • Some limited variation in use of tense and verb forms, not always secure.	• I can rewrite sentences to make my autobiographical text more personal. • I can use powerful language to improve my autobiographical text. • I can identify and rewrite sentences to improve my autobiographical text.

Unit 1 Biography and autobiography

Learning outcomes	Assessment opportunity and evidence	Assessment focuses (AFs)		Success criteria
		Level 4	Level 5	
Phase ① activities pages 84–86				
Biography or autobiography? Children can understand the terms 'biography' and 'autobiography' and can use them appropriately.	• Group activity where children suggest biographical and autobiographical features to be added to a chart. • Children's oral responses, discussion and written work. • Teacher's notes.	**Reading AF7** • Features common to different texts or versions of the same text identified, with simple comment. • Simple comment on the effect that the reader's or writer's context has on the meaning of texts.	**Reading AF7** • Some simple connections between texts identified. • Recognition of some features of the context of texts.	• I can identify the features of a biography. • I can identify the features of an autobiography.
Tanni Grey-Thompson's timeline Children can extract and interpret information effectively from biographical and autobiographical sources.	• Supported group activity where children create a timeline of Tanni Grey-Thompson. • Children's oral responses and observational notes. • Written timelines.	**Reading AF2** • Some relevant points identified. • Comments supported by some generally relevant textual reference or quotation.	**Reading AF2** • Most relevant points clearly identified, including those selected from different places in the text. • Comments generally supported by relevant textual reference or quotation, even when points made are not always accurate.	• I can extract information from a range of sources. • I can select relevant information to create a timeline of a person's life.
Reliable accounts Children can evaluate the reliability and usefulness of biographical information from different sources.	• Paired activity where children rank accounts from least to most reliable. • Children's oral responses. • Completed photocopiables.	**Reading AF6** • Main purpose identified. • Simple comments show some awareness of writer's viewpoint. • Simple comment on overall effect on reader.	**Reading AF6** • Main purpose clearly identified, often through general overview. • Viewpoints in texts clearly identified, with some, often limited, explanation. • General awareness of effect on the reader, with some, often limited, explanation.	• I can evaluate information for its reliability, bias and usefulness. • I can give information a score out of 10 for reliability and justify my reasons.
Phase ② activities pages 87–88				
Key question checklists Children can research, prepare and present orally a reasoned account of a particular life.	• Group activity where children agree a set of key questions that could be used to help a writer research the life of a person. • Children's oral responses and discussion. • Feedback and written checklists. • Teacher's notes.	**Reading AF2** • Some relevant points identified. • Comments supported by some generally relevant textual reference or quotation. **Writing AF2** • Main purpose of writing is clear but not always consistently maintained. • Main features of selected form are clear and appropriate to purpose. • Style generally appropriate to task, though awareness of reader not always sustained.	**Reading AF2** • Most relevant points clearly identified, including those selected from different places in the text. • Comments generally supported by relevant textual reference or quotation, even when points made are not always accurate. **Writing AF2** • Main purpose of writing is clear and consistently maintained. • Features of selected form clearly established with some adaptation to purpose. • Appropriate style clearly established to maintain reader's interest throughout.	• I can debate and agree to a set of key questions for researching a person's life. • I can use a list of key questions to help me research a person's life. • I can evaluate how well a set of key questions helped me to research a person.

Unit 1 Biography and autobiography

Learning outcomes	Assessment opportunity and evidence	Assessment focuses (AFs)		Success criteria
		Level 4	Level 5	
Presentations Children can research, prepare and present orally a reasoned account of a particular life.	• Group activity where children prepare and present a short oral presentation. • Children's oral responses and discussion. • Feedback and written notes.	**Writing AF1** • Relevant ideas and content chosen. • Some ideas and material developed in detail. • Straightforward viewpoint generally established and maintained.	**Writing AF1** • Relevant ideas and material developed with some imaginative detail. • Development of ideas and material appropriately shaped for selected form. • Clear viewpoint established, generally consistent, with some elaboration.	• I can debate and agree to the resources and materials needed for a presentation. • I can present orally an account of a life of a chosen person. • I can evaluate a presentation about a chosen person.

Phase ③ activities pages 89–90

Chronological order Children can recognise the structure and language, organisational and presentational features of different forms of biography and autobiography.	• Independent or paired activity where children put extracts in chronological order. • Children's oral responses and discussion. • Completed interactives.	**Reading AF4** • Some structural choices identified with simple comment. • Some basic features of organisation at text level identified.	**Reading AF4** • Comments on structural choices show some general awareness of writer's craft. • Various features relating to organisation at text level, including form, are clearly identified, with some explanation.	• I can understand how important events in a biography are often ordered chronologically. • I can put biographical sentences in chronological order.
Marie Curie's account Children can recognise the structure and language, organisational and presentational features of different forms of biography and autobiography.	• Independent activity where children re-write a part of Marie Curie's biography into an autobiography. • Children's oral responses and discussion. • Children's written accounts.	**Writing AF1** • Relevant ideas and content chosen. • Some ideas and material developed in detail. • Straightforward viewpoint generally established and maintained.	**Writing AF1** • Relevant ideas and material developed with some imaginative detail. • Development of ideas and material appropriately shaped for selected form. • Clear viewpoint established, generally consistent, with some elaboration.	• I can rewrite a biography as an autobiography. • I can use autobiographical features in a text.

Phase ④ activities pages 91–92

Biography checklist Children can write an effective biography or autobiography selecting language, form, format and content to suit a particular audience and purpose.	• Paired activity where children evaluate each other's biographies. • Children's oral responses and discussion. • Children's written biographies and checklists. • Teacher's notes.	**Reading AF2** • Some relevant points identified. • Comments supported by some generally relevant textual reference or quotation.	**Reading AF2** • Most relevant points clearly identified, including those selected from different places in the text. • Comments generally supported by relevant textual reference or quotation, even when points made are not always accurate.	• I can identify biographical features in a text. • I can evaluate my partner's biographical text.
Autobiographical sentences Children can write an effective biography or autobiography selecting language, form, format and content to suit a particular audience and purpose.	• Independent activity where children look at how they can write more personal and expressive sentences. • Children's oral responses. • Children's revised written autobiographies. • Teacher's notes.	**Writing AF5** • Some variety in length, structure or subject of sentences. • Use of some subordinating connectives. • Some variation, generally accurate, in tense and verb forms.	**Writing AF5** • A variety of sentence lengths, structures and subjects provides clarity and emphasis. • Wider range of connectives used to clarify relationship between ideas. • Some features of sentence structure used to build up detail or convey shades of meaning.	• I can rewrite sentences to make my autobiographical text more personal. • I can use powerful language to improve my autobiographical text. • I can identify and rewrite sentences to improve my autobiographical text.

NON-FICTION

Phase ① Biography or autobiography?

Learning outcome
Children can understand the terms 'biography' and 'autobiography' and can use them appropriately.

Success criteria
● I can identify the features of a biography.
● I can identify the features of an autobiography.

Setting the context
Work with the children in levelled groups, one group at a time. Display the success criteria in the classroom. For children at levels 2–3, display the interactive activity 'Tanni Grey-Thompson' for the group to see. Explain that the children have to listen to and read the two extracts and decide whether they are biographical or autobiographical. For children working at levels 4–5, draw a table on a board with two columns titled 'Biography' and 'Autobiography'. Recap briefly on the main features of autobiographical accounts and record them in the table. Provide the children with a longer extract from a well-known person's biography, such as Tanni Grey-Thomson (see her website, www.tanni.co.uk) and then individually to write down examples of the biographical features.

Assessment opportunity
Children working at levels 2–3 can discuss why each extract in the interactive activity is biographical or autobiographical. Focus on simple features such as first and third person and use of personal language, and take notes of the children's individual responses as they discuss the features. When the children working at levels 4–5 have completed their individual biographical features lists, ask them to share their findings and quotes. Lists their examples in the table on the board. As a group, ask the children to compare and contrast biographical and autobiographical features identified in the table. Take notes of their discussion and responses. After the activity discuss with all the children what elements in the success criteria they feel they need more support with.

Assessment evidence
At levels 2–3, children should be able to identify and discuss the basic autobiographical and biographical features of each text. At levels 4–5, children should be able to evaluate and discuss the differences between biographical and autobiographical features - for example, the use of formal language in biographical texts and informal language in autobiographical accounts. Use the notes of the children's responses and any written work as evidence against Reading AF7.

Next steps
Support: To compare autobiographical and biographical features, focus on one area such as first and third person features. Encourage children to describe the week of the bad wolf from 'The Three Little Pigs' and follow it by writing the week in his own words.
Extension: Give children a range of material about a person and ask them to sort and classify the texts into autobiography and biography. What is the purpose and audience of each text? What feature examples can they extract as evidence?

Key aspects of learning
Information processing: Children will identify relevant information from a range of sources on paper and on screen and use this as a basis for both oral presentation and writing.
Communication: Children will develop their ability to discuss and debate issues in respect of both the form and the content of the biographical texts they are reading and writing. They will often work collaboratively in pairs and groups. They will communicate outcomes orally, in writing and through using other modes and media.

Phase ① Tanni Grey-Thompson's timeline

Learning outcome
Children can extract and interpret information effectively from biographical and autobiographical sources.

Success criteria
- I can extract information from a range of sources.
- I can select relevant information to create a timeline of a person's life.

Setting the context
Display the success criteria in the classroom. Explore how information can be taken out of biographical and autobiographical sources for a range of purposes, such as a timeline. Explain that the children are going to look through biographical materials about the disabled athlete Tanni Grey-Thompson to create a timeline of her life. Children at levels 2–3 can work in a group with adult support and use the photocopiable page 'Tanni Grey-Thomnson' to retrieve information. Children at levels 4–5 can work independently on finding information for their timeline using a range of materials, starting with the photocopiable page 'Tanni Grey-Thompson', and by accessing her website (see Resources for details).

Assessment opportunity
Give children at levels 2–3 copies of the photocopiable page 'Tanni Grey-Thompson'. As a group they should highlight dates and information needed for their timelines. Establish when Tanni was born and the main periods of her life. Help the children sort out the dates and events by writing them out in simple captions on a large piece of paper. Take notes of how they understand the information and use it. Give out ready-made strips with marks for every two years and encourage the children to write out their timelines. Note how children at levels 4–5 search for, collect and organise their information for the timeline. Give out strips of paper for them to complete the timelines. Once all the children have completed the timelines have a class plenary where children can show their timelines and read out their information. What did they find easy about the activity? What did they find difficult?

Assessment evidence
At levels 2–3, children should be able to identify dates and simple information. They should transfer the information they find onto a timeline and use it to talk about Tanni. At levels 4–5, children should be able to identify relevant information from a range of material for their timeline. They should be able to use the timelines to ask questions for further research. Use the notes on the children's responses, observation of their research skills and their written timelines as evidence against Reading AF2.

Next steps
Support: Encourage children to create a timeline of main events in their own lives. Discuss what evidence they could use, for example, memories from family members, photographs, leaflets and brochures of events they participated in or attended. Discuss how the timeline helps them look at what they have done and how they have developed.
Extension: Ask children to create a timeline of a famous historical figure as a homework assignment. When they have presented their timelines discuss the different range of materials they used and the need to record their sources.

Key aspects of learning
Enquiry: Children will identify their own key questions about a particular life, and then locate the evidence to answer it within a range of sources.
Information processing: Children will identify relevant information from a range of sources on paper and on screen and use this as a basis for both oral presentation and writing.
Communication: Children will develop their ability to discuss and debate issues in respect of both the form and the content of the biographical texts they are reading and writing. They will often work collaboratively in pairs and groups. They will communicate outcomes orally, in writing and through using other modes and media.

Phase ① Reliable accounts

Learning outcome
Children can evaluate the reliability and usefulness of biographical information from different sources.

Success criteria
● I can evaluate information for its reliability, bias and usefulness.
● I can give information a score out of 10 for reliability and justify my reasons.

Setting the context
Before this assessment, collect a range of material about a person's life that the children can study. Stress how some information about a person's life might not be totally reliable or accurate, such as newspaper reports. Explain to the children that they are going to look at a range of material about the chosen person's life to find evidence of reliability, bias and usefulness and then record the results on the photocopiable page 'Reliable accounts'. Children at levels 2-3 can work as a discussion group with an adult supporting them as a reader and scribing their responses on one copy of the photocopiable page. Children at levels 4-5 can work in pairs with one copy per pair.

Assessment opportunity
As the children work, make observational notes of the materials they have chosen and the evidence they are evaluating. Take note of the children's discussions on the ranking of least reliable to most reliable accounts. Ask discussion questions: *Why do you think the news report may be biased? Why is it less reliable than the biographical account?* Note the children's answers. Encourage children at levels 2-3 to discuss their findings. Children at levels 4-5 can share their findings with another pair. Take notes of their discussions. In a class plenary ask the children to justify their rankings for the least reliable and most reliable accounts.

Assessment evidence
At levels 2-3, children should be able to recognise straightforward biased information. They should be able to discuss and identify what information is useful to the reader. At levels 4-5, children should be able to analyse more complex material, such as autobiographical accounts. They should be able to identify the writers' viewpoints and be aware of how the same information can be presented in different ways. Use the children's photocopiable charts and notes of their responses as evidence against Reading AF6.

Next steps
Support: Describe a scenario such as a boy walking along the street sees a woman drop her purse. He picks it up and offers it back to the woman. Discuss the different reports eyewitnesses could give of the situation. Which ones are the most reliable? Which ones are biased?
Extension: Ask children to explore newspaper reports or magazine articles of famous people and grade them on their reliability and bias. How useful are they for writing a biography?

Key aspects of learning
Information processing: Children will identify relevant information from a range of sources on paper and on screen and use this as a basis for both oral presentation and writing.
Reasoning: Children will construct reasoned arguments based on available information and evidence.
Communication: Children will develop their ability to discuss and debate issues in respect of both the form and the content of the biographical texts they are reading and writing. They will often work collaboratively in pairs and groups. They will communicate outcomes orally, in writing and through using other modes and media.

Phase ② Key question checklists

Learning outcome
Children can research, prepare and present orally a reasoned account of a particular life.

Success criteria
● I can debate and agree to a set of key questions for researching a person's life.
● I can use a list of key questions to help me research a person's life.
● I can evaluate how well a set of key questions helped me to research a person.

Setting the context
Put the children into mixed ability groups. Discuss the need to research a range of different materials when writing a biographical account of someone. Explain to the children that a writer has been asked to write a biography. Make clear that the writer needs to identify key evaluative questions that will help explain the person's importance or their life, for example, 'Why was Henry VIII famous?' Explain that they will be working in their groups to create a key question checklist for the writer to use. Ask the children to choose a scribe from their group. Display the success criteria in the classroom.

Assessment opportunity
As they work, walk round the groups and take notes of individual children's responses as they debate and discuss which key questions to include on their checklist and why. Ask how their questions could help the writer learn more about the person. Encourage the groups to swap their completed checklists with another group and use them to research information on a chosen person. Suggest that the questions are split amongst the children in the group. Make observation notes on how the children use the questions to help them find information. Once the groups have found the answers have a class feedback session. Ask: *Which key questions enabled you to find more information? How? Which questions were not useful? Why?*

Assessment evidence
At levels 2–3, children should be able to suggest key questions that identify the chronological order of information and straightforward reasons for the person's actions, such as 'What year did Henry VIII become king? 'Why did he want to divorce Katherine of Aragon?' They should be able to find some specific information to answer straightforward questions. At levels 4–5, children should be able to suggest more in-depth questions such as 'What made Henry VIII turn his back on the Pope?' and give clear and concise evaluations. Use notes of the children's responses and the observational notes along with the written key question checklists as evidence against Reading AF2 and Writing AF2.

Next steps
Support: Ask children to find out about one element of a person's life, such as their school days. Encourage them to write down key questions to help them find out useful information.
Extension: Encourage children to create a key question list for different sections of a person's life. For example, childhood, school days, teenage years, work. Discuss how specific key questions help give research more of a focus.

Key aspects of learning
Enquiry: Children will identify their own key questions about a particular life, and then locate the evidence to answer it within a range of sources.
Information processing: Children will identify relevant information from a range of sources on paper and on screen and use this as a basis for both oral presentation and writing.
Communication: Children will develop their ability to discuss and debate issues in respect of both the form and the content of the biographical texts they are reading and writing. They will often work collaboratively in pairs and groups. They will communicate outcomes orally, in writing and through using other modes and media.

Phase ② Presentations

Learning outcome
Children can research, prepare and present orally a reasoned account of a particular life.

Success criteria
- I can debate and agree to the resources and materials needed for a presentation.
- I can present orally an account of a life of a chosen person.
- I can evaluate a presentation about a chosen person.

Setting the context
In a previous activity the children worked in mixed ability groups to research information about a chosen person's life. Put the children back in their mixed ability groups and explain that they are to use their researched information to prepare and present a short oral presentation of that person to the rest of the class. List on the board the areas they would need to consider during their preparation such as the information they want to impart to their audience, the method (timelines, quotes) and the resources needed (visual support, internet access, presentation software). Encourage them to debate and note down their preparation needs within their groups. Display the success criteria in the classroom.

Assessment opportunity
Allow time for the groups to prepare their presentations. Suggest they allocate tasks using the different skills of the children. Join the groups and look at their plans and notes. Make observational notes of their preparations. Encourage the children to explain the ideas behind their presentations. Ask: *When would you show the timeline? Would you talk about it or is it just to be displayed?* Identify areas that need more work. Before the groups present their accounts, have a class discussion to create success criteria for the presentations and write the criteria on the board. With the class, watch each presentation and take notes. Encourage the class to take notes to help in their evaluations. Identify good points in each presentation and ask for class feedback and the group's feedback matched to the agreed criteria.

Assessment evidence
At levels 2–3, children should be able to include appropriate ideas and content in their presentations and make some attempt to elaborate on basic information. At levels 4–5, children should be able to develop some ideas in detail and maintain a clear viewpoint. Use the observation notes made during the activity and the presentations as evidence against Writing AF1.

Next steps
Support: Encourage children to create a small presentation of a person to a younger age group. Discuss how they can present information simply, clearly and effectively, for example using posters, a picture or ICT presentations to explain something.
Extension: Have a presentation session of different people's lives and invite another class or parents. Encourage children to have multimodal materials such as timelines, props, posters and music on display.

Key aspects of learning
Enquiry: Children will identify their own key questions about a particular life, and then locate the evidence to answer it within a range of sources.
Information processing: Children will identify relevant information from a range of sources on paper and on screen and use this as a basis for both oral presentation and writing.
Communication: Children will develop their ability to discuss and debate issues in respect of both the form and the content of the biographical texts they are reading and writing. They will often work collaboratively in pairs and groups. They will communicate outcomes orally, in writing and through using other modes and media.

Phase ③ Chronological order

NON-FICTION

Learning outcome

Children can recognise the structure and language, organisational and presentational features of different forms of biography and autobiography.

Success criteria
- I can understand how important events in a biography are often ordered chronologically.
- I can put biographical sentences in chronological order.

Setting the context

Display several extracts from a well-known person's biography, such as Tanni Grey-Thompson (see her website, www.tanni.co.uk). Remind the children of the purpose of a biography. Encourage them to read the extracts and identify features of biographical writing in the texts. Explain that the main events in the texts are ordered chronologically and ask the children why this is important. Ask them what kind of non-fiction a biography is (a recount text). Children at levels 2–3 will work individually or in pairs to sequence a biography about Marie Curie, using version 1 of the interactive activity 'Chronological order'. Children at levels 4–5 can work individually or in pairs on version 2 of the interactive activity.

Assessment opportunity

As the children work on the activity, ask them questions about why they have chosen to put the events in a certain sequence. Ask: *What information does it give the reader about the person? Why would it be difficult to understand if the events were out of sequence? Why does it not matter so much with autobiographical writing (for example, memories or actions explained by the actual person may cause time shifts)?* Take notes of their choices and responses. Encourage the children to look at the success criteria and discuss their understanding of biographical features and where or how they may need future support.

Assessment evidence

At levels 2–3, children should notice cues such as date order, and language such as 'born', 'died'. They should be able to recognise how having the texts out of chronological order makes it difficult to understand the events of Marie Curie's life. At levels 4–5, children should also be able to identify the use of a conclusion to bring the information together. Use notes of the children's discussion and work on the activity as evidence against Reading AF4.

Next steps

Support: Give children a cut-up sequence of a well-known short story and ask them to put it into chronological order. Discuss how the text is a recount and recap its features.

Extension: Extend work on biographical organisation by looking more closely at how paragraphs create a flow and structure when writing a biography. Focus on extracts and examine their effect.

Key aspects of learning

Information processing: Children will identify relevant information from a range of sources on paper and on screen and use this as a basis for both oral presentation and writing.

Communication: Children will develop their ability to discuss and debate issues in respect of both the form and the content of the biographical texts they are reading and writing. They will often work collaboratively in pairs and groups. They will communicate outcomes orally, in writing and through using other modes and media.

NON-FICTION

Phase ③ Marie Curie's account

Learning outcome
Children can recognise the structure and language, organisational and presentational features of different forms of biography and autobiography.

Success criteria
● I can rewrite a biography as an autobiography.
● I can use autobiographical features in a text.

Setting the context
Encourage the children as a class to identify the features of an autobiography and list them on the board. Display the photocopiable page 'Marie Curie' and explain that it is an extract from a short biography of her life. With the children, identify the biographical features, such as the impersonal style, that it is written in third person. Explain to the children that you would like them to write the biographical account as an autobiographical account. Remind the children of the autobiographical features list from the board. Children at levels 2-3 can write a short passage of one part of the extract with adult support if needed. Children at levels 4-5 can rewrite the whole extract in autobiographical form. Display the success criteria in the classroom.

Assessment opportunity
As the children work, move around the class and take notes. Ask questions about their work: *In what ways are you turning the language from formal to informal? Have you used the third or first person? How would Marie Curie describe it?* Encourage the children to share their completed account with a response partner. Invite them to identify autobiographical features in their partner's accounts and then feed back their findings. Ask them to compare their accounts to the success criteria. All the children should come together at the end of the activity to read through their accounts. Praise and identify those who have used autobiographical features successfully.

Assessment evidence
At levels 2-3, children should write their autobiographical text in the first person and start using more adventurous words to create a more personal style. At levels 4-5, children should use a personal style, using a range of techniques including time connectives to show shifts of time, descriptive use of verbs, adjectives and adverbs. The text should also show some form of structure. Use the children's written autobiographical accounts along with their responses and feedback as evidence against Writing AF1.

Next steps
Support: With the children, look at their short autobiographical passage. Discuss how autobiographies help to see a life from that person's point of view, for example how the person feels about an event, their feelings about other people, their reasons for doing something.
Extension: Encourage children to find out more about Marie Curie's childhood. How did she come to be a great scientist in an age when women were rarely able to do well in academic areas?

Key aspects of learning
Information processing: Children will identify relevant information from a range of sources on paper and on screen and use this as a basis for both oral presentation and writing.
Empathy: Through discussing and writing simulated autobiography, children will need to imagine themselves in another person's position.

Phase ④ Biography checklist

Learning outcome
Children can write an effective biography or autobiography selecting language, form, format and content to suit a particular audience and purpose.

Success criteria
● I can identify biographical features in a text.
● I can evaluate my partner's biographical text.

Setting the context
Use this assessment activity once the children have completed researching and writing a short biography relating to the life of a chosen person. Explain to the children that they are going to use a biography checklist to evaluate each other's biographies for the correct structure and language. Children at levels 2–3 will work within a group with an adult acting as scribe, using version 1 of the photocopiable page 'Biography checklist'. As a group, read through the list and discuss the different checkpoints. For the children at levels 4–5, give out version 2 of the photocopiable page and ask them to read through the list.

Assessment opportunity
Ask all the children to swap their written biographies with another child. Children at levels 2–3 should pass their work to a child within their group. Ask all the children to read the biographies and use the checklists to record examples of biographical features. Children at levels 2–3 can feed back to their group while those at levels 4–5 feed back to their partner. Encourage all the children to discuss each part of their checklist. Allow the children to take notes of any areas that they feel need improving or revising. Move around the class, observing their discussions and oral feedback about their biographies. Ask questions such as: *How could you improve the structure? Who is your audience?* Encourage the children to self-assess their work by looking at the success criteria.

Assessment evidence
At levels 2–3, children should be able to use the checklist to select information and consolidate their knowledge of biographical features. At levels 4–5, children should be able to identify the features and discuss the text in more depth. Use the children's checklists along with notes of their responses as evidence against Reading AF2.

Next steps
Support: Display a published biographical text and read it out to the children. Encourage them to stop you when they hear or recognise a biographical feature. Allow them to highlight the text. Discuss whether it is a good biographical text.
Extension: Encourage children to use the checklists on published biographical materials. Have a competition where the children choose what they think is the best text and give justifications.

Key aspects of learning
Information processing: Children will identify relevant information from a range of sources on paper and on screen and use this as a basis for both oral presentation and writing.
Communication: Children will develop their ability to discuss and debate issues in respect of both the form and the content of the biographical texts they are reading and writing. They will often work collaboratively in pairs and groups. They will communicate outcomes orally, in writing and through using other modes and media.

NON-FICTION

Phase ④ Autobiographical sentences

Learning outcome
Children can write an effective biography or autobiography selecting language, form, format and content to suit a particular audience and purpose.

Success criteria
● I can rewrite sentences to make my autobiographical text more personal.
● I can use powerful language to improve my autobiographical text.
● I can identify and rewrite sentences to improve my autobiographical text.

Setting the context
Use this assessment activity during a writing session when the children are writing or revising a short autobiography about the life of a chosen person. Remind the children how autobiographical texts can be made more effective by making the language more personal and expressive. Display the photocopiable page 'Marie Curie - my life'. Show how Marie Curie's feelings and emotions are conveyed in the text using different sentences such as simple, compound and complex sentences, for example, 'Pierre put his burnt hands over his eyes and started to sob in despair'. Identify how the powerful verbs and adjectives also help convey how Marie Curie is feeling.

Assessment opportunity
Children at levels 2–3 can work in a small groups with adult support. Ask all the children to re-read their autobiographies and highlight or underline sentences that could be improved and mark places in the text where a new sentence could be added in. Encourage all the children to use small whiteboards or paper to experiment and create new sentences with more powerful language. Move around the class and ask questions such as: *What is the person feeling? How would you bring that across in a sentence? What verbs or adjectives could you use to indicate their emotions?* Take notes of the children's ideas and ability to construct effective sentences. Once they have revised the sentences, discuss with each of the children whether they feel they have achieved the success criteria.

Assessment evidence
At levels 2–3, children should be able to use simple sentences and basic compound sentences to create an effect. They should also be able to elaborate on basic information and make apt word choices. At levels 4–5, children should be able to use a wide range of sentence structures and develop some ideas with imaginative detail. Use the notes and children's revised written work as evidence against Writing AF5.

Next steps
Support: Work on constructing sentences to illustrate feelings and emotions by turning simple sentences into complex sentences. Look at the use of time connectives to link ideas and thoughts.
Extension: Look at the use of punctuation and how it indicates direct and indirect speech.

Key aspects of learning
Information processing: Children will identify relevant information from a range of sources on paper and on screen and use this as a basis for both oral presentation and writing.
Empathy: Through discussing and writing simulated autobiography, children will need to imagine themselves in another person's position.

■SCHOLASTIC

Periodic assessment

Reading

Learning outcome
Children can recognise the structure and language, organisational and presentational features of different forms of biography and autobiography.

Success criteria
- I can identify the features of an autobiographical text.
- I can analyse the features of an autobiographical text.
- I can understand the effects of an autobiographical text on the reader.

Setting the context
Put the children into their guided reading groups and work with one group at a time. Provide copies of the photocopiable page 'Non-fiction 1 Reading assessment text', which shows two text extracts from Tanni Grey-Thompson's autobiography. Read through the texts with each group. Identify that they are Tanni Grey-Thompson's account of two very important events. Discuss the success criteria and, with the children, identify examples of the language and organisational features that indicate they are autobiographical, for example, personal language, use of the first person, emotive language, sentence construction, past and present tense, time shifts.

Assessment opportunity
Take notes of the children's comments and responses. With children working at levels 2-3 you may want to just study one of the texts and look at one area, such as the use of personal language. Ask guided questions to encourage the children to focus and respond, for example: *What did Tanni say when she read the letter? Point to examples of text in the first person.* Encourage children working at levels 4-5 to highlight or underline words or sentences that indicate an autobiographical text. With each group discuss ways in which the text allows the reader to understand and experience Tanni's feelings and actions. Encourage the children to self-assess their progress using the success criteria.

Assessment evidence
The children at levels 2-3 should recognise the main features of an autobiography, such as the use of the past tense, and personal and emotive language. The children at levels 4-5 should recognise features such as the use of sentences and connectives to illustrate the emotion Tanni felt. They should also notice how the text sounds as though Tanni is talking directly to them: 'It was as if it was a school trip...' Record the children's understandings and needs and use them to make level judgements against Reading AF4, AF5 and AF6.

Periodic assessment

Writing

Learning outcome
Children can write an effective biography or autobiography selecting language, form, format and content to suit a particular audience or purpose.

Success criteria
● I can use the third person to change an autobiographical text into a biographical text.
● I can use impersonal language to write an effective biographical text.
● I can use chronological order to write an effective biographical text.

Setting the context
Display the autobiographical text extract from photocopiable page 'Non-fiction 1 Writing assessment' and read it to the class. Explain words that may be unknown to the children, such as 'pitchblende'. Explain that the extract is from the point when Marie Curie found a run-down shed to carry out experiments to discover pure radium. Explain to the children that they are going to rewrite the account as an effective biography. Give the children the photocopiable page 'Non-fiction 1 Writing assessment' and allow them to annotate the copies for planning and inspiration. Display the success criteria in the classroom.

Assessment opportunity
Move round the children taking notes of their progress. Discuss how they are going to write the sentences as they get to each one. Take notes of their responses and work. Do they use the past tense, the third person, impersonal language? Encourage the children to share their completed biographies with a response partner. Invite them to evaluate the texts and identify areas that may need extra work or improvement. Encourage them to discuss the success criteria. What areas are they satisfied with? What needs more support?

Assessment evidence
Children at levels 2–3 should turn each autobiographical sentence into a biographical sentence and write them below the extract. They should write straightforward biographical sentences using the past tense, the third person and some form of impersonal language. Children at levels 4–5 should show a good use of biographical features such as the use of impersonal language, chronological order, use of quotes and direct or indirect speech. Record the children's understandings and needs and use them to make level judgements against Writing AF1, AF2, AF7 and AF8.

Marie Curie

Marie Curie was born as Maria Sklodowski in Warsaw, Poland on 7 November 1867. The youngest of five children, Marie came from a happy and loving family. Both her parents were teachers who passed their love for learning onto their children. In 1874 tragedy struck, with the death of Marie's eldest sister of typhus and then, two years later, her mother died from tuberculosis.

Marie studied very hard at school and in 1883 she was awarded with the gold medal for the most outstanding pupil in her school. Marie wanted to go onto university to study like her brother but at that time women in Poland were forbidden to go on to higher education. Marie's sister, Bronia, also wanted to go to university and had discovered that women were accepted at universities in France. Marie and Bronia decided to take action. Bronia would go to Paris and get her degree whilst Marie got a job as a governess to support Bronia. They would then change roles.

In November 1891, Marie's long wait finally came to an end and she immediately signed up at the Sorbonne University in Paris, to study mathematics and physics. Marie studied very hard for the two degrees and came top in both of them.

In 1894 Marie met Pierre Curie, a brilliant young scientist. He was quiet and serious and, like Marie, dedicated to scientific research. Marie and Pierre found they had much in common and in 1895 they got married. It was the start of what became the most famous partnership in scientific history.

NON-FICTION
Unit 2 Journalistic writing

Literacy objectives

Speak and listen for a wide range of purposes in different contexts
Strand 1 Speaking
- Use a range of oral techniques to present persuasive arguments and engaging narratives.
- Use the techniques of dialogic talk to explore ideas, topics or issues.

Strand 2 Listening and responding
- Make notes when listening for a sustained period and discuss how note-taking varies depending on context and purpose.

Strand 4 Drama
- Improvise using a range of drama strategies and conventions to explore themes such as hopes, fears and desires.

Read and write for a range of purposes on paper and on screen
Strand 6 Word structure and spelling
- Spell familiar words correctly and employ a range of strategies to spell difficult and unfamiliar words.
- Use a range of appropriate strategies to edit, proofread and correct spelling in their own work, on paper and on screen.

Strand 7 Understanding and interpreting texts
- Appraise a text quickly, deciding on its value, quality or usefulness.
- Recognise rhetorical devices used to argue, persuade, mislead and sway the reader.

Strand 8 Engaging with and responding to texts
- Sustain engagement with longer texts using different techniques to make the text come alive.
- Compare how writers from different times and places present experiences and use language.

Strand 9 Creating and shaping texts
- Use different narrative techniques to engage and entertain the reader.
- Select words and language drawing on their knowledge of literary features and formal and informal writing.
- Integrate words, images and sounds imaginatively for different purposes.

Strand 10 Text structure and organisation
- Use varied structures to shape and organise text coherently.

Strand 11 Sentence structure and punctuation
- Express subtle distinctions of meaning, including hypothesis, speculation and supposition, by constructing sentences in varied ways.

Key aspects of learning

Enquiry
- Children will learn to ask: Who? What? Where? When? and Why? in researching a news story for a written or oral report.

Unit 2 Journalistic writing

NON-FICTION

Key aspects of learning (contd)

Evaluation
- Children will read, compare and evaluate news from a variety of sources. When presenting news reports orally and in writing, they will discuss success criteria, give feedback to others and judge the effectiveness of their own work.

Empathy
- In discussing and writing about real or simulated events, children will need to imagine themselves in another person's situation.

Communication
- Children will develop their ability to discuss and debate issues in respect of both the content and the presentation of the news reports they are reading and writing. They will often work collaboratively in pairs and groups. They will communicate outcomes orally (in the stye of radio broadcasts), in writing and through using other modes and media.

Assessment focuses

Reading
AF2 (understand, describe, select or retrieve information, events or ideas from texts and use quotation and reference to text).
AF4 (identify and comment on the structure and organisation of text, including grammatical and presentation features at text level).
AF6 (identify and comment on writers' purposes and viewpoints, and the overall effect of the text on the reader).

Writing
AF2 (produce texts which are appropriate to task, reader and purpose).

Speaking and listening
Speaking (speak with clarity, intonation and pace).
Listening and responding (understand and recall the main points; responds appropriately).
Drama (take and sustain different roles).

Resources

Phase 1 activities
Photocopiable page, 'The five 'W' questions'
Phase 2 activities
Website, http://news.bbc.co.uk/1/hi/entertainment/7600126.stm
Interactive activity, 'News reports'
Video, 'La Machine'
Phase 3 activities
Photocopiable page, 'News report features' (versions 1 and 2)
Phase 4 activities
Photocopiable page, 'Self-assessment checklist'
Periodic assessment
Interactive activity, 'Non-fiction 2 Reading assessment'
Photocopiable page, 'Non-fiction 2 Writing assessment'

Unit 2 ◻ Journalistic writing

Learning outcomes	Assessment opportunity and evidence	Assessment focuses (AFs)		Success criteria
		Level 2	Level 3	
Phase ① activities pages 102-103				
The five 'W' questions Children have experience of a wide range of news reporting, on paper and in other media, and can understand what is being communicated, why and how. They can evaluate its effectiveness in terms of informing and engaging its audience.	● Paired activity where children answer the five 'W' questions for a range of different news reports. ● Children's oral responses. ● Teacher's notes. ● Completed photocopiables.	**Reading AF2** ● Some specific, straightforward information recalled. ● Generally clear idea of where to look for information. **Reading AF6** ● Some awareness that writers have viewpoints and purposes. ● Simple statements about likes and dislikes in reading, sometimes with reasons.	**Reading AF2** ● Simple, most obvious points identified though there may also be some misunderstanding. ● Some comments include quotations from or references to text, but not always relevant. **Reading AF6** ● Comments identify main purpose. ● Express personal response but with little awareness of writer's viewpoint or effect on reader.	● I can identify the five 'W' questions in a range of different news reports. ● I can record information to answer questions. ● I can compare different news reports.
Impact survey Children are aware of the power and potential of different communication modalities and media.	● Supported group activity where children agree to create a criteria list to help them evaluate the impact of different news reports and give them a rating out of ten. ● Children's oral responses and discussion. ● Teacher's notes.	**Reading AF6** ● Some awareness that writers have viewpoints and purposes. ● Simple statements about likes and dislikes in reading, sometimes with reasons.	**Reading AF6** ● Comments identify main purpose. ● Express personal response but with little awareness of writer's viewpoint or effect on reader.	● I can identify the different ways information is communicated by different media. ● I can compare different journalistic forms.
Phase ② activities pages 104-106				
The Liverpool spider Children can listen attentively to an aural news report and make notes for specific purposes.	● Group activity where children focus on one area of a spoken news report, take effective notes, collate their notes and present them to the class. ● Children's oral responses and discussion. ● Children's written notes. ● Teacher's notes.	**Reading AF2** ● Some specific, straightforward information recalled. ● Generally clear idea of where to look for information.	**Reading AF2** ● Simple, most obvious points identified though there may also be some misunderstanding. ● Some comments include quotations from or references to text, but not always relevant.	● I can listen attentively to a news report. ● I can make notes on one focus of the news report. ● I can discuss one area of a news report using my notes.
News reports Children understand some key features of the way radio news programmes are structured and presented to inform and engage particular audiences.	● Group activity where children identify and discuss the key features of different news report scripts and the targeted audiences. ● Children's oral responses. ● Children's written notes. ● Teacher's notes.	**Reading AF6** ● Some awareness that writers have viewpoints and purposes. ● Simple statements about likes and dislikes in reading, sometimes with reasons.	**Reading AF6** ● Comments identify main purpose. ● Express personal response but with little awareness of writer's viewpoint or effect on reader.	● I can recognise some key features of radio news programmes. ● I can identify a news report aimed at a specific audience.

Unit 2 📖 Journalistic writing

Learning outcomes	Assessment opportunity and evidence	Assessment focuses (AFs)		Success criteria
		Level 2	Level 3	
Questions for the bride Children can use discussion and drama techniques to explore a particular event, incident or situation and its protagonists.	• Group activity where children debate and choose interview questions, followed by hot seating. • Children's oral responses. • Children's interview questions. • Drama session feedback.	**Writing AF2** • Some basic purpose established. • Some appropriate features of the given form used. • Some attempts to adopt appropriate style.	**Writing AF2** • Purpose established at a general level. • Main features of selected form sometimes signalled to the reader. • Some attempts at appropriate style, with attention to reader.	• I can empathise with a person in a particular situation. • I can create and ask questions to find out how a person feels about a situation. • I can use drama to try and find out how a person feels about a situation.

Phase ③ activity page 107

Learning outcomes	Assessment opportunity and evidence	Level 2	Level 3	Success criteria
Newspaper report features Children can recognise the structure and language features of journalistic reports, both as written text and as scripts for oral presentation.	• Supported group activity where children read a newspaper report, identify examples of features of newspaper report writing and add them to a checklist. • Children's oral responses. • Children's written checklists.	**Reading AF4** • Some awareness of use of features of organisation.	**Reading AF4** • A few basic features of organisation at text level identified, with little or no linked comment.	• I can identify the structure features of journalistic reports. • I can identify the language features of journalistic reports.

Phase ④ activities pages 108–109

Learning outcomes	Assessment opportunity and evidence	Level 2	Level 3	Success criteria
Self-assessment checklist Children can write an effective news article in journalistic style, selecting language, form, format and content to suit a particular audience and purpose.	• Group activity where children evaluate, redraft and edit different elements of their work. • Children's oral responses. • Children's checklists.	**Writing AF2** • Some basic purpose established. • Some appropriate features of the given form used. • Some attempts to adopt appropriate style.	**Writing AF2** • Purpose established at a general level. • Main features of selected form sometimes signalled to the reader. • Some attempts at appropriate style, with attention to reader.	• I can plan and write an effective news article. • I can use structural and language features of journalistic writing. • I can evaluate, redraft and edit my news article.
News broadcasts Children can use a news article as the basis for a script and present it orally in the style of a radio news item in a way which is informative and engaging.	• Supported activity where children plan and perform a news broadcast with a written script, make notes on the script for presentation cues and evaluate them to agreed criteria. • Children's written notes on scripts. • Teacher's notes on class discussions, evaluations and performances.	**Writing AF2** • Some basic purpose established. • Some appropriate features of the given form used. • Some attempts to adopt appropriate style.	**Writing AF2** • Purpose established at a general level. • Main features of selected form sometimes signalled to the reader. • Some attempts at appropriate style, with attention to reader.	• I can make notes on my news broadcast script to help with its presentation. • I can present an effective broadcast using presentational skills. • I can evaluate a news broadcast using set criteria.

Unit 2 ◖ Journalistic writing

Learning outcomes	Assessment opportunity and evidence	Assessment focuses (AFs)		Success criteria
		Level 4	Level 5	

Phase ① activities pages 102-103

Learning outcomes	Assessment opportunity and evidence	Level 4	Level 5	Success criteria
The five 'W' questions Children have experience of a wide range of news reporting, on paper and in other media, and can understand what is being communicated, why and how. They can evaluate its effectiveness in terms of informing and engaging its audience.	• Paired activity where children answer the five 'W' questions for a range of different news reports. • Children's oral responses. • Teacher's notes. • Completed photocopiables.	**Reading AF2** • Some relevant points identified. • Comments supported by some generally relevant textual reference or quotation. **Reading AF6** • Main purpose identified. • Simple comments show some awareness of writer's viewpoint. • Simple comment on overall effect on reader.	**Reading AF2** • Most relevant points clearly identified, including those selected from different places in the text. • Comments generally supported by relevant textual reference or quotation, even when points made are not always accurate. **Reading AF6** • Main purpose clearly identified, often through general overview. • Viewpoints in texts clearly identified, with some, often limited, explanation. • General awareness of effect on the reader, with some, often limited, explanation.	• I can identify the five 'W' questions in a range of different news reports. • I can record information to answer questions. • I can compare different news reports.
Impact survey Children are aware of the power and potential of different communication modalities and media.	• Paired activity where children agree to create a criteria list to help them evaluate the impact of different news reports and give them a rating out of ten. • Children's oral responses and discussion. • Teacher's notes.	**Reading AF6** • Main purpose identified. • Simple comments show some awareness of writer's viewpoint. • Simple comment on overall effect on reader.	**Reading AF6** • Main purpose clearly identified, often through general. • Viewpoints in texts clearly identified, with some, often limited, explanation. • General awareness of effect on the reader, with some, often limited, explanation.	• I can identify the different ways information is communicated by different media. • I can compare different journalistic forms.

Phase ② activities pages 104-106

Learning outcomes	Assessment opportunity and evidence	Level 4	Level 5	Success criteria
The Liverpool spider Children can listen attentively to an aural news report and make notes for specific purposes.	• Group activity where children focus on one area of a spoken news report, take effective notes, collate their notes and present them to the class. • Children's oral responses and discussion. • Children's written notes. • Teacher's notes.	**Reading AF2** • Some relevant points identified. • Comments supported by some generally relevant textual reference or quotation.	**Reading AF2** • Most relevant points clearly identified, including those selected from different places in the text. • Comments generally supported by relevant textual reference or quotation, even when points made are not always accurate.	• I can listen attentively to a news report. • I can make notes on one focus of the news report. • I can discuss one area of a news report using my notes.
News reports Children understand some key features of the way radio news programmes are structured and presented to inform and engage particular audiences.	• Group activity where children identify and discuss the key features of different news report scripts and the targeted audiences. • Children's oral responses. • Children's written notes. • Teacher's notes.	**Reading AF6** • Main purpose identified. • Simple comments show some awareness of writer's viewpoint. • Simple comment on overall effect on reader.	**Reading AF6** • Main purpose clearly identified, often through general. • Viewpoints in texts clearly identified, with some, often limited, explanation. • General awareness of effect on the reader, with some, often limited, explanation.	• I can recognise some key features of radio news programmes. • I can identify a news report aimed at a specific audience.

Unit 2 ▢ Journalistic writing

Learning outcomes	Assessment opportunity and evidence	Assessment focuses (AFs)		Success criteria
		Level 4	Level 5	
Questions for the bride Children can use discussion and drama techniques to explore a particular event, incident or situation and its protagonists.	• Group activity where children debate and choose interview questions, followed by hot seating. • Children's oral responses. • Children's interview questions. • Drama session feedback.	**Writing AF2** • Main purpose of writing is clear but not always consistently maintained. • Main features of selected form are clear and appropriate to purpose. • Style generally appropriate to task, though awareness of reader not always sustained.	**Writing AF2** • Main purpose of writing is clear and consistently maintained. • Features of selected form clearly established with some adaptation to purpose. • Appropriate style clearly established to maintain reader's interest throughout.	• I can empathise with a person in a particular situation. • I can create and ask questions to find out how a person feels about a situation. • I can use drama to try and find out how a person feels about a situation.

Phase ③ activity page 107

Learning outcomes	Assessment opportunity and evidence	Level 4	Level 5	Success criteria
Newspaper report features Children can recognise the structure and language features of journalistic reports, both as written text and as scripts for oral presentation.	• Independent activity where children examine a range of news reports for examples of typical features. • Children's oral responses. • Children's written checklists.	**Reading AF4** • Some structural choices identified with simple comment. • Some basic features of organisation at text level identified.	**Reading AF4** • Comments on structural choices show some general awareness of writer's craft. • Various features relating to organisation at text level, including form, are clearly identified, with some explanation.	• I can identify the structure features of journalistic reports. • I can identify the language features of journalistic reports.

Phase ④ activities pages 108–109

Learning outcomes	Assessment opportunity and evidence	Level 4	Level 5	Success criteria
Self-assessment checklist Children can write an effective news article in journalistic style, selecting language, form, format and content to suit a particular audience and purpose.	• Paired activity where children evaluate, redraft and edit different elements of their work. • Children's oral responses. • Children's checklists.	**Writing AF2** • Main purpose of writing is clear but not always consistently maintained. • Main features of selected form are clear and appropriate to purpose. • Style generally appropriate to task, though awareness of reader not always sustained.	**Writing AF2** • Main purpose of writing is clear and consistently maintained. • Features of selected form clearly established with some adaptation to purpose. • Appropriate style clearly established to maintain reader's interest throughout.	• I can plan and write an effective news article. • I can use structural and language features of journalistic writing. • I can evaluate, redraft and edit my news article.
News broadcasts Children can use a news article as the basis for a script and present it orally in the style of a radio news item in a way which is informative and engaging.	• Independent activity where children plan and perform a news broadcast with a written script, make notes on the script for presentation cues and evaluate them to agreed criteria. • Children's written notes on scripts. • Teacher's notes on class discussions, evaluations and performances.	**Writing AF2** • Main purpose of writing is clear but not always consistently maintained. • Main features of selected form are clear and appropriate to purpose. • Style generally appropriate to task, though awareness of reader not always sustained.	**Writing AF2** • Main purpose of writing is clear and consistently maintained. • Features of selected form clearly established with some adaptation to purpose. • Appropriate style clearly established to maintain reader's interest throughout.	• I can make notes on my news broadcast script to help with its presentation. • I can present an effective broadcast using presentational skills. • I can evaluate a news broadcast using set criteria.

NON-FICTION

Phase ① The five 'W' questions

Learning outcome
Children have experience of a wide range of news reporting, on paper and in other media, and can understand what is being communicated, why and how. They can evaluate its effectiveness in terms of informing and engaging its audience.

Success criteria
● I can identify the five 'W' questions in a range of different news reports.
● I can record information to answer questions.
● I can compare different news reports.

Setting the context
Display the success criteria in the classroom. Use this activity once the children have had experience in exploring and comparing journalistic writing and other mediums. Revise the five 'W' questions: Who? What? Where? When? and Why? Arrange workstations around the classroom to represent different types of news reports, for example, internet reports, radio reports, newspapers, and so on. Put the children into mixed ability pairs. Give the pairs a copy of the photocopiable 'The five "W" questions' to use at each workstation. The pairs read or listen to the news reports and then write examples of the five 'W' questions on the sheet. Give the children several minutes at each workstation to complete the sheet and then move on to the next one. Make sure they keep their sheets as they progress. Children at levels 2-3 may need to work with adult support.

Assessment opportunity
Observe and make notes of the children as they work. Ensure they put the type of news report at the top of each sheet. As they complete the sheets ask guided questions, such as: *What is the purpose and audience of the report? What is the effect on the reader or listener?* Once they have visited all the workstations, bring the class together and encourage the children to discuss and compare their results. Examine the differences between the types of report and link that to their purpose and audience. Ask: *Which report do you think was most effective in getting the five 'W' questions across to the audience? Why?*

Assessment evidence
At levels 2-3, children should be able to identify the five 'W' questions in clear, straightforward news reports. They may need support on identifying 'W' questions in more wordy reports. Children at levels 4-5 should be able to listen or read carefully and extract the five 'W' questions and record their examples. They should discuss their effect on the audience. Use the children's written sheets along with your observation notes as evidence against Reading AF2 and AF6.

Next steps
Support: Some children may find it hard to focus on all five 'W' questions when scanning a news report. Give the children a copy of a newspaper and, with support, use a highlighter to find examples of one question such as 'Who?' or 'What?' Discuss the information and how it is presented.
Extension: As a homework challenge children to explore and investigate the way the five 'Ws' are presented in different styles of journalistic reports, such as a celebrity interview, a headline news report, a travel report, or a local community report.

Key aspects of learning
Evaluation: Children will read, compare and evaluate news from a variety of sources. When presenting news reports orally and in writing, they will discuss success criteria, give feedback to others and judge the effectiveness of their own work.
Communication: Children will develop their ability to discuss and debate issues in respect of both the content and the presentation of the news reports they are reading and writing. They will often work collaboratively in pairs and groups. They will communicate outcomes orally (in the style of radio broadcasts), in writing and through using other modes and media.

Phase ① Impact survey

Learning outcome
Children are aware of the power and potential of different communication modalities and media.

Success criteria
● I can identify the different ways information is communicated by different media.
● I can compare different journalistic forms.

Setting the context
Put children at levels 2-3 in small groups with an adult support as a scribe and children at levels 4-5 into pairs. With the class, revise how journalistic reports come in many forms. List a few examples. Discuss how each form has its own impact and effect on the reader, viewer or listener, for example, the use of word or sentence construction. With the children, create agreed criteria against which to evaluate the impact of a range of news reports and display them on the board. Ask the children to use the criteria to give a range of news reports a rating of one to ten for impact.

Assessment opportunity
Give out a selection of different news reports and set up aural and visual mediums for the children to access. As the children use the criteria to evaluate the reports, move round the class and ask guided questions, such as: *How clear is the purpose of the text? How well is the information conveyed? Is the style memorable? What score would you give out of ten for its impact?* Take notes of their responses and comments. Once the children have completed their evaluations have a class debate about their findings and ratings. Which reports had the most impact? Why?

Assessment evidence
At levels 2-3, children should be able to recognise simple sentences and descriptive vocabulary, such as 'devastated' and 'astonished' and discuss the impact they may have on the reader. At levels 4-5, children should be able to explain why the journalist chose certain words and sentence constructions to create the right effect. Use the children's comments as evidence towards Reading AF6.

Next steps
Support: Encourage children to collate the ratings from the class and, with support, create a ratings graph. Use the graph to ask guided questions about why certain news reports had more impact than others.
Extension: Ask children to write out and keep the evaluation criteria to use as a guide to help judge and evaluate future news reports that are read or listened to, in or outside of the classroom.

Key aspects of learning
Evaluation: Children will read, compare and evaluate news from a variety of sources. When presenting news reports orally and in writing, they will discuss success criteria, give feedback to others and judge the effectiveness of their own work.
Reasoning: Children will construct reasoned arguments based on available information and evidence.
Communication: Children will develop their ability to discuss and debate issues in respect of both the content and the presentation of the news reports they are reading and writing. They will often work collaboratively in pairs and groups. They will communicate outcomes orally (in the style of radio broadcasts), in writing and through using other modes and media.

Phase ② The Liverpool spider

Learning outcome
Children can listen attentively to an aural news report and make notes for specific purposes.

Success criteria
- I can listen attentively to a news report.
- I can make notes on one focus of the news report.
- I can discuss one area of a news report using my notes.

Setting the context
With the class revise how to make notes of a radio or TV news report, for example: have a clear focus, noting only key words and information. Put the children into mixed ability groups and give each group one aspect to focus on during the report about the Liverpool spider (also referred to as La Machine or La Princesse). For example, the groups could focus and take notes on one of the five 'W' questions, the type of language used and the structure of the report. The report is found at: http://news.bbc.co.uk/1/hi/entertainment/7600126.stm. Play the report through so the children can listen to the whole story and then repeat it a couple of times for note-taking. Display the success criteria in the classroom.

Assessment opportunity
Walk around the groups and take observational notes as they work together. Once the children have completed their note-taking, encourage them to work as a group to discuss and collate their ideas into a group report of their findings. Observe their discussions and debates and take notes to identify those who may need extra support and those who have a good understanding of the activity. Have a plenary session to discuss each group's notes and findings. Play back the report and encourage the class to focus on each group's results. Were the notes effective? Look at the success criteria and talk with each child about their progress and how they could improve their note-taking skills.

Assessment evidence
At levels 2–3, children should be able to listen to the report and take notes of basic facts. At levels 4–5, children should be able to make informative notes based on information from the entire news report. Use your observational notes and the children's own notes as evidence against Reading AF2.

Next steps
Support: Work with children in pairs or in small groups. Listen to a news report in advance and create a tick sheet for one area of information, such as certain descriptive words. Let the children listen to the report and tick off the information as they listen.
Extension: As a homework challenge, ask children to listen to a radio or TV news programme and take notes of a chosen focus. How much of the information have they collected? How could they improve their note-taking for the next report?

Key aspects of learning
Information processing: Children will identify relevant information from a range of sources on paper and on screen and use this as a basis for both oral and written reporting.
Evaluation: Children will read, compare and evaluate news from a variety of sources. When presenting news reports orally and in writing, they will discuss success criteria, give feedback to others and judge the effectiveness of their own work.
Communication: Children will develop their ability to discuss and debate issues in respect of both the content and the presentation of the news reports they are reading and writing. They will often work collaboratively in pairs and groups. They will communicate outcomes orally (in the style of radio broadcasts), in writing and through using other modes and media.

Phase ② News reports

Learning outcome
Children understand some key features of the way radio news programmes are structured and presented to inform and engage particular audiences.

Success criteria
- I can recognise some key features of radio news programmes.
- I can identify a news report aimed at a specific audience.

Setting the context
Work with the children in levelled groups. Remind them of previous activities where they have investigated and compared the style, content, presentation and structure of news programmes, including radio news programmes. Discuss and compare various examples, such as reports aimed at children compared to news reports aimed at adults. Explain to the children that they are going to look at four small news report extracts to decide on their intended audience and to write notes on their key features.

Assessment opportunity
Within each group display the interactive activity 'News reports' on a screen. Ask each child in the group whether the news reports are aimed at a local audience or a national audience. Take notes of their responses. Encourage the children to note any features that give clues to the audience, such as names of local organisations. Identify the use of words and, with children at levels 4- 5, look at the sentence structure. Ask all the children to write notes on the key features of radio news programmes demonstrated within the four extracts. Have a group discussion on the features and whether the reports target the right audience effectively.

Assessment evidence
At levels 2–3, children should be able to recognise that the extracts for local news have references to local places and people and is of more interest to a local community. At levels 4-5, children should be able to recognise the more informal language of local news compared with the formal language of the national reports. These features should be present in their own work. Use the notes of the children's comments as evidence against Reading AF6.

Next steps
Support: If children find it hard to compare news reports, go back to focusing on one type. Use the internet to find news reports aimed at children. Focus on one area, such as the structure or the simple explanatory language.
Extension: Encourage children to read out the scripts from the interactive activity as if they were newsreaders on the radio. Discuss how they can use expression and intonation to give the reports impact.

Key aspects of learning
Information processing: Children will identify relevant information from a range of sources on paper and on screen and use this as a basis for both oral and written reporting.
Evaluation: Children will read, compare and evaluate news from a variety of sources. When presenting news reports orally and in writing, they will discuss success criteria, give feedback to others and judge the effectiveness of their own work.
Communication: Children will develop their ability to discuss and debate issues in respect of both the content and the presentation of the news reports they are reading and writing. They will often work collaboratively in pairs and groups. They will communicate outcomes orally (in the style of radio broadcasts), in writing and through using other modes and media.

Phase ② Questions for the bride

Learning outcome
Children can use discussion and drama techniques to explore a particular event, incident or situation and its protagonists.

Success criteria
- I can empathise with a person in a particular situation.
- I can create and ask questions to find out how a person feels about a situation.
- I can use drama to try and find out how a person feels about a situation.

Setting the context
Show the children the video 'La Machine' from the CD-ROM. Focus on the situation with the wedding party. Discuss what had happened to the bride during the event with the spider machine. Put the children into small mixed ability groups. Ask them to imagine what the bride must have felt when her car got caught in the crowds, when she was told she had to walk to the church and the response from the crowds as she passed them. Explain to the children that they are going to interview the bride about the event and her feelings for a news report. Display the success criteria in the classroom.

Assessment opportunity
Encourage the children to think of ten interview questions. As the groups debate and decide on their questions, ask questions, such as: *What do you think she thought of the spider? Was she late for the wedding? Who was she marrying? Who made the decision to walk? How did she feel walking through the streets?* Once the groups have drafted and written their questions, pair them up with another group and choose two children to act as the bride for a hot-seat session. Once the session is over, ask each group how effective their questions were? Did they get the bride's side of the story? Did they get enough information? How could they improve the questions?

Assessment evidence
At levels 2–3, children should be able to construct their questions correctly and elicit key facts from the bride. They should begin to understand how to find out and present how she feels. At levels 4–5, children should be able to create questions that elicit a full version of the story from the bride and find out her feelings and views in more detail. Use the children's questions and your notes on the group discussions and drama session as evidence against Writing AF2.

Next steps
Support: To get a sense of chronology of the event with the bride, encourage children to create a sequence of freeze-frame tableaux of the event. Emphasise the bride's different expressions and body language.
Extension: Encourage children to use their interview questions to write up a report with a catchy headline. Focus on the use of quotations and punctuation in the report.

Key aspects of learning
Enquiry: Children will learn to ask: Who? What? Where? When? and Why? in researching a news story for a written or oral report.
Empathy: In discussing and writing about real or simulated events, children will need to imagine themselves in another person's situation.
Communication: Children will develop their ability to discuss and debate issues in respect of both the content and the presentation of the news reports they are reading and writing. They will often work collaboratively in pairs and groups. They will communicate outcomes orally (in the style of radio broadcasts), in writing and through using other modes and media.

Phase ③ Newspaper report features

Learning outcome
Children can recognise the structure and language features of journalistic reports, both as written text and as scripts for oral presentation.

Success criteria
● I can identify the structure features of journalistic reports.
● I can identify the language features of journalistic reports.

Setting the context
Remind the children how newspaper and radio/TV reports have distinct structural and language features. Briefly revise some examples, such as headlines, short sentences and descriptive language. Put the children into ability groups. Explain to the children that they are going to initially look at a newspaper report to identify and record structural and language features. Children at levels 2-3 can work as a discussion group with adult support to complete version 1 of the photocopiable page 'News report features' using one copy of a newspaper report. Children at levels 4-5 can work independently with their own newspaper report and version 2 of the photocopiable page.

Assessment evidence
Enable children in the levels 2-3 groups to read through the newspaper report with their adult support. Encourage them to identify examples of the report features. The adult can write down the children's comments on the checklist along with their name. Children at levels 4-5 should individually record their newspaper report information directly onto their sheets. Give out another copy of the sheets to all the children and ask them to listen to or watch a radio/TV news report and list its features. Once all the children have completed the sheets, have a class plenary for the children to report back their findings and discuss the effect of the news report features on the reader or listener.

Assessment opportunity
At levels 2-3, children should recognise a range of news report features, such as newspaper layout with headlines and captions, the use of language and facts and figures. At levels 4-5, children should be able to identify examples of features, such as different length sentence structures to create impact or give information, and be able to discuss how the structure and language creates an impact or effect on the reader or listener. Use the children's written checklists along with the observation notes of the children's comments and responses as evidence against Reading AF4.

Next steps
Support: Working independently or in pairs give the children a suitable newspaper report and encourage them to identify and then cut out examples of given features such as subheadings, short, informative sentences, descriptive vocabulary and then stick them onto paper as a collage.
Extension: Ask the children to look closely at a newspaper report and focus on one area, such as the use of punctuation. What effect does punctuation have on the text? Can they find more examples? How does it compare with other reports? Why is punctuation so important in reports?

Key aspects of learning
Enquiry: Children will learn to ask: Who? What? Where? When? and Why? in researching a news story for a written or oral report.
Information processing: Children will identify relevant information from a range of sources on paper and on screen and use this as a basis for both oral and written reporting.
Communication: Children will develop their ability to discuss and debate issues in respect of both the content and the presentation of the news reports they are reading and writing. They will often work collaboratively in pairs and groups. They will communicate outcomes orally (in the style of radio broadcasts), in writing and through using other modes and media.

NON-FICTION

NON-FICTION

Phase ④ Self-assessment checklist

Learning outcome
Children can write an effective news article in journalistic style, selecting language, form, format and content to suit a particular audience and purpose.

Success criteria
- I can plan and write an effective news article.
- I can use structural and language features of journalistic writing.
- I can evaluate, redraft and edit my news article.

Setting the context
Use this assessment during a writing activity where the children are planning and writing their own news articles. At each stage of the process of writing the news report - note-taking, devising layout, the use of quotations, headlines - encourage the children to evaluate their work with a response partner and then redraft or edit their work. Use the photocopiable page 'Self-assessment checklist' as an aid to record the children's progress and to identify areas that may need extra support. Display the success criteria in the classroom.

Assessment opportunity
Note down observations as the children work collaboratively on their news articles over a period of time. As they plan and write the article, encourage them to focus on different areas of their text, such as the use of short, informative sentences, paragraph layout or use of punctuation. Allow them to use their response partner or group to evaluate and discuss their work in those focus areas. They can use the photocopiable page 'Self-assessment checklist' to aid their understanding of the skills required. Create success criteria for each session to allow the children to focus on their achievements and areas in need of support.

Assessment evidence
At levels 2-3, children should use the main features of a news article in their writing, with a headline and the five 'W' questions in separate paragraphs or sentences. At levels 4-5, children should show a good use of language, sentence structures and use of media to convey information effectively to the reader. Use the checklists as evidence against Writing AF2.

Next steps
Support: Use the checklist to give support to the children who are struggling with their writing. Set them success criteria and enable them to explore and investigate different ways to improve and evaluate their writing.
Extension: Encourage the children to think of ways of improving their news report to give it more impact. Give examples such as quotations from others, and language effects such as puns, use of powerful verbs, and so on.

Key aspects of learning
Enquiry: Children will learn to ask: Who? What? Where? When? and Why? in researching a news story for a written or oral report.
Evaluation: Children will read, compare and evaluate news from a variety of sources. When presenting news reports orally and in writing, they will discuss success criteria, give feedback to others and judge the effectiveness of their own work.
Communication: Children will develop their ability to discuss and debate issues in respect of both the content and the presentation of the news reports they are reading and writing. They will often work collaboratively in pairs and groups. They will communicate outcomes orally (in the style of radio broadcasts), in writing and through using other modes and media.

Phase ④ News broadcasts

Learning outcome

Children can use a news article as the basis for a script and present it orally in the style of a radio news item in a way which is informative and engaging.

Success criteria
- I can make notes on my news broadcast script to help with its presentation.
- I can present an effective broadcast using presentational skills.
- I can evaluate a news broadcast using set criteria.

Setting the context
Display the success criteria in the classroom. Explain to the children that they are going to present an oral performance of a news report they have written in a past activity for a radio broadcast. Review the skills needed to make an effective presentation and, with the children's input, list them on the board, for example, the use of modulation, pace, emphasis, expression and volume in their voice. Display one of the children's reports and model how to make notes on the report as presentational cues and guidelines for the presenter. Before the children perform the broadcasts, debate and agree with the class on criteria to evaluate the effectiveness of the broadcast.

Assessment opportunity
Give the children time to look at their news reports and make notes for their presentations. Use adult support to help children at levels 2–3 mark their reports if needed. Let the children practise their presentations with a partner, revising their notes as they go along. Walk around the class to make observational notes. Bring the children together and invite them to all take turns to perform their broadcasts to the class. After each one, encourage the children to evaluate the performance against the agreed criteria. Ask questions such as: *How clear was the main focus of the report? Was the language to the point and informative? How could the performance be improved?* Encourage the children to edit and redraft their work in light of evaluations.

Assessment evidence
At levels 2–3, children should be able to use some features of note-making form, namely, simple marks to annotate their news reports. At levels 4–5, children should be able to write more detailed notes and present their reports effectively. Use your notes of class discussions and evaluations, along with observations of the content and effectiveness of the performances, as evidence against Writing AF2.

Next steps
Support: Encourage children to record their presentations and play them back. What do they think works? How could they improve the presentation? How could they improve the script to create more impact?

Extension: Encourage children to make a TV news broadcast using autocues taken from their scripts. What would they add to the cues to guide the news reporter? How would the news reporter present the report effectively?

Key aspects of learning
Evaluation: Children will read, compare and evaluate news from a variety of sources. When presenting news reports orally and in writing, they will discuss success criteria, give feedback to others and judge the effectiveness of their own work.

Communication: Children will develop their ability to discuss and debate issues in respect of both the content and the presentation of the news reports they are reading and writing. They will often work collaboratively in pairs and groups. They will communicate outcomes orally (in the style of radio broadcasts), in writing and through using other modes and media.

Periodic assessment

Reading

Learning outcome
Children can recognise the structure and language features of journalistic reports, both as written text and as scripts for oral presentation.

Success criteria
- I can understand how paragraphs are used to structure a newspaper report.
- I can explain why paragraphs are in a certain order in a newspaper report.

Setting the context
As a class, explore the layout of paragraphs in a newspaper article. Discuss the information sequence of the paragraphs. Ask: *Why are they put in that order? Does it matter if they are in any order?* Children at levels 2–3 work in pairs or small groups with support on the interactive activity 'Non-fiction 2 Reading assessment', where they put paragraphs in the right order. Children at levels 4–5 work in pairs to put a cut-up newspaper article into the correct sequence.

Assessment opportunity
Take notes of the children working at levels 2–3 as they sort out the paragraph order on the interactive activity. Discuss the reasons for their choices and order. Ask: *Which paragraphs cover the five 'W' questions? Which paragraph introduces the news article? Why would the paragraph with the boy's quote not work in the first part of the article?* Ask the children at levels 4–5 to select a report from a newspaper and note down the order of the paragraphs before cutting them out. The pairs swap their paragraphs with another pair and challenge them to put the paragraphs back in the correct sequence. Walk round the pairs, observing their discussions. Ask questions such as: *Why is that paragraph used to introduce the news report? How do some of the sentences at the end of the paragraphs give clues to the next paragraph subject? How does the layout of the paragraphs give the news impact? Which paragraph is used to end the report? Why?* Encourage the pairs to discuss their findings in a group or class plenary. Encourage all the children to self-assess their abilities using the success criteria. Where do they need more support?

Assessment evidence
Children at levels 2–3 should identify how the five paragraphs are structured to create a flowing report. They should recognise some of the five 'W' questions within the paragraphs. Children at levels 4–5 should identify paragraphs in a report and arrange them into the right order. They should notice the range of techniques to indicate a flow of logical information, such as connectives, sentence constructions and clues in the text. Record children's understandings and needs and use them to make level judgements against Reading AF2 and AF4.

Periodic assessment

Writing

Learning outcomes
● Children can use discussion and drama techniques to explore a particular event, incident or situation, and its protagonists.
● Children can write an effective news article in journalistic style, selecting language, form, format and content to suit a particular audience and purpose.
● Children can use this as the basis for a script and present it orally in the style of a radio news item in a way which is informative and engaging.

Success criteria
● I can use drama techniques to gather information from people in an event.
● I can use information I have collected to create a simple script for a radio bulletin.
● I can evaluate radio news bulletins about an event.

Setting the context
Put the children into mixed ability groups and give each child a copy of the photocopiable page 'Non-fiction 2 Writing assessment'. Explain to the children that they are going to use drama to explore a situation and then use the information to produce a simple script for a one-minute radio news bulletin. Introduce the scenario: a child has been knocked over outside the school gates at home time. Ask each of the groups to create a sequence of the possible events using a number of freeze-frame tableaux to perform to another group. Encourage the children watching the tableaux to interview the main characters (the driver, the parent, the child and bystanders) for their viewpoints about what happened, and to write notes and quotes on the sheet. Children at levels 2–3 may need adult support. Display the success criteria in the classroom.

Assessment opportunity
Take notes of the children's work and responses to your questions, such as: *Have you added in information about the character's feelings and quotes to highlight points?* Using their notes as guidance, invite the children to create their own scripts for a radio bulletin. Encourage the children to stand up and perform their one-minute script to the class who can evaluate their effect. Ask: *Is the script true to the events? Does it give clear information on the five 'W' questions? What sentences are used to create impact? How? What sentences are used to give information? How could the script be improved?* Encourage the children to self-assess their work against the success criteria.

Assessment evidence
Children at levels 2–3 should note the basic five 'W' questions of events connected to the accident. They should contribute towards the radio bulletin by suggesting straightforward, effective sentences that convey the information. Children at levels 4–5 should use the interviews of the accident's participants to create a more rounded radio bulletin with quotes and facts. Use the children's notes and scripts and observations of their group work and radio bulletins to make level judgements against Writing AF1, AF3 and AF5.

NON-FICTION
Unit 3 Argument

Literacy objectives

Speak and listen for a wide range of purposes in different contexts
Strand 1 Speaking
- Use a range of oral techniques to present persuasive arguments and engaging narratives.
- Participate in whole-class debate using the conventions and language of debate, including standard English.

Strand 2 Listening and responding
- Analyse and evaluate how speakers present points effectively through use of language and gesture.
- Listen for language variation in formal and informal contexts.
- Identify the ways spoken language varies according to differences in the context and purpose of its use.

Read and write for a range of purposes on paper and on screen
Strand 6 Word structure and spelling
- Use a range of appropriate strategies to edit, proofread and correct spelling in their own work, on paper and on screen.

Strand 7 Understanding and interpreting texts
- Recognise rhetorical devices used to argue, persuade, mislead and sway the reader.

Strand 8 Engaging with and responding to texts
- Compare how writers from different times and places present experiences and use language.

Strand 9 Creating and shaping texts
- In non-narrative, establish, balance and maintain viewpoints.

Strand 10 Text structure and organisation
- Use varied structures to shape and organise text coherently.
- Use paragraphs to achieve pace and emphasis.

Strand 11 Sentence structure and punctuation
- Use punctuation to clarify meaning in complex sentences.

Key aspects of learning

Enquiry
- Children will identify the particular information, ideas and opinions offered in different texts, asking questions such as: 'What does this particular writer think, and why?' 'Do others think the same?'

Information processing
- Children will source, collate and analyse information, ideas and opinions offered in different texts and media presentations.

Evaluation
- Children will examine a variety of arguments and discussions, weighing up evidence and evaluating both effectiveness and appropriateness for context. The same elements will then be explored in terms of their own speaking and writing.

Key aspects of learning (contd)

Reasoning
- Children will follow and evaluate the arguments of others, and then construct and evaluate their own reasoning both orally and in writing.

Communication
- They will develop their ability to discuss and debate issues from both a biased and a balanced standpoint. They will often work collaboratively in pairs and groups. They will communicate ideas and opinions orally, in writing and through using other modes and media.

Assessment focuses

Reading
AF3 *(deduce, infer or interpret information, events or ideas from texts).*
AF4 *(identify and comment on the structure and organisation of texts, including grammatical and presentational features at text level).*
AF5 *(explain and comment on writers' use of language, including grammatical and literary features at word and sentence level).*
AF6 *(identify and comment on writers' purposes and viewpoints, and the overall effect of the text on the reader).*

Writing
AF2 *(produce texts which are appropriate to task, reader and purpose).*
AF3 *(organise and present whole texts effectively, sequencing and structuring information, ideas and events).*
AF7 *(select appropriate and effective vocabulary).*

Speaking and listening
Speaking (speak with clarity, intonation and pace; use standard English).
Listening and responding (understand and recall main points; respond appropriately).

Resources

Phase 1 activities
Photocopiable page, 'Children watch too much television'
Photocopiable page, 'Fact or opinion?'
Interactive activity, 'Formal or informal?'
Photocopiable page, 'The TV debate'
Phase 3 activities
Interactive activity, 'Persuasive phrases'
Interactive activity, 'Connective types' (versions 1 and 2)
Photocopiable page, 'Should fireworks be banned?'
Phase 4 activities
Photocopiable page, 'How to write a persuasive text'
Photocopiable page, 'A persuasive letter'
Photocopiable page, 'Writing a balanced argument planning sheet'
Periodic assessment
Photocopiable page, 'Non-fiction 3 Writing assessment'

Unit 3 ▢ Argument

Learning outcomes	Assessment opportunity and evidence	Assessment focuses (AFs)		Success criteria
		Level 2	Level 3	
Phase ① activities pages 118-119				
Fact or opinion? Children can identify bias when considering a controversial issue	• Supported group activity where children discuss whether statements are fact or opinion. • Children's oral responses, choices and reasons.	**Reading AF3** • Simple, plausible inference about events and information, using evidence from text. • Comments made on textual cues, sometimes misunderstood.	**Reading AF3** • Straightforward inference based on a single point of reference in the text. • Responses to text show meaning established at a literal level.	• I can identify a persuasive argument. • I can tell the difference between fact and opinion.
Formal and informal Children can identify when it is appropriate to use formal and impersonal language.	• Independent or paired activity where children sort extracts into examples of formal and informal language. • Children's oral responses and discussion.	**Reading AF6** • Some awareness that writers have viewpoints and purposes. • Simple statements about likes and dislikes in reading, sometimes with reasons.	**Reading AF6** • Comments identify main purpose. • Express personal response but with little awareness of writer's viewpoint or effect on reader.	• I can identify and explore for, against and balanced texts for an issue. • I can identify the use of formal and informal language.
Phase ② activities pages 120-121				
School uniforms Children can use clear language and appropriate presentational features both to present a particular case (argument) and to provide a balanced overview (discussion).	• Paired activity where children present points of view. • Children's oral responses, discussions and feedback. • Children's presentations.	**Writing AF2** • Some basic purpose established. • Some appropriate features of the given form used. • Some attempts to adopt appropriate style.	**Writing AF2** • Purpose established at a general level. • Main features of selected form sometimes signalled to the reader. • Some attempts at appropriate style, with attention to reader.	• I can use clear language features to present a case. • I can use appropriate presentational features to present a case. • I can evaluate and feed back on other persuasive presentations.
A balanced discussion Children can use clear language and appropriate presentational features both to present a particular case (argument) and to provide a balanced overview (discussion).	• Group activity where children present opposing views of an issue and a fair summary. • Children's oral responses and discussions. • Children's presentations.	**Writing AF2** • Some basic purpose established. • Some appropriate features of the given form used. • Some attempts to adopt appropriate style.	**Writing AF2** • Purpose established at a general level. • Main features of selected form sometimes signalled to the reader. • Some attempts at appropriate style, with attention to reader.	• I can use clear language features to provide a balanced discussion. • I can use appropriate presentational features to provide a balanced discussion. • I can evaluate presentations using set criteria.
Phase ③ activities pages 122-124				
Persuasive phrases Children can recognise the structure and language features of both a persuasive argument and of a balanced discussion.	• Supported group activity where children identify persuasive phrases and questions in a persuasive text. • Children's oral responses and discussions.	**Reading AF5** • Some effective language choices noted. • Some familiar patterns of language identified. **Writing AF7** • Simple, often speech-like vocabulary conveys relevant meanings. • Some adventurous word choices.	**Reading AF5** • A few basic features of writer's use of language identified, but with little or no comment. **Writing AF7** • Simple, generally appropriate vocabulary used, limited in range. • Some words selected for effect or occasion.	• I can identify phrases used in a persuasive text. • I can understand how phrases and questions can be used effectively in a persuasive text. • I can create a persuasive phrase.

Unit 3 ▢ Argument

Learning outcomes	Assessment opportunity and evidence	Assessment focuses (AFs)		Success criteria
		Level 2	Level 3	
Connectives Children can recognise the structure and language features of both a persuasive argument and of a balanced discussion.	• Supported group activity where children identify connectives in a discussion text. • Children's oral responses and discussions.	**Reading AF4** • Some awareness of use of features of organisation.	**Reading AF4** • A few basic features of organisation at text level identified, with little or no linked comment.	• I can identify how different types of connectives help structure a balanced argument. • I can understand how connectives link ideas. • I can use connectives to create balanced statements for an argument.
Formal sentences Children can understand and apply impersonal and formal language when appropriate.	• Supported group activity where children redraft sentences that are not written in formal language. • Children's oral responses and discussions. • Children's redrafted sentences.	**Reading AF5** • Some effective language choices noted. • Some familiar patterns of language identified.	**Reading AF5** • A few basic features of writer's use of language identified, but with little or no comment.	• I can identify impersonal and formal language in a discussion text. • I can use formal language to write effective sentences.

Phase ④ activities pages 125-126

Learning outcomes	Assessment opportunity and evidence	Level 2	Level 3	Success criteria
Playground persuasive letter Children can write both an effective argument for a particular case and a balanced discussion of an issue, selecting language, form, format and content to suit a particular audience and purpose.	• Supported independent activity where children plan and write a three-point persuasive letter within a frame and evaluate their use of persuasive features. • Teacher's notes. • Children's written plans and letters.	**Writing AF2** • Some basic purpose established. • Some appropriate features of the given form used. • Some attempts to adopt appropriate style.	**Writing AF2** • Purpose established at a general level. • Main features of selected form sometimes signalled to the reader. • Some attempts at appropriate style, with attention to reader.	• I can set out my arguments clearly, using evidence to support my ideas. • I can structure and use persuasive language in my letter to present my case effectively. • I can evaluate persuasive texts.
Zoos - balanced arguments Children can write both an effective argument for a particular case and a balanced discussion of an issue, selecting language, form, format and content to suit a particular audience and purpose.	• Supported group activity where children write a balanced argument about the need for zoos and evaluate their own and each others' work. • Children's oral responses and ideas. • Children's written arguments.	**Writing AF3** • Some basic sequencing of ideas or material. • Openings and/or closings sometimes signalled.	**Writing AF3** • Some attempt to organise ideas with related points placed next to each other. • Openings and closings usually signalled. • Some attempt to sequence ideas or material logically.	• I can plan a balanced discussion. • I can write a balanced argument using features of discussion.

Unit 3 ◻ Argument

Learning outcomes	Assessment opportunity and evidence	Assessment focuses (AFs)		Success criteria
		Level 4	Level 5	
Phase ① activities pages 118-119				
Fact or opinion? Children can identify bias when considering a controversial issue.	• Independent activity where children highlight and record statements that are fact or opinion. • Children's oral responses and completed photocopiables.	**Reading AF3** • Comments make inferences based on evidence from different points in the text. • inferences often correct, but comments are not always rooted securely in the text or repeat narrative or content.	**Reading AF3** • Comments develop inferred meanings drawing on evidence across the text. • Comments make inferences and deductions based on textual evidence.	• I can identify a persuasive argument. • I can tell the difference between fact and opinion.
Formal and informal Children can identify when it is appropriate to use formal and impersonal language.	• Paired activity where children identify and highlight examples of formal or informal language. • Children's discussions and highlighted texts.	**Reading AF6** • Main purpose identified. • Simple comments show some awareness of writer's viewpoint. • Simple comment on overall effect on reader.	**Reading AF6** • Main purpose clearly identified, often through general overview. • Viewpoints in texts clearly identified, with some, often limited, explanation. • General awareness of effect on the reader, with some, often limited.	• I can identify and explore for, against and balanced texts for an issue. • I can identify the use of formal and informal language.
Phase ② activities pages 120-121				
School uniforms Children can use clear language and appropriate presentational features both to present a particular case (argument) and to provide a balanced overview (discussion).	• Paired activity where children present points of view. • Children's oral responses, discussions and feedback. • Children's presentations.	**Writing AF2** • Main purpose of writing is clear but not always consistently maintained. • Main features of selected form are clear and appropriate to purpose. • Style generally appropriate to task, though awareness of reader not always sustained.	**Writing AF2** • Main purpose of writing is clear and consistently maintained. • Features of selected form clearly established with some adaptation to purpose. • Appropriate style clearly established to maintain reader's interest throughout.	• I can use clear language features to present a case. • I can use appropriate presentational features to present a case. • I can evaluate and feed back on other persuasive presentations.
A balanced discussion Children can use clear language and appropriate presentational features both to present a particular case (argument) and to provide a balanced overview (discussion).	• Group activity where children present opposing views of an issue and a fair summary. • Children's oral responses and discussions. • Children's presentations.	**Writing AF2** • Main purpose of writing is clear but not always consistently maintained. • Main features of selected form are clear and appropriate to purpose. • Style generally appropriate to task, though awareness of reader not always sustained.	**Writing AF2** • Main purpose of writing is clear and consistently maintained. • Features of selected form clearly established with some adaptation to purpose. • Appropriate style clearly established to maintain reader's interest throughout.	• I can use clear language features to provide a balanced discussion. • I can use appropriate presentational features to provide a balanced discussion. • I can evaluate presentations using set criteria.
Phase ③ activities pages 122-124				
Persuasive phrases Children can recognise the structure and language features of both a persuasive argument and of a balanced discussion.	• Independent activity where children identify persuasive phrases and questions in a persuasive text. • Children's oral responses and discussions. • Children's persuasive sentences.	**Reading AF5** • Some basic features of writer's use of language identified. • Simple comments on writer's choices. **Writing AF7** • Some evidence of deliberate vocabulary choices. • Some expansion of general vocabulary to match topic.	**Reading AF5** • Various features of writer's use of language identified, with some explanation. • Comments show some awareness of the effect of writer's language choices. **Writing AF7** • Vocabulary chosen for effect. • Reasonably wide vocabulary used, though not always appropriately.	• I can identify phrases used in a persuasive text. • I can understand how phrases and questions can be used effectively in a persuasive text. • I can create a persuasive phrase.

Unit 3 ☐ Argument

Learning outcomes	Assessment opportunity and evidence	Assessment focuses (AFs)		Success criteria
		Level 4	Level 5	
Connectives Children can recognise the structure and language features of both a persuasive argument and a balanced discussion.	● Supported group activity where children identify connectives in a discussion text. ● Children's oral responses and discussions.	**Reading AF4** ● Some structural choices identified with simple comment. ● Some basic features of organisation at text level identified.	**Reading AF4** ● Comments on structural choices show some general awareness of writer's craft. ● Various features relating to organisation at text level, including form, are clearly identified, with some explanation.	● I can identify how different types of connectives help structure a balanced argument. I can understand how connectives link ideas. ● I can use connectives to create balanced statements for an argument.
Formal sentences Children can understand and apply impersonal and formal language when appropriate.	● Group activity where children redraft sentences that are not written in formal language. ● Children's oral responses and discussions. ● Children's rewritten sentences.	**Reading AF5** ● Some basic features of writer's use of language identified. ● Simple comments on writer's choices.	**Reading AF5** ● Various features of writer's use of language identified, with some explanation. ● Comments show some awareness of the effect of writer's language choices.	● I can identify impersonal and formal language in a discussion text. ● I can use formal language to write effective sentences.

Phase ④ activities pages 125–126

Learning outcomes	Assessment opportunity and evidence	Assessment focuses (AFs)		Success criteria
		Level 4	Level 5	
Playground persuasive letter Children can write both an effective argument for a particular case and a balanced discussion of an issue, selecting language, form, format and content to suit a particular audience and purpose.	● Independent activity where children put persuasive ideas on a chart, use it to write a persuasive letter to the local council and evaluate their letters. ● Children's oral feedback and discussions. ● Children's planning charts and written letters.	**Writing AF2** ● Main purpose of writing is clear but not always consistently maintained. ● Main features of selected form are clear and appropriate to purpose. ● Style generally appropriate to task, though awareness of reader not always sustained.	**Writing AF2** ● Main purpose of writing is clear and consistently maintained. ● Features of selected form clearly established with some adaptation to purpose. ● Appropriate style clearly established to maintain reader's interest throughout.	● I can set out my arguments clearly, using evidence to support my ideas. ● I can structure and use persuasive language in my letter to present my case effectively. ● I can evaluate persuasive texts.
Zoos – balanced arguments Children can write both an effective argument for a particular case and a balanced discussion of an issue, selecting language, form, format and content to suit a particular audience and purpose.	● Independent activity where children write a balanced argument about the need for zoos and evaluate their own and each others' work. ● Children's oral feedback and discussion. ● Children's planning sheets and written arguments.	**Writing AF3** ● Ideas organised by clustering related points or by time sequence. ● Ideas are organised simply with a fitting opening and closing, sometimes linked. ● Ideas or material generally in logical sequence but overall direction of writing not always clearly signalled.	**Writing AF3** ● Material is structured clearly, with sentences organised into appropriate paragraphs. ● Development of material is effectively managed across text. ● Overall direction of the text supported by clear links between paragraphs.	● I can plan a balanced discussion. ● I can write a balanced argument using features of discussion.

NON-FICTION

Phase ① Fact or opinion?

Learning outcome
Children can identify bias when considering a controversial issue.

Success criteria
● I can identify a persuasive argument.
● I can tell the difference between fact and opinion.

Setting the context
Have a brief discussion on the ongoing debate about whether children watch too much television. Explain to the children that they are going to read or listen to an article about the issue and underline statements which are either fact or opinion. Discuss briefly the difference between fact and opinion/bias. Put the children working at levels 2-3 into a group with adult support as a reader and a recorder of the children's responses using the text extract from the photocopiable page 'Children watch too much television'. Children at levels 4-5 will work independently on 'Fact or opinion?' Give out the photocopiable pages along with two colouring pencils to all the children. Tell them which colour is to be used for fact and which colour is to be used for opinion.

Assessment opportunity
The children at levels 2-3 listen to each statement being read out by an adult and underline the statement on their copy to show whether they think it is a fact or opinion. Once it has been read out, go back through the article as a group and discuss each of the children's choices. Note down their reasons. Ask the children at levels 4-5 to read through the article to identify fact and opinion and then record them under the two headings 'Fact' or 'Opinion'. Once the children have finished, encourage them to discuss their findings with a partner. Listen to the discussions and record the children's comments. Ask: *Is the article biased? Who do you think the article is aimed at?*

Assessment evidence
At levels 2-3, children should be able to recognise the difference between clear facts and obvious opinions. At levels 4-5, children should be able to analyse the statements in greater depth. Use the photocopiable pages and the notes of the children's responses as evidence against Reading AF3.

Next steps
Support: For children, who may find it hard to decide whether a statement is fact or opinion, encourage them to look for clues within a statement, such as 'It's a fact...' or 'A recent survey...', 'We must stop...', 'Everyone knows...'.
Extension: Ask children to imagine they are putting the writer of the article in the hot seat. Encourage them to work in pairs to think of questions they would like to ask about the article.

Key aspects of learning
Enquiry: Children will identify the particular information, ideas and opinions offered in different texts, asking questions such as: 'What does this particular writer think, and why?' 'Do others think the same?'
Evaluation: Children will examine a variety of arguments and discussions, weighing up evidence and evaluating both effectiveness and appropriateness for context. The same elements will then be explored in terms of their own speaking and writing.

Phase ① Formal and informal

Learning outcome
Children can identify when it is appropriate to use formal and impersonal language.

Success criteria
- I can identify and explore for, against and balanced texts for an issue.
- I can identify the use of formal and informal language.

Setting the context
This activity should be used once the children have had experience with studying texts using formal and informal language. Explain to the children that they are going to study two texts about whether or not children watch too much TV and identify examples of formal and informal language. Briefly go through the definitions and features of formal and informal language. Children at levels 2–3 can work independently or in pairs on the interactive activity 'Formal or informal?' Have an adult as reading support, to ask questions during the activity and to take notes of the children's responses. Children working at levels 4–5 will work in pairs by highlighting copies of two different types of text. They should use one highlighter colour for formal text and another for informal.

Assessment opportunity
The children at levels 2–3 working on the interactive activity should decide which two texts have formal or informal language and then discuss their reasons for their choice. Prompt the children to explain when it is appropriate to use formal or informal language. Ask questions such as: *What clues in the first text help you to work out whether it is personal or impersonal? Would you use the word 'brilliant' in an impersonal text?* For the children working at levels 4–5 give out copies of the texts 'Children watch too much television' and 'The TV debate' to each pair. Ask the children to read a text each and highlight examples of formal or informal language. Encourage the children to share their findings. Move round the pairs and take notes of their discussion. Ask them to give you examples of personal or impersonal language.

Assessment evidence
At levels 2–3, children should be able to recognise clues in the texts to show whether they are informal or formal. For example, they may identify that the informal text uses personal names, is in the first person and uses powerful words. At levels 4–5, children should highlight impersonal examples such as present tense, the third person, use of phrases and nouns. The children should notice the effects informal and formal language have on a text. Use the notes of all the children's responses and the highlighted text copies as evidence against Reading AF6.

Next steps
Support: Some children may still struggle to recognise the difference between formal and informal texts. Choose a text or create a passage and write it in formal language. Read it out and ask the children how they could convert it using everyday conversational language.
Extension: Encourage children to find out more about the debate on children watching too much TV. Ask them to collect evidence from both sides of the argument and present a balanced report of the issue to the rest of the class.

Key aspects of learning
Enquiry: Children will identify the particular information, ideas and opinions offered in different texts, asking questions such as: 'What does this particular writer think, and why?' 'Do others think the same?'
Evaluation: Children will examine a variety of arguments and discussions, weighing up evidence and evaluating both effectiveness and appropriateness for context. The same elements will then be explored in terms of their own speaking and writing.

NON-FICTION

Phase ② School uniforms

Learning outcome
Children can use clear language and appropriate presentational features both to present a particular case (argument) and to provide a balanced overview (discussion).

Success criteria
● I can use clear language features to present a case.
● I can use appropriate presentational features to present a case.
● I can evaluate and feed back on other persuasive presentations.

Setting the context
Display the success criteria in the classroom. Introduce the debate about whether school uniform should be compulsory for all schools. Discuss the different points of view with the children, noting their points on the board. Explain that the children are going to present a case for supporting or not supporting uniform. Discuss ways of presenting a case, such as using persuasive and emotive vocabulary, clear points, an introduction and summing up, and personal style. As a class, create agreed criteria on evaluating a persuasive presentation and write them on the board.

Assessment opportunity
Put the children into mixed ability groups of four. Ask them to split into pairs and give each pair one side of the argument to present to the other pair. Give each pair time to put their case together. Walk round the groups and take observation notes of their preparations. Once the pairs are ready, ask one pair to present their case to the second pair in the group. The second pair can write evaluation notes of the presentation using the agreed criteria. The pairs then swap roles. Take observation notes. As a class or within groups encourage the children to discuss their evaluations. Ask: *Which presentations were persuasive? In what way? How could they be improved?*

Assessment evidence
At levels 2–3, children should try to bring across their argument using clear and emotive language with a short introduction and a good summing up. They should discuss and make simple evaluation notes of other presentations. At levels 4–5, children should be able to present their points clearly with examples using persuasive language and take informative evaluation notes for presentation feedback. All the children should be able to use body language to bring over their feelings of the issue to the audience. Use the presentations and the children's notes and feedback as evidence against Writing AF2.

Next steps
Support: Let children film their presentations. Play them back and encourage the children to self-evaluate their performances. Write down their new targets and encourage them to revise their work.
Extension: Encourage children to find out more about the school uniform issue. Invite the children to collate evidence from the children in their own school and from other sources to enhance their different points of view. Does their evidence make a difference to the argument?

Key aspects of learning
Evaluation: Children will examine a variety of arguments and discussions, weighing up evidence and evaluating both effectiveness and appropriateness for context. The same elements will then be explored in terms of their own speaking and writing.
Reasoning: Children will follow and evaluate the arguments of others, and then construct and evaluate their own reasoning both orally and in writing.
Communication: They will develop their ability to discuss and debate issues from both a biased and a balanced standpoint. They will often work collaboratively in pairs and groups. They will communicate ideas and opinions orally, in writing and through using other modes and media.

Phase ② A balanced discussion

Learning outcome
Children can use clear language and appropriate presentational features both to present a particular case (argument) and to provide a balanced overview (discussion).

Success criteria
- I can use clear language features to provide a balanced discussion.
- I can use appropriate presentational features to provide a balanced discussion.
- I can evaluate presentations using set criteria.

Setting the context
Display the success criteria in the classroom. With the children, revise the purpose of discussions about an issue, for example, to present arguments from differing points of view fairly and effectively. Introduce the discussion topic, such as: 'Houses need to be built but where is best?' There are two opposing communities so a balanced discussion is needed to judge where is best. Discuss the criteria needed for a balanced discussion – for example, opening statements, summing up of both arguments and fair summary of arguments. Write them on the board. Explain to the children that they are going to work in groups to present and summarise the opposing views of the discussion.

Assessment opportunity
Put the children into mixed ability groups of three. Two children prepare and present the cases for the two opposing views while the third child listens and takes notes. The three children can then use the notes to present a summary of their discussion using appropriate language and presentation features. Ask the children to check the summary against the criteria on the board. Sit with groups as they conduct their discussions. Identify those who may need future support. Encourage each group to present the summaries of their discussions to the class or to other groups. Ask: *Did they bring over a fair and balanced overview of the discussion? Was the summary impartial or was one side stronger? How could it be improved?*

Assessment evidence
At levels 2–3, children should be able to structure their notes into a balanced summary of their argument. At levels 4–5, children should show more well-developed evidence of a clear introduction, well set-out points and examples for and against the issue, and a balanced summing up. Identify children who were able to give the summary constructive feedback highlighting both use of language and structure. Use the group summaries and class discussions along with the children's responses as evidence against Writing AF2.

Next steps
Support: Some children may find it hard to create a fair summary of the different arguments. Have a session where the children can add simple statements or words in a 'pros and cons' table of one issue and then write a fair summary of the argument in a few sentences.
Extension: Have two groups of children present opposing sides of an issue while another group of children, acting as diplomats, summarise the problems and come up with a compromise for both sides to accept.

Key aspects of learning
Evaluation: Children will examine a variety of arguments and discussions, weighing up evidence and evaluating both effectiveness and appropriateness for context. The same elements will then be explored in terms of their own speaking and writing.
Reasoning: Children will follow and evaluate the arguments of others, and then construct and evaluate their own reasoning both orally and in writing.
Communication: They will develop their ability to discuss and debate issues from both a biased and a balanced standpoint. They will often work collaboratively in pairs and groups. They will communicate ideas and opinions orally, in writing and through using other modes and media.

NON-FICTION

Phase ③ Persuasive phrases

Learning outcome
Children can recognise the structure and language features of both a persuasive argument and of a balanced discussion.

Success criteria
● I can identify phrases used in a persuasive text.
● I can understand how phrases and questions can be used effectively in a persuasive text.
● I can create a persuasive phrase.

Setting the context
Use this interactive assessment within a literacy session on persuasive texts. Children at levels 2–3 can work as a group with support. Children at levels 4–5 can work on the interactive activity independently within the lesson. First, remind all the children how language in persuasive arguments is used to encourage people to agree. Give examples of emotive phrases, such as 'This is obviously...' With the children at levels 4–5 discuss how rhetorical questions can also be used to effect, such as 'Are we to believe that...?' Explain to the children that they are going to try to identify more persuasive phrases in an interactive activity 'Persuasive phrases'.

Assessment opportunity
Display the interactive activity for all the children working at levels 2–3 to see. Read out the phrases or questions one at a time and ask each child whether they think it is a persuasive phrase/question or not, noting their reasons. Once all the children have answered, show the result on the screen and reinforce the reasons. At the end of the activity ask them to create one persuasive phrase each. Write down their suggestions. With the children at levels 4–5, take notes of their progress while they are engaged in the activity. Do they recognise the effect that certain phrases or questions would have in a persuasive argument? Encourage them to write six new persuasive phrases and questions.

Assessment evidence
At levels 2–3, children should recognise most of the persuasive phrases in the activity. They may comment on the use of emotive words such as 'devastated' and 'hurt' and the biased nature of the phrases. Their own phrases or questions may use emotive words. At levels 4–5, children should highlight the use of rhetorical questions and the sentence structure of the persuasive phrase to create an emotive effect. They should assess the persuasive effect of their own phrases and questions. Use the notes of the children's responses and their sentences as evidence against Reading AF5 and Writing AF7.

Next steps
Support: Give children an issue such as 'Fireworks should be banned'. Give them a list of simple phrases and ask them to think of how they could turn the phrases into complete sentences to illustrate the issue. Record their responses.
Extension: Encourage children to create a persuasive word and phrase bank. They could collect their ideas from reading through persuasive texts for examples or adding their own ideas.

Key aspects of learning
Enquiry: Children will identify the particular information, ideas and opinions offered in different texts, asking questions such as: 'What does this particular writer think, and why?' 'Do others think the same?'
Information processing: Children will source, collate and analyse information, ideas and opinions offered in different texts and media presentations.

Unit 3 **Argument**

NON-FICTION

Phase ③ Connectives

Learning outcome
Children can recognise the structure and language features of both a persuasive argument and of a balanced discussion.

Success criteria
- I can identify how different types of connectives help structure a balanced argument.
- I can understand how connectives link ideas.
- I can use connectives to create balanced statements for an argument.

Setting the context
Use this assessment activity during literacy sessions that focus on balanced arguments. Work with levelled groups one at a time while the rest of the class are working on another activity. Display and read the text from the photocopiable page 'The TV debate' to the group. Focus on the use of connectives within the text, such as 'therefore' and 'however'. With the children at levels 2–3, discuss how connectives can be used in a balanced argument to sequence points and to link an example to a point. With the children at levels 4–5, discuss how connectives can be used to contrast two points of view, to show a cause and effect, to show logical conclusions or to explain a point further. Display the success criteria on the board.

Assessment opportunity
Display version 1 of the interactive activity 'Connective types' for the children in the levels 2–3 groups to see. Point out the words 'Sequencing' and 'To give examples' over the two boxes. Go through the list of connectives one at a time and ask each child their choice. Note down responses. At the end of the activity, encourage each child to think of a balanced statement using sequencing and example connectives. Write them on the board and discuss them with the group. Display version 2 of the interactive activity to the levels 4–5 groups. Follow the same process as with the levels 2–3 group activity. Ask for further balanced statements using connectives for sequencing, to give examples, to compare and contrast, for cause and effect and to explain a reason. Write the examples on the board. Encourage all the children to look at the success criteria and evaluate their work. Do they need more work to help with their understanding of connectives in a discussion? How?

Assessment evidence
At levels 2–3, children should be able to sort out the connectives into the 'Sequencing' and 'To give examples' boxes. They may be able to recognise that these connectives link points in a balanced argument and suggest more, such as 'secondly' or 'to sum up'. At levels 4–5, children should be able to identify and discuss the different uses of the connectives and how they link ideas. They should list similar connectives such as 'although', 'furthermore' or 'since'. Use the children's discussion and oral responses during and after the activities, and their connective sentences as evidence against Reading AF4.

Next steps
Support: For children who struggle with identifying connectives in a balanced discussion, help them collect a bank of connective words and discuss how they could be used effectively within a discussion.
Extension: Encourage children to collect a bank of connectives that could be used in balanced discussions and sort them into groups: cause and effect, sequencing, compare and contrast, to summarise and to give examples.

Key aspects of learning
Enquiry: Children will identify the particular information, ideas and opinions offered in different texts, asking questions such as: 'What does this particular writer think, and why?' 'Do others think the same?'
Information processing: Children will source, collate and analyse information, ideas and opinions offered in different texts and media presentations.

Phase ③ Formal sentences

Learning outcome
Children can understand and apply impersonal and formal language when appropriate.

Success criteria
● I can identify impersonal and formal language in a discussion text.
● I can use formal language to write effective sentences.

Setting the context
Use this assessment activity within guided reading sessions. Work with one group at a time taking notes of the children's responses. Remind the children in the group of the features of formal and impersonal language, for example, use of the third person, formal phrases and connectives. Display the discussion text on the photocopiable page 'Should fireworks be banned?' Explain that the text is a discussion argument and should be written using formal language, but the writer has made a few mistakes and used some informal language. Ask the children to see if they can find the mistakes.

Assessment opportunity
Encourage the children to find and highlight the sentences written in an informal, personal style. Discuss the effect the informal language has on the text, for example, it is no longer balanced. With children working at levels 2–3, choose a few of the sentences and encourage them to help you redraft the sentences into a formal style. Give a sentence to each child working at levels 4–5 and ask them to redraft the sentence into a formal style using mini whiteboards. Encourage all the children to share their ideas and evaluate their effect in the context of the original text. Ask the children to link their sentences to the success criteria.

Assessment evidence
At levels 2–3, children should be aware of some of the informal language used in the text and should be able to rewrite informal language in simple, formal style. At levels 4–5, children should identify most of the informal text and explain how they would change it back to formal. Use the notes, children's discussion and responses and their rewritten sentences as evidence against Reading AF5.

Next steps
Support: Give children a set of formal language word cards and encourage them to create formal sentences. Explore the different variations and their effect.
Extension: Encourage children to create a formal writing checklist poster which includes examples by each point. Display this in the class or allow the children to publish it on the computer and give out copies for children to keep in their writing books.

Key aspects of learning
Enquiry: Children will identify the particular information, ideas and opinions offered in different texts, asking questions such as: 'What does this particular writer think, and why?' 'Do others think the same?'
Evaluation: Children will examine a variety of arguments and discussions, weighing up evidence and evaluating both effectiveness and appropriateness for context. The same elements will then be explored in terms of their own speaking and writing.

Phase ④ Playground persuasive letter

NON-FICTION

Learning outcome
Children can write both an effective argument for a particular case and a balanced discussion of an issue, selecting language, form, format and content to suit a particular audience and purpose.

Success criteria
● I can set out my arguments clearly, using evidence to support my ideas.
● I can structure and use persuasive language in my letter to present my case effectively.
● I can evaluate persuasive texts.

Setting the context
Ask the children to imagine that their school is on the list to receive new playground equipment, along with other local schools. Explain that the children need to write a persuasive letter to the local council to argue why they should have the equipment. Briefly model on the board, with the children's input, the layout of a formal letter. Display the photocopiable page 'How to write a persuasive text' and go through the different points in relation to the letter. Draw a table on the board with three columns, 'Main point', 'Explanation' and 'Examples/evidence', and model how to use it by listing a couple of issues that could be included in the letter. Display the success criteria in the classroom.

Assessment opportunity
Children at levels 2-3 can use the photocopiable page 'A persuasive letter' to plan and write a simple three-point letter within a frame. Ask children at levels 4-5 to draw out the table plan and add in their own argument points for the letter. Having completed their plan, encourage them to write their letter. Move around the class taking notes as the children work on their letters. Discuss their ideas. Ask questions such as: *What persuasive words or phrases could be used to get that point over? Where is your example for this point?* Once all the children have finished, encourage them to work with a response partner to evaluate their letters against the checklist and the success criteria. Encourage them to ask: *Would the council find it persuasive enough to give the school the equipment? Did it use various persuasive features?*

Assessment evidence
At levels 2-3, children should write a straightforward introduction, clear points and a summary using persuasive language in sentences that may use connectives to link ideas. At levels 4-5, children should plan out their letters and use the notes to create a persuasive letter with a good structure, emotive language and a range of connectives to create the desired effect. Use the notes of the children's responses and their evaluations along with their written work as evidence against Writing AF2.

Next steps
Support: In a group, put children in pairs. Ask each pair to present a persuasive speech on a given issue to the rest of the group. Ask the group to listen for examples of persuasive words and phrases. Record the examples on the board and discuss their effect.
Extension: Encourage children to refine and redraft their persuasive letters. Encourage them to explore and experiment with persuasive language. Are there other words or phrases that might highlight a point more powerfully?

Key aspects of learning
Evaluation: Children will examine a variety of arguments and discussions, weighing up evidence and evaluating both effectiveness and appropriateness for context. The same elements will then be explored in terms of their own speaking and writing.
Communication: They will develop their ability to discuss and debate issues from both a biased and a balanced standpoint. They will often work collaboratively in pairs and groups. They will communicate ideas and opinions orally, in writing and through using other modes and media.

Phase ④ Zoos – balanced arguments

Learning outcome
Children can write both an effective argument for a particular case and a balanced discussion of an issue, selecting language, form, format and content to suit a particular audience and purpose.

Success criteria
● I can plan a balanced discussion.
● I can write a balanced argument using features of discussion.

Setting the context
Discuss with the children the debate about whether or not zoos are good for animals. Explain to the children that they are going to plan and write a balanced discussion text about the need for zoos. Revise the features of a balanced discussion text. Remind them that a discussion text should be unbiased and consider both sides of the argument. Discuss possible purposes of their discussion text, such as a summing-up after a debate or a news report. Children at levels 2–3 will work in a discussion group with adult support acting as scribe on one displayed copy of 'Writing a balanced argument planning sheet'. Each child working at levels 4–5 can work independently on their own copy.

Assessment opportunity
Encourage children at levels 2–3 to think of reasons for and against zoos and write their ideas and examples in the correct sections of the photocopiable page. Make a note of each child's contribution. With children at levels 4–5, discuss their points for and against zoos. Do they have good examples to back up their points? Take notes of their responses. Once all the children have completed their plans, ask them to write out their individual balanced arguments on a piece of paper. Remind the children of balanced text features such as connectives and impersonal language. Invite the children to read out their finished texts to the class. Ask: *Have you presented a balanced discussion of the issues? Have you got an effective introduction and conclusion?*

Assessment evidence
At levels 2–3, children should be able to write a logical, structured, balanced discussion text with an introduction, several points for and against, and a conclusion. At levels 4–5, children should show that they have researched their points and have accompanying figures and examples. They should be able to create a well-structured and logical, balanced text showing both sides of the argument without bias. Use the notes of the children's responses and feedback along with their written work as evidence against Writing AF3.

Next steps
Support: Some children may find it hard to write out a balanced argument. In a group, let the children choose an issue and then think of arguments from one point of view. Model writing simple, formal, unbiased sentences and repeat with the opposite point of view.
Extension: Children can use their texts to have a discussion about zoos. Discuss presentation skills and how to bring over the points fairly and without emotion. Encourage the children to evaluate the presentations.

Key aspects of learning
Evaluation: Children will examine a variety of arguments and discussions, weighing up evidence and evaluating both effectiveness and appropriateness for context. The same elements will then be explored in terms of their own speaking and writing.
Reasoning: Children will follow and evaluate the arguments of others, and then construct and evaluate their own reasoning both orally and in writing.
Communication: They will develop their ability to discuss and debate issues from both a biased and a balanced standpoint. They will often work collaboratively in pairs and groups. They will communicate ideas and opinions orally, in writing and through using other modes and media.

Periodic assessment

Reading

Learning outcomes
● Children can identify bias when considering a controversial issue.
● Children can use clear language and appropriate presentational features both to present a particular case (argument) and to provide a balanced (overview) discussion.

Success criteria
● I can present a case clearly using persuasive language and features.
● I can present a balanced discussion using appropriate language and features.
● I can evaluate a persuasive presentation and a balanced discussion.

Setting the context
Display the success criteria in the classroom. Ask the children to imagine that they are a famous person in a hot air balloon with three other famous people. The balloon is rapidly sinking to the ground. One person can be saved if *all* the other people jump out. Explain that they have to present a case, in character, of why that person should be saved. With the children, write agreed criteria on the board to evaluate each presentation and help decide which characters should go.

Assessment opportunity
Give each of the children a famous person's name and a piece of paper, and then allow them a few minutes to plan their case. Walk round the class and make observation notes. Ask four children to come up and individually present their case. Ask the rest of the class to evaluate the presentations and then vote, giving reasons for their choice. What was the purpose of the presentation? What was the presentor's viewpoint? Was their argument balanced? How did the presentation make you feel? Why do you think this was? Whose presentation was more believable? Why were they more believable? Put the children into pairs and give them one of the famous people. Ask them to present a balanced argument for why that person should and shouldn't stay. Ask: *Is the presentation fair and impartial?* Discuss the differences in language and the way it is presented. Evaluate each presentation against the agreed criteria.

Assessment evidence
Walk round the children as they make notes or practise their presentations. Take observation notes of discussions and responses. Note down the presentations of each child. Have they achieved the activity's success criteria? Discuss the criteria with the child. What do they feel they have achieved? Where do they need to improve? How? Use the assessment as evidence against Reading AF6.

Periodic assessment

Writing

Learning outcome
Children can write an effective argument for a particular case, selecting language, form, format and content to suit a particular audience and purpose.

Success criteria
- I can plan and write a persuasive argument for a purpose and audience.
- I can use persuasive vocabulary to create an effect.
- I can evaluate my argument and those of others.

Setting the context
Choose a controversial issue, such as the wearing of school uniform. Put children at levels 2–3 in a group with adult support. Put the children working at levels 4–5 into pairs. At the beginning of the activity introduce the issue to the whole class and briefly discuss the pros and cons of the argument. Explain to the children that they are going to plan and write an effective argument about one side of the issue. Explore the use of persuasive vocabulary and informal language to create an effective argument, giving examples on the board. Explain that after they have completed their argument they are going to evaluate how persuasive and effective their text is with their partner or members of their group. Display the success criteria in the classroom.

Assessment opportunity
Give the children a copy each of the photocopiable page 'Non-fiction 3 Writing assessment'. Encourage them to suggest three reasons 'for' the argument and three 'against' as an adult records them on a large sheet of paper. Ask them to use the photocopiable page to plan reasons for one side of the argument and then write out the text on paper. Walk round and discuss their choice of words. Encourage them to evaluate their written texts with their response partner. Encourage all the children to compare their work against the success criteria. What do they need to work on? What did they do successfully?

Assessment evidence
Children at levels 2–3 should give three clear reasons for and against an argument and write out their chosen reasons using informal language in the first person. They should be able to use simple persuasive vocabulary and connectives. Children at levels 4–5 should show that they can use persuasive phrases and connectives to create a good argument. Use the planning sheets and the children's argument texts as evidence against Writing AF2.

NON-FICTION

Name	Date

Fact or opinion?

Do children watch too much television?

Children definitely watch too much television these days. A recent survey showed that quite young children are watching over four hours of television a day. This is obviously damaging to their health. Everyone knows that children today take far less exercise and the television must be to blame. There is nothing worth watching anyway and children who watch television don't do well at school. It's a fact that children who watch television don't read. They see bad behaviour on the television and this makes

them immediately go out and do the same. The advertisements for toys and food tempt them and they're not satisfied until they get what they want. We must stop our children from watching this dreadful machine.

Fact	Opinion

Photograph © 2009, JupiterImages Corporation. Text © 1995, Diane Bentley & Dee Reid.

Red
Amber
Green

I can identify a persuasive argument. ☐
I can tell the difference between fact or opinion. ☐

NON-FICTION
UNIT 4 Formal/impersonal writing

Literacy objectives

Speak and listen for a wide range of purposes in different contexts
Strand 1 Speaking
- Use the techniques of dialogic talk to explore ideas, topics or issues.

Strand 2 Listening and responding
- Identify the ways spoken language varies according to differences in the context and purpose of its use.

Strand 3 Group discussion and interaction
- Understand and use a variety of ways to criticise constructively and respond to criticism.

Read and write for a range of purposes on paper and on screen
Strand 6 Word structure and spelling
- Use a range of appropriate strategies to edit, proofread and correct spelling in their own work, on paper and on screen.

Strand 7 Understanding and interpreting texts
- Understand how writers use different structures to create coherence and impact.

Strand 8 Engaging with and responding to texts
- Compare how writers from different times and places present experiences and use language.

Strand 9 Creating and shaping texts
- Set their own challenges to extend achievement and experience in writing.
- Select words and language drawing on their knowledge of literary features and formal and informal writing.
- Integrate words, images and sounds imaginatively for different purposes.

Strand 10 Text structure and organisation
- Use varied structures to shape and organise text coherently.

Strand 11 Sentence structure and punctuation
- Express subtle distinctions of meaning, including hypothesis, speculation and supposition, by constructing sentences in varied ways.
- Use punctuation to clarify meaning in complex sentences.

Strand 12 Presentation
- Select from a wide range of ICT programs to present text effectively and communicate information and ideas.

Key aspects of learning

Enquiry
- Children will seek the answers to their own and others' questions in their activity throughout this unit.

Information processing
- Children will identify relevant information from a range of sources and use this as a basis for writing or presentation. They will explore and tease out the elements involved in combined, conflated and multimodal text types.

Key aspects of learning (contd)

Evaluation
● Children will compare and evaluate the effectiveness of a wide range of non-fiction texts and presentations. They will share their own writing and presentation outcomes, discuss success criteria, give feedback to others and judge the effectiveness of their own work.

Communication
● Children will develop their ability to discuss effective communication in respect of both the form and the content of the non-fiction texts they are reading and creating. They will often work collaboratively in pairs and groups. They will communicate outcomes orally and in writing.

Assessment focuses

Reading
AF4 *(identify and comment on the structure and organisation of texts, including grammatical and presentational features at text level).*
AF5 *(explain and comment on writers' use of language, including grammatical and literary features at word and sentence level).*
AF6 *(identify and comment on writers' purposes and viewpoints and the overall effect of the text on the reader).*
AF7 *(relate texts to their social, cultural and historical contexts and literary traditions).*

Writing
AF2 *(produce texts which are appropriate to task, reader and purpose).*
AF3 *(organise and present whole texts effectively, sequencing and structuring information, ideas and events).*
AF5 *(vary sentences for clarity, pupose and effect).*
AF6 *(write with technical accuracy of sytnax and punctuation in phrases, clauses and sentences).*

Speaking and listening
Speaking (speak with clarity intonation and pace).
Listening and responding (respond appropriately).
Group discussion and interaction (make contributions to sustain the activity).

Resources

Phase 1 activities
Photocopiable page, 'Information text features'
Photocopiable page, 'Non-fiction text types' (versions 1 and 2)
Interactive activity, 'Missing words!' (versions 1 and 2)
Photocopiable page, 'Evaluating non-fiction texts'
Phase 4 activities
Photocopiable page, 'Information text features'
Periodic assessment
Photocopiable page, 'Non-fiction 4 Reading assessment'

Unit 4 ◾ Formal/impersonal writing

Learning outcomes	Assessment opportunity and evidence	Assessment focuses (AFs)		Success criteria
		Level 2	Level 3	
Phase ① activities pages 136–138				
Non-fiction text types Children can understand how non-fiction information can be presented in a number of formats combining modes, media and text types with reference to specific purposes and audiences.	• Supported group activity where children revise features of non-fiction texts and highlight examples on suitable non-fiction texts. • Children's oral responses. • Teacher's notes. • Completed photocopiables.	**Reading AF7** • General features of a few text types identified. • Some awareness that books are set in different times and places.	**Reading AF7** • Some simple connections between texts identified. • Recognition of some features of the context of texts.	• I can identify and record examples of different non-fiction text types used in guides. • I can understand how non-fiction information can be presented.
Missing words! Children can evaluate the effectiveness of the language, organisation and presentational features of specific non-fiction texts.	• Group activity where children choose the correct non-chronological words to complete a passage. • Children's oral responses and discussions. • Teacher's notes. • Completed interactives.	**Reading AF4** • Some awareness of use of features of organisation. **Reading AF5** • Some effective language choices noted. • Some familiar patterns of language identified.	**Reading AF4** • A few basic features of organisation at text level identified, with little or no linked comment. **Reading AF5** • A few basic features of writer's use of language identified, but with little or no comment.	• I can identify language features in a non-chronological text. • I can analyse how non-chronological features are used for effect in a text.
Evaluating non-fiction texts Children can evaluate the effectiveness of the language, organisation and presentational features of specific non-fiction texts.	• Supported group activity where children choose simple statements, add them to a criteria frame and pool ideas to create a criteria list. • Children's oral responses and discussions. • Teacher's notes. • Completed written criteria.	**Reading AF4** • Some awareness of use of features of organisation. **Reading AF6** • Some awareness that writers have viewpoints and purposes. • Simple statements about likes and dislikes in reading, sometimes with reasons.	**Reading AF4** • A few basic features of organisation at text level identified, with little or no linked comment. **Reading AF6** • Comments identify main purpose. • Express personal response but with little awareness of writer's viewpoint or effect on reader.	• I can debate and agree to criteria that will evaluate the effectiveness of non-fiction texts. • I can use criteria to evaluate the effectiveness of features used in non-fiction texts.
Phase ② activity page 139				
Star-rating presentations Children can use a wide range of discussion and role-taking techniques to explore non-fiction subject matter.	• Group activity where children prepare and present a case to win a star rating for visitor information and vote on other presentations using an agreed criteria. • Children's oral responses and discussions. • Teacher's notes. • Children's presentations.	**Writing AF2** • Some basic purpose established. • Some appropriate features of the given form used. • Some attempts to adopt appropriate style.	**Writing AF2** • Purpose established at a general level. • Main features of selected form sometimes signalled to the reader. • Some attempts at appropriate style, with attention to reader.	• I can plan, prepare and present a presentation using a range of non-fiction information. • I can debate and evaluate a presentation about a non-fiction matter.

Unit 4 📖 Formal/impersonal writing

Learning outcomes	Assessment opportunity and evidence	Assessment focuses (AFs)		Success criteria
		Level 2	Level 3	
Phase ③ activities pages 140–141				
Resources revision Children can research and assemble information from a variety of paper-based, electronic and live sources.	• Group activity where children create a checklist of resources that they have used and then re-evaluate and add notes to them. • Teacher's notes. • Children's checklists.	**Writing AF3** • Some basic sequencing of ideas or material. • Openings and/or closings sometimes signalled.	**Writing AF3** • Some attempt to organise ideas with related points placed next to each other. • Openings and closings usually signalled. • Some attempt to sequence ideas or material logically.	• I can explain why, when and how chosen resources will be used in my project. • I can evaluate and revise the effectiveness of my resources.
Organising plans Children can plan a presentation of non-fiction information that combines writing with different modes of communication into an interactive ICT text.	• Supported group activity where children choose a suitable planner to plan out their presentations and add information keeping in mind how, why and when it is used. • Children's oral responses, evaluations and written plans. • Teacher's notes.	**Writing AF3** • Some basic sequencing of ideas or material. • Openings and/or closings sometimes signalled.	**Writing AF3** • Some attempt to organise ideas with related points placed next to each other. • Openings and closings usually signalled. • Some attempt to sequence ideas or material logically.	• I can understand how, why and when information is used for my presentation. • I can organise and plan my non-fiction information and resources effectively.
Phase ④ activity page 143				
Evaluating language features Children can evaluate their own work and that of others against agreed criteria.	• Supported group activity where children revise and discuss information text features then go through their texts and identify and revise language features of the different non-fiction texts used. • Children's oral responses and discussions. • Teacher's notes. • Children's written notes and redrafted texts.	**Writing AF5** • Some variation in sentence openings. • Mainly simple sentences with *and* used to connect clauses. • Past and present tense generally consistent. **Writing AF6** • Clause structure mostly grammatically correct. • Sentence demarcation with capital letters and full stops usually accurate. • Some accurate use of question and exclamation marks, and commas in lists.	**Writing AF5** • Reliance mainly on simply structured sentences, variation with support. • Some limited variation in use of tense and verb forms, not always secure. **Writing AF6** • Straightforward sentences usually demarcated accurately with full stops, capital letters, question and exclamation marks. • Some, limited, use of speech punctuation. • Comma splicing evident, particularly in narrative.	• I can identify language features that need editing within non-fiction texts. • I can revise and evaluate language features in non-fiction texts.

Learning outcomes	Assessment opportunity and evidence	Assessment focuses (AFs)		Success criteria
		Level 4	Level 5	
Phase ① activities pages 136–138				
Non-fiction text types Children can understand how non-fiction information can be presented in a number of formats combining modes, media and text types with reference to specific purposes and audiences.	• Paired activity where children revise features of non-fiction texts and highlight examples on suitable non-fiction texts. • Children's oral responses. • Teacher's notes. • Completed photocopiables	**Reading AF7** • Features common to different texts or versions of the same text identified, with simple comment. • Simple comment on the effect that the reader's or writer's context has on the meaning of texts.	**Reading AF7** • Comments identify similarities and differences between texts, or versions, with some explanation. • Some explanation of how the contexts in which texts are written and read contribute to meaning.	• I can identify and record examples of different non-fiction text types used in guides. • I can understand how non-fiction information can be presented.

Unit 4 📖 Formal/impersonal writing

Learning outcomes	Assessment opportunity and evidence	Assessment focuses (AFs)		Success criteria
		Level 4	**Level 5**	
Missing words! Children can evaluate the effectiveness of the language, organisation and presentational features of specific non-fiction texts.	• Group activity where children choose the correct non-chronological words to complete a passage and discuss their reasons. • Children's oral responses and discussions. • Teacher's notes. • Completed interactives.	**Reading AF4** • Some structural choices identified with simple comment. • Some basic features of organisation at text level identified. **Reading AF5** • Some basic features of writer's use of language identified. • Simple comments on writer's choices.	**Reading AF4** • Comments on structural choices show some general awareness of writer's craft. • Various features relating to organisation at text level, including form, are clearly identified, with some explanation. **Reading AF5** • Various features of writer's use of language identified, with some explanation. • Comments show some awareness of the effect of writer's language choices.	• I can identify language features in a non-chronological text. • I can analyse how non-chronological features are used for effect in a text.
Evaluating non-fiction texts Children can evaluate the effectiveness of the language, organisation and presentational features of specific non-fiction texts.	• Group activity where children agree and produce written criteria that can be used to evaluate the effectiveness of a range of non-fiction texts. • Children's oral responses and discussions. • Teacher's notes. • Completed written criteria.	**Reading AF4** • Some structural choices identified with simple comment. • Some basic features of organisation at text level identified. **Reading AF6** • Main purpose identified. • Simple comments show some awareness of writer's viewpoint. • Simple comment on overall effect on reader.	**Reading AF4** • Comments on structural choices show some general awareness of writer's craft. • Various features relating to organisation at text level, including form, are clearly identified, with some explanation. **Reading AF6** • Main purpose clearly identified, often through general overview. • Viewpoints in texts clearly identified, with some, often limited, explanation. • General awareness of effect on the reader, with some, often limited, explanation.	• I can debate and agree to criteria that will evaluate the effectiveness of non-fiction texts. • I can use criteria to evaluate the effectiveness of features used in non-fiction texts.

Phase ② activity page 139

Learning outcomes	Assessment opportunity and evidence	Level 4	Level 5	Success criteria
Star-rating presentations Children can use a wide range of discussion and role-taking techniques to explore non-fiction subject matter.	• Group activity where children prepare and present a case to win a star rating for visitor information and vote on other presentations using an agreed criteria. • Children's oral responses and discussions. • Teacher's notes. • Children's presentations.	**Writing AF2** • Main purpose of writing is clear but not always consistently maintained. • Main features of selected form are clear and appropriate to purpose. • Style generally appropriate to task, though awareness of reader not always sustained.	**Writing AF2** • Main purpose of writing is clear and consistently maintained. • Features of selected form clearly established with some adaptation to purpose. • Appropriate style clearly established to maintain reader's interest throughout.	• I can plan, prepare and present a presentation using a range of non-fiction information. • I can debate and evaluate a presentation about a non-fiction matter.

Unit 4 📖 Formal/impersonal writing

Learning outcomes	Assessment opportunity and evidence	Assessment focuses (AFs)		Success criteria
		Level 4	**Level 5**	
Phase ③ activities pages 140–141				
Resources revision Children can research and assemble information from a variety of paper-based, electronic and live sources.	• Group activity where children create a checklist of resources that they have used and then re-evaluate and add notes to them. • Teacher's notes. • Children's checklists.	**Writing AF3** • Ideas organised by clustering related points or by time sequence. • Ideas are organised simply with a fitting opening and closing, sometimes linked. • Ideas or material generally in logical sequence but overall direction of writing not always clearly signalled.	**Writing AF3** • Material is structured clearly, with sentences organised into appropriate paragraphs. • Development of material is effectively managed across text. • Overall direction of the text supported by clear links between paragraphs.	• I can explain why, when and how chosen resources will be used in my project. • I can evaluate and revise the effectiveness of my resources.
Organising plans Children can plan a presentation of non-fiction information that combines writing with different modes of communication into an interactive ICT text.	• Group activity where children choose a suitable planner to plan out their presentations and add information keeping in mind how, why and when it is used. • Children's oral responses, evaluations and written plans. • Teacher's notes.	**Writing AF3** • Ideas organised by clustering related points or by time sequence. • Ideas are organised simply with a fitting opening and closing, sometimes linked. • Ideas or material generally in logical sequence but overall direction of writing not always clearly signalled.	**Writing AF3** • Material is structured clearly, with sentences organised into appropriate paragraphs. • Development of material is effectively managed across text. • Overall direction of the text supported by clear links between paragraphs.	• I can understand how, why and when information is used for my presentation. • I can organise and plan my non-fiction information and resources effectively.
Phase ④ activity page 142				
Evaluating language features Children can evaluate their own work and that of others against agreed criteria.	• Group activity where children revise and discuss information text features then go through their texts and identify and revise language features of the different non-fiction texts used. • Children's oral responses and discussions. • Teacher's notes. • Children's written notes and redrafted texts.	**Writing AF5** • Some variety in length, structure or subject of sentences. • Use of some subordinating connectives. • Some variation, generally accurate, in tense and verb forms. **Writing AF6** • Sentences demarcated accurately throughout the text, including question marks. • Speech marks to denote speech generally accurate, with some other speech punctuation. • Commas used in lists and occasionally to mark clauses, although not always accurate.	**Writing AF5** • A variety of sentence lengths, structures and subjects provides clarity and emphasis. • Wider range of connectives used to clarify relationship between ideas. • Some features of sentence structure used to build up detail or convey shades of meaning. **Writing AF6** • Full range of punctuation used accurately to demarcate sentences, including speech punctuation. • Syntax and punctuation within the sentence generally accurate including commas to mark clauses, though some errors occur where ambitious structures are attempted.	• I can identify language features that need editing within non-fiction texts. • I can revise and evaluate language features in non-fiction texts.

Phase ① Non-fiction text types

Learning outcome
Children can understand how non-fiction information can be presented in a number of formats combining modes, media and text types with reference to specific purposes and audiences.

Success criteria
● I can identify and record examples of different non-fiction text types used in guides.
● I can understand how non-fiction information can be presented.

Setting the context
Use this activity once the children have explored a range of different guidebooks of one particular location. Put the children into pairs. Children at levels 2–3 can work as a discussion group with adult support. As a class, discuss how guidebooks can use a range of different non-fiction text types to convey information to a visitor. Display the photocopiable page 'Information text features'. Go through each one and discuss possible examples, such as recounts of an historical person's life. Give out version 1 of the photocopiable page 'Non-fiction text types' for children at levels 2–3 and version 2 for children at levels 4–5. Ask the children to go through a selection of guides to find and record examples of non-fiction text types. Display the success criteria in the classroom.

Assessment opportunity
Children at levels 2–3 can look at easy-read guides, maps and trails and record their findings on the photocopiable page with adult support. Make notes of the children's discussions. Children at levels 4–5 should work in pairs to record examples of non-fiction text types in a range of the guides. Give each pair a particular type of guide, for example, an audio guide, children's guidebook or self-guided trail and encourage them to record text examples and the purpose of each section. Once they have completed the worksheet, ask them to compare and contrast their findings with another pair. Have a class plenary where all the children discuss their findings. Which text type is most used? How, when and where and to what effect?

Assessment evidence
At levels 2–3, children should be able to identify language features of a range of texts, such as technical, descriptive and persuasive language. They should also be able to discuss the way each text is presented and its use. At levels 4–5, children should be able to identify the type of non-fiction text and record language and structural examples. They should discuss how the presentation of each text identifies its purpose and audience. Use the children's completed photocopiable pages along with notes of their responses as evidence against Reading AF7.

Next steps
Support: Choose one non-fiction text type, for example non-chronological reports, and encourage children to identify different features, such as its use of the third person or formal and impersonal language.
Extension: Encourage children to collect and explore just one type of non-fiction text type in a range of guides, such as persuasive texts or instruction texts and diagrams. How do they compare and contrast? How, where and when are they used in the guides and to what effect?

Key aspects of learning
Information processing: Children will identify relevant information from a range of sources and use this as a basis for writing or presentation. They will explore and tease out the elements involved in combined, conflated and multimodal text types.
Evaluation: Children will compare and evaluate the effectiveness of a wide range of non-fiction texts and presentations. They will share their own writing and presentation outcomes, discuss success criteria, give feedback to others and judge the effectiveness of their own work.
Communication: Children will develop their ability to discuss effective communication in respect of both the form and the content of the non-fiction texts they are reading and creating. They will often work collaboratively in pairs and groups. They will communicate outcomes orally and in writing.

Phase ① Missing words!

Learning outcome
Children can evaluate the effectiveness of the language, organisation and presentational features of specific non-fiction texts.

Success criteria
- I can identify language features in a non-chronological text.
- I can analyse how non-chronological features are used for effect in a text.

Setting the context
Work with the children in their guided reading groups. Discuss how non-fiction texts have specific language, organisational and presentational features. With each group briefly go through a few examples. Display version 1 of the interactive activity 'Missing words!' to children at levels 2–3, and version 2 of the interactive activity to children at levels 4–5. Explain that it is an extract from a museum guide and that there are important words missing from the text. Explain that as the group goes through the extract they have to choose each correct missing word from a choice of three.

Assessment opportunity
Read out the extract and stop at a missing word. Read out the three options to the group. Ask each child in turn what word they would choose and why. Allow a child to reveal the right answer and discuss the reason, such as the use of the present tense, third person, technical and descriptive language. Take notes of each of the children's choices and reasons. Once all the correct missing words have been put in place, read through the extract and discuss its intended audience. Ask: *Is the extract effective in conveying information to the reader? How could you organise and present the extract to make it more interesting and include more information?*

Assessment evidence
At levels 2–3, children should be able to identify and choose present tense words, connectives and relevant descriptive words and give reasons for their answers. At levels 4–5, children should be able to recognise the tenses, technical, descriptive and impersonal language. They should discuss the introduction and conclusion, and the ways the information is presented to the intended audience. Use the notes of the children's responses and word choices as evidence against Reading AF4 and AF5.

Next steps
Support: Continue the above activity by choosing material from a non-fiction text that children may need extra support in understanding. Delete various words that use the past or present tense and ask them to think of what they may be. Discuss their reasons.
Extension: Encourage children to explore the differences between formal and informal language within texts. Give them a range of formal and informal texts and ask them to identify differences and make a chart recording the two examples.

Key aspects of learning
Information processing: Children will identify relevant information from a range of sources and use this as a basis for writing or presentation. They will explore and tease out the elements involved in combined, conflated and multimodal text types.
Communication: Children will develop their ability to discuss effective communication in respect of both the form and the content of the non-fiction texts they are reading and creating. They will often work collaboratively in pairs and groups. They will communicate outcomes orally and in writing.

Unit 4 Formal/impersonal writing

Phase ① Evaluating non-fiction texts

Learning outcome
Children can evaluate the effectiveness of the language, organisation and presentational features of specific non-fiction texts.

Success criteria
● I can debate and agree to criteria that will evaluate the effectiveness of non-fiction texts.
● I can use criteria to evaluate the effectiveness of features used in non-fiction texts.

Setting the context
Put the children into their guided reading groups. Give each group a range of guides or specific non-fiction texts that the class may have been studying. In their groups, ask the children to debate and agree to criteria that can be used to successfully evaluate the effectiveness of the non-fiction texts. Discuss briefly the areas that should be evaluated, for example, language, organisation and presentation, as well as different methods of recording the criteria, such as a checklist of questions, a chart with headings and space for text examples, or simple statements with a tick sheet. Children at levels 2–3 can work with adult support on the photocopiable page 'Evaluating non-fiction texts'.

Assessment opportunity
With level 2–3 groups, read out the list of criteria statements from the photocopiable page 'Evaluating non-fiction texts' and ask each child to choose one statement they would like to add to the criteria list. Encourage them to discuss their reasons and take notes of their responses. Ask them to copy their chosen statement into the criteria frame. Ask each child in the level 4–5 groups to contribute two criteria statements and then select one statement per group member through debate and discussion. Take notes of each child's responses and suggestions. Once the children have agreed their criteria, encourage them to create their criteria sheets. Ask all the groups to use the criteria to evaluate a few non-fiction texts. Ask: *Which texts were the most effective? Why? Did your criteria evaluate the texts effectively? How could you improve it?*

Assessment evidence
At levels 2–3, children should choose a criteria statement and discuss why it would be useful in effectively evaluating a non-fiction text. At levels 4–5, children should debate a range of criteria statements. All the children should be able to discuss how effective their criteria lists are in evaluations. Use notes of the children's discussion and responses along with the written criteria as evidence against Reading AF4 and AF6.

Next steps
Support: Encourage children to use their criteria sheets on a range of texts and compare the different results. Discuss which texts they found the easiest to evaluate and why.
Extension: Ask children to create and produce criteria sheets for a range of non-fiction resources, such as maps, audio guides, reports, visitor questionnaires. Display the results and discuss their differences.

Key aspects of learning
Enquiry: Children will seek the answers to their own and others' questions in their activity throughout this unit.
Information processing: Children will identify relevant information from a range of sources and use this as a basis for writing or presentation. They will explore and tease out the elements involved in combined, conflated and multimodal text types.
Evaluation: Children will compare and evaluate the effectiveness of a wide range of non-fiction texts and presentations. They will share their own writing and presentation outcomes, discuss success criteria, give feedback to others and judge the effectiveness of their own work.

Phase ② Star-rating presentations

Learning outcome
Children can use a wide range of discussion and role-taking techniques to explore non-fiction subject matter.

Success criteria
● I can plan, prepare and present a presentation using a range of non-fiction information.
● I can debate and evaluate a presentation about a non-fiction matter.

Setting the context
Use this activity once the children have started working on their guided tours and when they have had time to discuss and use role play to explore ways to attract visitors to their chosen site. Put the children into their working groups and explain that they are going to make a presentation to try to win a tourism star rating, using agreed criteria, for useful visitor information. Discuss known ratings such as AA hotels, or tourism boards. Encourage the children to debate and agree to the criteria and write it on the board. Identify a range of presentational methods, such as role-playing visitors, presentations using ICT, display of materials such as maps and children's trails. Briefly revise the structure of a persuasive argument and text.

Assessment opportunity
Go round the groups and ask questions such as: *What will be your main persuasive statements or achievements? What is your evidence for these? Have you got visitors to back up your statements? What form do your statements take (for example, written comments or interviews)? What is your closing statement?* Take notes of the children's individual responses. Bring all the groups together for the presentations. As a group presents, encourage the other groups to decide on the star rating (with the lowest rating as one star and the highest as five stars) using the set visitor information criteria. Discuss and debate the presentations, given ratings and evaluations. Which presentations were impressive? Why? What areas needed more work? How? Take notes of the children's discussions.

Assessment evidence
At levels 2-3, children should be able to use some basic features of a persuasive text and make some attempt to adopt the appropriate style. At levels 4-5, children should be able to produce written and oral work using persuasive arguments effectively and use a good range of resources to present their case. Use the notes of the children's responses and their presentations as evidence against Writing AF2.

Next steps
Support: Have a drama session where the children hot seat visitors who are 'very happy', 'satisfied' and 'not happy' with the visitor information. How would they bring over their comments? What would the visitor site owners do or say in response?
Extension: Have a question-and-answer session after the groups' presentations. Let the other groups take notes during the presentation and ask questions, for example to a visitor, about the owner's future plans for the site.

Key aspects of learning
Enquiry: Children will seek the answers to their own and others' questions in their activity throughout this unit.
Evaluation: Children will compare and evaluate the effectiveness of a wide range of non-fiction texts and presentations. They will share their own writing and presentation outcomes, discuss success criteria, give feedback to others and judge the effectiveness of their own work.
Communication: Children will develop their ability to discuss effective communication in respect of both the form and the content of the non-fiction texts they are reading and creating. They will often work collaboratively in pairs and groups. They will communicate outcomes orally and in writing.

Phase ③ Resources revision

Learning outcome
Children can research and assemble information from a variety of paper-based, electronic and live sources.

Success criteria
● I can explain why, when and how chosen resources will be used in my project.
● I can evaluate and revise the effectiveness of my resources.

Setting the context
Use this activity once the children have researched information from a range of sources and then created their own resources for their project. Put the children into their working project groups. Explain to the class that they are going to create a checklist of the resources they have covered. Give each group a large piece of paper and with one member as scribe encourage the groups to list all their resources using a chart or mind map under headings such as 'Visual' (maps, diagrams, photographs, video), 'Audio' , 'ICT', 'Written text' (bullet points, non-chronological information, instructions) and so on.

Assessment opportunity
Ask the children to re-evaluate their resources in their groups. Encourage them to consider how, when and why the resources are used. Ask: *Is there something else that could be added, such as café menus or a children's worksheet? Is there a way that a resource could be improved, such as making the map clearer or changing text that is too long or too short?* Encourage the children to write notes of their revision ideas on the checklists. Take notes of each child's responses and discussion within the groups. Let two groups swap and look at each others' work to compare findings and evaluate their work. With each child, look at the success criteria and help them as they self-assess their own contributions to the group's work. Discuss future development and support.

Assessment evidence
At levels 2–3, children should be able to write notes on the reasons why, how and when the resources will be used, such as 'We are drawing a children's trail with simple pictures to make it easier to follow.' At levels 4–5, children be able to include, for example, 'We want to show how the machine works so we are going to have a diagram with the text.' Use the group's checklists and notes of the children's responses and discussions as evidence against Writing AF3.

Next steps
Support: Encourage children who may need reading or writing support to be in charge of visual or audio resources, such as photographs, maps or recordings.
Extension: Encourage children to build up a system to record their sources and their resources for easy filing and planning.

Key aspects of learning
Evaluation: Children will compare and evaluate the effectiveness of a wide range of non-fiction texts and presentations. They will share their own writing and presentation outcomes, discuss success criteria, give feedback to others and judge the effectiveness of their own work.
Communication: Children will develop their ability to discuss effective communication in respect of both the form and the content of the non-fiction texts they are reading and creating. They will often work collaboratively in pairs and groups. They will communicate outcomes orally and in writing.

Phase ③ Organising plans

Learning outcome
Children can plan a presentation of non-fiction information that combines writing with different modes of communication into an interactive ICT text.

Success criteria
- I can understand how, why and when information is used for my presentation.
- I can organise and plan my non-fiction information and resources effectively.

Setting the context
The children will need to have experience in using ICT presentational software. Put the children into their project groups with access to computers. Remind them that the elements they want to use in their presentations need to be organised to give the reader or visitor effective information. Remind the groups to think of how, why and when the information is presented. Encourage them to plan out their presentations or guides using ICT. Identify different forms such as spidergrams, flat plans or ICT-screen diagram plans. Children working at levels 2–3 may need support.

Assessment opportunity
Work with individual groups and discuss their plans for their presentations. Ask each group the three questions about organising the information: how is it to be presented, why is it to be presented (purpose and audience) and when? Discuss their choice of planner. Does it help them organise their information effectively? Does it give the group an overall view of how the information is organised? Make notes of the children's individual responses. Invite the groups to present and discuss their on-screen plans to the class. Encourage the class to ask questions and evaluate each group's work. Allow each child to use the success criteria to self-assess their own contribution to their group's work and what areas need more support.

Assessment evidence
At levels 2–3, children should be able to create a plan that shows they understand the purpose of their presentation and that they have thought about how to sequence their ideas logically. At levels 4–5, children should be able to explain how, why and when their information will be presented and be able to create a clearly structured plan that includes a series of linked ideas. Use your observations and notes of children's comments and oral feedback, along with their written plans, as evidence against Writing AF3.

Next steps
Support: Work with children who need support by creating a template to show how each page of their guides or non-fiction writing could look. Encourage them to move their work round until they are happy with the layout.
Extension: Ask children to produce an interactive planner or use PowerPoint® to create a plan of a colourful, easy-to-follow map with information captions for a fictional theme park with six differently themed areas.

Key aspects of learning
Evaluation: Children will compare and evaluate the effectiveness of a wide range of non-fiction texts and presentations. They will share their own writing and presentation outcomes, discuss success criteria, give feedback to others and judge the effectiveness of their own work.
Communication: Children will develop their ability to discuss effective communication in respect of both the form and the content of the non-fiction texts they are reading and creating. They will often work collaboratively in pairs and groups. They will communicate outcomes orally and in writing.

Phase ④ Evaluating language features

Learning outcome
Children can evaluate their own work and that of others against agreed criteria.

Success criteria
- I can identify language features that need editing within non-fiction texts.
- I can revise and evaluate language features in non-fiction texts.

Setting the context
Use this activity as the children work in groups to create and write their non-fiction presentations. In advance of the activity look at the groups' work and select different language features that need revising and allocate them to specific members of the group, for example, correcting tenses or more descriptive words for children at levels 2–3, impersonal language, persuasive phrasing for children at levels 4–5. Display the photocopiable page 'Information text features' to the class or groups. Briefly revise the features. Display or read out the success criteria to the children. Choose a piece of work and model editing the text to improve language features. Give the groups their work and explain to each child what revision task and text they have to work on. Children at levels 2–3 may need support.

Assessment opportunity
Walk round the groups and take notes of each of the children as they identify words or sentences that may need revising. Using adult support, children at levels 2–3 can use individual whiteboards to discuss or explore different ways of writing the text. With children at levels 4–5, ask guided questions such as: *Does the language style and form of the text match the purpose and targeted audience? If not, what needs to be improved or changed?* Once the children have established what needs to be changed, encourage them to suggest new words or sentences. Allow them time to redraft and refine their texts. Once all the children have completed their tasks, encourage them to share their revised texts with the group. Children can also self-assess their work using the success criteria

Assessment evidence
At levels 2–3, children should be able to go through the given texts and identify and change tenses and non-fiction language, for example, 'The words "had" and "wanted" should be "has" and "want" to make sense'. At levels 4–5, children should be able to change sentences and text, for example, 'The text is too informal and chatty. I will change it into the third person and use more technical words.' Use the notes of the children's comments along with their redrafted texts as evidence against Writing AF5 and AF6.

Next steps
Support: Some children may find it hard to look through texts and identify words or sentences that may need revising. Create sentences to be displayed on a whiteboard that have language errors in one or two areas and work with them to revise the text. Discuss the overall text once it has been revised.
Extension: Encourage children to explore ways to revise the language of non-fiction texts. Give them a text and ask them to rewrite it for a different purpose or audience, for example from adult to under seven year olds.

Key aspects of learning
Enquiry: Children will seek the answers to their own and others' questions in their activity throughout this unit.
Evaluation: Children will compare and evaluate the effectiveness of a wide range of non-fiction texts and presentations. They will share their own writing and presentation outcomes, discuss success criteria, give feedback to others and judge the effectiveness of their own work.
Communication: Children will develop their ability to discuss effective communication in respect of both the form and the content of the non-fiction texts they are reading and creating. They will often work collaboratively in pairs and groups. They will communicate outcomes orally and in writing.

Periodic assessment

Reading

Learning outcome
Children can evaluate the effectiveness of the language, organisation and presentational features of specific non-fiction texts.

Success criteria
● I can identify and analyse the features of different non-fiction text types.
● I can understand and evaluate the effectiveness of non-fiction text features in different texts.

Setting the context
This activity is a revision and assessment to gauge the children's understanding of the different features of non-fiction text types. Show a non-fiction text from a guide book to the class. With the children discuss its text type, its purpose and audience, examples of language and organisational features and a ratings score out of five for effectiveness where one is the lowest score and five is the highest. Explain to the children that they are going to do the same to two more non-fiction text examples. Give out the copies of the photocopiable page 'Non-fiction 4 Reading assessment'.

Assessment opportunity
Allow the children to complete the photocopiable page individually. Encourage them to use highlighters or underline features within the text. Walk round the class and discuss the children's work. Record their responses. Once all the children have finished ask them to read through the sheet again to check they have recorded everything. Encourage all the children to look at the success criteria and consider their progress and areas that need improvement or more support.

Assessment evidence
Children at levels 2–3 should identify that the first text is persuasive – for example, 'There are descriptive words such as "fabulous" and "fantastic" that make you want to visit the place'. Children at levels 4–5 should discuss further the features and effectiveness of the texts – for example, 'I think the first text was very persuasive. It uses language such as alliteration and persuasive phrases to encourage people to visit'. 'The last text was an information text which uses information to entice people to the tower'. Record children's understandings and needs and use them to make level judgements against Reading AF3, AF4 and AF6.

Periodic assessment

Writing

Learning outcome
Children can plan and create an information leaflet using non-fiction text types and ICT.

Success criteria
● I can identify the effectiveness of the language and structure of visitor leaflets.
● I can plan a range of information to be included in a visitor leaflet.
● I can write a visitor leaflet which effectively presents a range of different information.

Setting the context
This assessment activity may need to be carried out over a number of days. The children will need access to computers and a suitable desktop publishing program. Show some examples of A4 or A3 folded visitor leaflets to the class. Explore how the information is laid out, for example with front and back covers, maps, general visitor information (opening times, refreshments, disabled access, where it is, exhibit information and so on). Explore the use of different texts types, such as persuasive or non-chronological. Explain to the children that they are going to plan and then write an information leaflet for a new aquarium on A3 paper or, if they prefer, using ICT. Explain that there are lots of other visitor attractions in the fictional seaside town, such as a pier and a theme park, so the leaflet has to encourage tourists to visit the aquarium.

Assessment opportunity
Put the children at levels 2–3 into small groups with support and children at levels 4–5 into pairs. Give out paper for planning notes and leaflet examples for reference. Walk round the pairs or groups to take observation notes of their planning process. What kind of planners do they use (for example, spidergrams, tables, mind maps)? Once the children are happy with their plans, ask them to write the first drafts of each information section. Give a section each to the children working in a group. Ask the children to evaluate their drafts before they write them up in best. Are the language and organisational features effective? Encourage the children who are confident in using ICT to create their final leaflets using the desktop publishing program. Once they have created their leaflets, encourage the children to use the success criteria to self-assess their understanding and progress.

Assessment evidence
Children at levels 2–3 should plan and write a simple visitor leaflet for the intended audience with information on where it is, when it opens, what is there. They should also use different non-fiction texts and language features and so on. Children at levels 4–5 should plan and present their leaflet information using a wide range of non-fiction texts and features and understand their effect and use on the reader. Record children's understandings and needs and use them to make level judgements against Writing AF2, AF3 and AF7.

Name	Date

Evaluating non-fiction texts

◼ Read the statements below the table.

◼ Discuss and select six statements that could be used to evaluate the effectiveness of a non-fiction text.

◼ Copy the chosen statements into the table below.

Criteria statements to evaluate a non-fiction text	Yes ✔	No ✗

The purpose of the information is clear.

The intended audience of the information is clear.

There is a good opening statement.

There is a good closing statement.

The text is set out clearly.

The information uses typical features of a non-fiction text.

The tenses are correct.

The vocabulary is effective.

The text gives the reader information.

The text makes the reader want to read on.

The information is visually attractive.

The layout attracts the intended audience.

Red / Amber / Green

I can debate and agree to criteria that will evaluate non-fiction texts. ◻

I can use criteria to evaluate features used in non-fiction texts. ◻

POETRY
UNIT 1 The power of imagery

Literacy objectives

Speak and listen for a wide range of purposes in different contexts
Strand 1 Speaking
- Use a range of oral techniques to present persuasive arguments and engaging narratives.

Strand 2 Listening and responding
- Analyse and evaluate how speakers present points effectively through use of language and gesture.

Strand 3 Group discussion and interaction
- Understand and use a variety of ways to criticise constructively and respond to criticism.

Strand 4 Drama
- Consider the overall impact of a live or recorded performance, identifying dramatic ways of conveying characters' ideas and building tension.

Read and write for a range of purposes on paper and on screen
Strand 6 Word structure and spelling
- Use a range of appropriate strategies to edit, proofread and correct spelling in their own work, on paper and on screen.

Strand 7 Understanding and interpreting texts
- Understand underlying themes, causes and points of view.
- Understand how writers use different structures to create coherence and impact.

Strand 8 Engaging with and responding to texts
- Read extensively and discuss personal reading with others, including in reading groups.
- Compare how writers from different times and places present experiences and use language.

Strand 9 Creating and shaping texts
- Select words and language drawing on their knowledge of literary features and formal and informal writing.

Strand 10 Text structure and organisation
- Use varied structures to shape and organise text coherently.

Key aspects of learning

Enquiry
- Children will seek the answers to their own and others' questions in their reading.

Information processing
- Children will explore and tease out the information communicated through the language and forms of poetry.

Reasoning
- Children will identify, explore and generate the mental connections represented within various forms of powerful imagery (simile and metaphor) – a vital aspect of thinking, reasoning and understanding.

Key aspects of learning (contd)

Empathy
- In discussing and writing about the poems and their images, children will need to imagine themselves in another person's position. They will explore techniques that facilitate this process.

Self-awareness
- Children will discuss and reflect on their personal responses to the texts.

Assessment focuses

Reading
AF4 *(identify and comment on the structure and organisation of texts, including grammatical and presentational features at text level).*
AF5 *(explain and comment on writers' uses of language, including grammatical and literary features at word and sentence level).*

Writing
AF1 *(write imaginative, interesting and thoughtful texts).*
AF7 *(select appropriate and effective vocabulary).*

Speaking and listening
Speaking (speak with clarity intonation and pace).
Listening and responding (understand main points; responds appropriately).
Group discussion and interaction (make contributions to sustain the activity).
Drama (evaluate performances).

Resources

Phase 1 activities
Photocopiable page, 'The River's Story'
Interactive activity, 'Find the verb'
Photocopiable page, 'The River's Story – analysis sheet'
Image, 'River (a–c)'
Photocopiable page, 'Five senses of a river'
Photocopiable page, 'River poem frame'
Phase 2 activities
Photocopiable page, 'Some Aunts and Uncles'
Photocopiable page, 'Animal images'
Photocopiable page, 'Guided questions checklist' (versions 1 and 2)
Image, 'Stag'
Interactive activity, 'Stag poem'
Photocopiable page, 'My stag poem'
Phase 3 activities
Photocopiable page, 'The Painting Lesson'
Photocopiable page, 'An amusing day' (versions 1 and 2)
Photocopiable page, 'My Dad is Amazing!'
Photocopiable page, 'My Dad is Amazing! – analysis sheet'
Photocopiable page, 'Well-known sayings'
Photocopiable page, 'Who is amazing?'
Periodic assessment
Photocopiable page, 'Poetry 1 Reading assessment text'
Photocopiable page, 'Poetry 1 Reading assessment'
Photocopiable page, 'Poetry 1 Writing assessment'

Unit 1 ▢ The power of imagery

Learning outcomes	Assessment opportunity and evidence	Assessment focuses (AFs)		Success criteria
		Level 2	Level 3	
Phase ① activities pages 152–154				
The river's story Children understand how poets can use personification to communicate with their readers.	• Supported paired activity where children find the right verbs to re-create the personification used in a poem. • Children's oral responses and. completed interactives.	**Reading AF5** • Some effective language choices noted. • Some familiar patterns of language identified.	**Reading AF5** • A few basic features of writer's use of language identified, but with little or no comment.	• I can identify and explain the use of personification in a poem. • I can identify the use and effect of powerful verbs within the poem. • I can identify the use and effect of powerful adjectives within the poem.
Personification of a river Children can write a poem that begins to use personification effectively.	• Supported group activity where children describe the five senses of a river. • Children's oral responses and completed photocopiables.	**Writing AF7** • Simple, often speech-like vocabulary conveys relevant meanings. • Some adventurous word choices.	**Writing AF7** • Simple, generally appropriate vocabulary used, limited in range. • Some words selected for effect or occasion.	• I can plan a poem that uses personification to describe a river. • I can choose powerful verbs and images to start creating a poem.
River poem Children can write a poem that begins to use personification effectively.	• Supported group activity where children select their best five senses ideas and write them within a given poem frame. • Children's oral responses and completed photocopiables.	**Writing AF1** • Mostly relevant ideas and content, sometimes repetitive or sparse. • Some apt word choices create interest. • Brief comments, questions about events or actions suggest viewpoint.	**Writing AF1** • Some appropriate ideas and content included. • Some attempt to elaborate on basic information or events. • Attempt to adopt viewpoint, though often not maintained or inconsistent.	• I can select and use my ideas to create a poem. • I can write a poem that uses personification. • I can evaluate my poem and improve it where necessary.
Phase ② activities pages 155–157				
Aunts and uncles Children understand how poets can use powerful images to communicate with their readers.	• Group activity where children answer guided questions about a poem's powerful imagery and words. • Children's oral responses and completed pictures. • Teacher's notes.	**Reading AF5** • Some effective language choices noted. • Some familiar patterns of language identified.	**Reading AF5** • A few basic features of writer's use of language identified, but with little or no comment.	• I can identify how a poet can use powerful imagery to change a person into something else. • I can evaluate the imagery in a poem.
Animal images Children understand how poets can use powerful images to communicate with their readers.	• Supported group activity where children explore the use of metaphors and similes. • Children's oral responses and checklist comments. • Teacher's notes.	**Reading AF5** • Some effective language choices noted. • Some familiar patterns of language identified.	**Reading AF5** • A few basic features of writer's use of language identified, but with little or no comment.	• I can identify and explain how metaphors are used to create powerful images. • I can identify and explain how similes are used to create powerful images.
Stag poem Children can write a poem that begins to use powerful imagery effectively.	• Supported group or paired activity where children select metaphorical descriptions to complete a stag poem. • Children's oral responses and completed interactives.	**Writing AF1** • Mostly relevant ideas and content, sometimes repetitive or sparse. • Some apt word choices create interest. • Brief comments, questions about events or actions suggest viewpoint.	**Writing AF1** • Some appropriate ideas and content included. • Some attempt to elaborate on basic information or events. • Attempt to adopt viewpoint, though often not maintained or inconsistent.	• I can write a poem using metaphors effectively to describe a stag. • I can create a poem which uses powerful imagery effectively.

Unit 1 ◻ The power of imagery

Learning outcomes	Assessment opportunity and evidence	Assessment focuses (AFs)		Success criteria
		Level 2	Level 3	
Phase ③ activities pages 158-161				
The Painting Lesson Children understand how poets can use surreal, surprising and amusing images to communicate with their readers.	● Group activity where children respond, analyse and evaluate a poem. ● Children's oral responses and discussions.	**Reading AF4** ● Some awareness of use of features of organisation. **Reading AF5** ● Some effective language choices noted. ● Some familiar patterns of language identified.	**Reading AF4** ● A few basic features of organisation at text level identified, with little or no linked comment. **Reading AF5** ● A few basic features of writer's use of language identified, but with little or no comment.	● I can identify and explain surprising and amusing images within poems. ● I can respond to and analyse a poem that uses surprising and amusing images.
An amusing day poem Children can write a poem that begins to use surreal, surprising and amusing imagery effectively.	● Supported activity where children plan and write a poem about an everyday situation with an amusing and surprising ending. ● Children's oral responses, photocopiables and written poems.	**Writing AF1** ● Mostly relevant ideas and content, sometimes repetitive or sparse. ● Some apt word choices create interest. ● Brief comments, questions about events or actions suggest viewpoint.	**Writing AF1** ● Some appropriate ideas and content included. ● Some attempt to elaborate on basic information or events. ● Attempt to adopt viewpoint, though often not maintained or inconsistent.	● I can create amusing and surprising images. ● I can write a poem that uses surprising and amusing imagery.
My Dad is Amazing! Children understand how poets can use surreal, surprising and amusing images to communicate with their readers.	● Supported group activity where children highlight the real meanings of a poem's sayings and the surreal images of the sayings. ● Children's oral responses and completed photocopiables.	**Reading AF5** ● Some effective language choices noted. ● Some familiar patterns of language identified.	**Reading AF5** ● A few basic features of writer's use of language identified, but with little or no comment.	● I can identify surreal images within a poem. ● I can explain the meaning behind surreal images within a poem. ● I can understand the surreal images effect on the reader.
Who is amazing? Children can write a poem that begins to use surreal, surprising and amusing imagery effectively.	● Supported activity where children choose ten examples from a list of sayings and decide on surreal images to use for their own poem. ● Children's oral responses, notes and written poems.	**Writing AF1** ● Mostly relevant ideas and content, sometimes repetitive or sparse. ● Some apt word choices create interest. ● Brief comments, questions about events or actions suggest viewpoint.	**Writing AF1** ● Some appropriate ideas and content included. ● Some attempt to elaborate on basic information or events. ● Attempt to adopt viewpoint, though often not maintained or inconsistent.	● I can create surreal images. ● I can write a poem using surreal imagery for effect.
Phase ④ activity page 162				
Poem reviews Children value their own poems and those of others and enjoy sharing them.	● Supported paired activity where children create lists of qualities needed in a poem. ● Children's oral responses, lists and poetry review sheets.	**Reading AF5** ● Some effective language choices noted. ● Some familiar patterns of language identified.	**Reading AF5** ● A few basic features of writer's use of language identified, but with little or no comment.	● I can create a list of qualities that make up a good poem. ● I can work with others to create agreed criteria to review and evaluate poems.

Unit 1 The power of imagery

Learning outcomes	Assessment opportunity and evidence	Assessment focuses (AFs)		Success criteria
		Level 4	Level 5	
Phase ① activities pages 152-154				
The river's story Children understand how poets can use personification to communicate with their readers.	• Group activity where children read and analyse a poem, highlight the poem text and use examples and quotes on a photocopiable to show personification. • Children's oral responses and completed photocopiables.	**Reading AF5** • Some basic features of writer's use of language identified. • Simple comments on writer's choices.	**Reading AF5** • Various features of writer's use of language identified, with some explanation. • Comments show some awareness of the effect of writer's language choices.	• I can identify and explain the use of personification in a poem. • I can identify the use and effect of powerful verbs within the poem. • I can identify the use and effect of powerful adjectives within the poem.
Personification of a river Children can write a poem that begins to use personification effectively.	• Paired activity where children annotate a photo of a river to give it human characteristics. • Children's oral responses and written work.	**Writing AF7** • Some evidence of deliberate vocabulary choices. • Some expansion of general vocabulary to match topic.	**Writing AF7** • Vocabulary chosen for effect. • Reasonably wide vocabulary used, though not always appropriately.	• I can plan a poem that uses personification to describe a river. • I can choose powerful verbs and images to start creating a poem.
River poem Children can write a poem that begins to use personification effectively.	• Independent activity where children write a personification river poem. • Children's oral responses and discussions. • Children's completed poems.	**Writing AF1** • Relevant ideas and content chosen. • Some ideas and material developed in detail. • Straightforward viewpoint generally established and maintained.	**Writing AF1** • Relevant ideas and material developed with some imaginative detail. • Development of ideas and material appropriately shaped for selected form. • Clear viewpoint established, generally consistent, with some elaboration.	• I can select and use my ideas to create a poem. • I can write a poem that uses personification. • I can evaluate my poem and improve it where necessary.
Phase ② activities pages 155-157				
Aunts and uncles Children understand how poets can use powerful images to communicate with their readers.	• Group activity where children answer questions about a poem's powerful imagery and then write a review of the poem. • Children's oral responses, reviews, and teacher's notes.	**Reading AF5** • Some basic features of writer's use of language identified. • Simple comments on writer's choices.	**Reading AF5** • Various features of writer's use of language identified, with some explanation. • Comments show some awareness of the effect of writer's language choices.	• I can identify how a poet can use powerful imagery to change a person into something else. • I can evaluate the imagery in a poem.
Animal images Children understand how poets can use powerful images to communicate with their readers.	• Group activity where children explore the use of metaphors and similes. • Children's oral responses and discussions. • Children's checklist comments. • Teacher's notes.	**Reading AF5** • Some basic features of writer's use of language identified. • Simple comments on writer's choices.	**Reading AF5** • Various features of writer's use of language identified, with some explanation. • Comments show some awareness of the effect of writer's language choices.	• I can identify and explain how metaphors are used to create powerful images. • I can identify and explain how similes are used to create powerful images.
Stag poem Children can write a poem that begins to use powerful imagery effectively.	• Independent activity where children look at a photo of a stag and write ideas for metaphors on the photocopiable. • Children's oral responses and completed poems.	**Writing AF1** • Relevant ideas and content chosen. • Some ideas and material developed in detail. • Straightforward viewpoint generally established and maintained.	**Writing AF1** • Relevant ideas and material developed with some imaginative detail. • Development of ideas and material appropriately shaped for selected form. • Clear viewpoint established, generally consistent, with some elaboration.	• I can write a poem using metaphors effectively to describe a stag. • I can create a poem which uses powerful imagery effectively.

Unit 1 📖 The power of imagery

POETRY

Learning outcomes	Assessment opportunity and evidence	Assessment focuses (AFs)		Success criteria
		Level 4	Level 5	
Phase ③ activities page 158-161				
The Painting Lesson Children understand how poets can use surreal, surprising and amusing images to communicate with their readers.	• Group activity where children respond, analyse and evaluate a poem. • Children's oral responses and discussions.	**Reading AF4** • Some structural choices identified with simple comment. • Some basic features of organisation at text level identified. **Reading AF5** • Some basic features of writer's use of language identified. • Simple comments on writer's choices.	**Reading AF4** • Comments on structural choices show some general awareness of writer's craft. • Various features relating to organisation at text level, including form, are clearly identified, with some explanation. **Reading AF5** • Various features of writer's use of language identified, with some explanation. • Comments show some awareness of the effect of writer's language choices.	• I can identify and explain surprising and amusing images within poems. • I can respond to and analyse a poem that uses surprising and amusing images.
Phase ① activities pages 158-161				
An amusing day poem Children can write a poem that begins to use surreal, surprising and amusing imagery effectively.	• Independent activity where children plan and write a poem about an everyday situation with an amusing and surprising ending. • Children's oral responses, photocopiables and written poems.	**Writing AF1** • Relevant ideas and content chosen. • Some ideas and material developed in detail. • Straightforward viewpoint generally established and maintained.	**Writing AF1** • Relevant ideas and material developed with some imaginative detail. • Development of ideas and material appropriately shaped for selected form. • Clear viewpoint established, generally consistent, with some elaboration.	• I can create amusing and surprising images. • I can write a poem that uses surprising and amusing imagery.
My Dad is Amazing! Children understand how poets can use surreal, surprising and amusing images to communicate with their readers.	• Independent activity where children highlight the real meanings of a poem's sayings and the surreal images of the sayings. • Children's oral responses and photocopiables.	**Reading AF5** • Some basic features of writer's use of language identified. • Simple comments on writer's choices.	**Reading AF5** • Various features of writer's use of language identified, with some explanation. • Comments show some awareness of the effect of writer's language choices.	• I can identify surreal images within a poem. • I can explain the meaning behind surreal images. • I can understand the surreal images' effect on the reader.
Who is amazing? Children can write a poem that begins to use surreal, surprising and amusing imagery effectively.	• Independent activity where children find ten sayings that give a surreal twist and use them to write a poem in a similar style. • Children's oral responses and discussions. • Children's notes and written poems.	**Writing AF1** • Relevant ideas and content chosen. • Some ideas and material developed in detail. • Straightforward viewpoint generally established and maintained.	**Writing AF1** • Relevant ideas and material developed with some imaginative detail. • Development of ideas and material appropriately shaped for selected form. • Clear viewpoint established, generally consistent, with some elaboration.	• I can create surreal images. • I can write a poem using surreal imagery for effect.
Phase ④ activity page 162				
Poem reviews Children value their own poems and those of others and enjoy sharing them.	• Paired activity where children list qualities needed in a poem, and use the list to evaluate their poems. • Children's oral responses, lists and review sheets.	**Reading AF5** • Some basic features of writer's use of language identified. • Simple comments on writer's choices.	**Reading AF5** • Various features of writer's use of language identified, with some explanation. • Comments show some awareness of the effect of writer's language choices.	• I can create a list of qualities that make up a good poem. • I can work with others to create agreed criteria to review and evaluate poems.

SCHOLASTIC

100 LITERACY ASSESSMENT LESSONS • YEAR 6   **151**

Phase ① The river's story

Learning outcome
Children understand how poets can use personification to communicate with their readers.

Success criteria
● I can identify and explain the use of personification in a poem.
● I can identify the use and effect of powerful verbs within the poem.
● I can identify the use and effect of powerful adjectives within the poem.

Setting the context
Children should understand personification and be able to identify examples. Children at levels 2-3 should work in pairs with adult support. They will listen to the poem 'The River's Story' by Brian Patten from photocopiable page and use the interactive activity 'Find the verb' to identify the right verb to complete personifications used in the poem. Record their attempts and comments. Children at levels 4-5 can work in their guided reading groups. Give out copies of 'The River's Story'. Ask them to read it through individually and complete the photocopiable page 'The River's Story - analysis sheet' using examples from the poem, highlighting the text as an aid. Display the success criteria in the classroom.

Assessment opportunity
Once the children at levels 2-3 have completed the interactive activity, discuss how the verbs create strong images of the river. Once the children at levels 4-5 have completed the photocopiable page, ask them to discuss their findings with a partner using the think-pair-share technique. Encourage them to compare their findings and discuss the use of powerful verbs and adjectives and their impact and effect on the poem. The pairs can then share their views with the rest of their group. Share all the children's findings with the class. Ask: *How did you visualise the river in the first part of the poem? How did you visualise the river at the end? Why do you think the poet used personification in the poem? Did it have an effect on you?*

Assessment evidence
At levels 2-3, children should recognise powerful verbs within the poem and discuss the images they conjured up. They should think of simple vocabulary to convey their ideas and include some adventurous word choices. At levels 4-5, children should find and record examples of personification and discuss the images created. They should discuss the use of powerful verbs and adjectives. Use the children's completed sheets and their oral responses as evidence against Reading AF5.

Next steps
Support: Choose some personification phrases and write them out. Discuss the images and verbs used and have children draw the image they imagine above each phrase.
Extension: Ask children to create a pictorial version for each part of the poem. Encourage them to think how they would show, for example, 'laughing and gurgling through woods'. Invite them to write the poem underneath their pictures.

Key aspects of learning
Information processing: Children will explore and tease out the information communicated through the language and forms of poetry.
Reasoning: Children will identify, explore and generate the mental connections represented within various forms of powerful imagery (simile and metaphor) - a vital aspect of thinking, reasoning and understanding.
Empathy: In discussing and writing about the poems and their images, children will need to imagine themselves in another person's position. They will explore techniques that facilitate this process.
Self-awareness: Children will discuss and reflect on their personal responses to the texts.

Phase ① Personification of a river

Learning outcome
Children can write a poem that begins to use personification effectively.

Success criteria
- I can plan a poem that uses personification to describe a river.
- I can choose powerful verbs and images to start creating a poem.

Setting the context
Re-read the poem 'The River's Story' to the class. Remind the children how personification is used to give the river human characteristics. Explain that they are going to start writing a poem about a river. Show one of the 'River' images from the CD-ROM and model how to annotate the photograph with ideas of the river's human characteristics. With the children's help list some questions they would ask to guide them. Who would the river be? What does it feel? What does it want? How does it move? What does it like? Display the success criteria in the classroom.

Assessment opportunity
Children working at levels 2-3 work, with an adult, in a supported group. Give out the photocopiable page 'Five senses of a river' and copies of the images 'River (a–c)'. Encourage them to think of words and phrases, including verbs, that describe the river within the five senses boxes. Children working at levels 4-5 will work in pairs. Print off copies or display the three images on a screen. Allow each pair to focus on one photograph. Ensure each child has access to a dictionary or thesaurus. Using the board questions, ask them to study the images. Working individually, ask the children to write down their personification ideas, including the use of verbs and adjectives and then compare and discuss their findings with their response partner. At the end of the session, have a class discussion to celebrate some of the children's work. Praise children's personification ideas, words and phrases.

Assessment evidence
Children at levels 2-3 should create words or phrases about the image, for example, 'The river feels like playing hide and seek through the bridge'. Children at levels 4-5 should create effective words and phrases, including powerful verbs or adjectives, to conjure up images of the river, for example, 'As it tripped and skipped through the bridge, the river felt its heart soar'. Use the children's written planning sheets and their responses during discussions as evidence against Writing AF7.

Next steps
Support: Choose just one or two senses and, with an adult as scribe, encourage children to think of as many verbs, adjectives, adverbs and nouns related to those senses. Ask them to then select the best examples to describe an object.
Extension: Encourage children to write a question list to help poets think of how to make their object have human characteristics.

Key aspects of learning
Reasoning: Children will identify, explore and generate the mental connections represented within various forms of powerful imagery (simile and metaphor) - a vital aspect of thinking, reasoning and understanding.
Empathy: In discussing and writing about the poems and their images, children will need to imagine themselves in another person's position. They will explore techniques that facilitate this process.
Self-awareness: Children will discuss and reflect on their personal responses to the texts.

POETRY

Phase ① River poem

Learning outcome
Children can write a poem that begins to use personification effectively.

Success criteria
● I can select and use my ideas to create a poem.
● I can write a poem that uses personification.
● I can evaluate my poem and improve it where necessary.

Setting the context
Display the images 'River (a–c)' and give out the children's notes for their personification river poem. Explain that they are going to select the best of their ideas to create a river poem. Remind the children that they need to think about what they want to express in the poem, such as the way the river moves. Encourage them to re-read their notes and look at the river images again before they start to form the poem. Children at levels 2-3 can work in a small group with an adult to help them select their best five senses ideas and to write their poems on the photocopiable 'River poem frame'. Display the success criteria in the classroom.

Assessment opportunity
The children can choose their best ideas and develop their river poem. Walk round the class and encourage them to evaluate and discuss whether or not their personification matches what they want to express. Allow them to read out their poem to a response partner or within their group. Ask: *Does the poem have the right effect? Are there any clichéd images? Are the personified images clear and powerful? Are the verbs or adjectives effective?* Encourage the need to revise. Take notes of the children's revision process and discuss how and why they are improving the poem. The children can write out their completed poem in best or on the photocopiable page 'River poem frame' and perform it to the class. Ask the children to look at the success criteria to see what they have achieved. Discuss what they would like to improve and how.

Assessment evidence
At levels 2-3, children should be able to choose five ideas they think are the most effective from the five senses areas and arrange them into a short poem. At levels 4-5, children should be able to select words and phrases to create an effective personification poem. Use the written poems and drafts along with notes of children's responses as evidence for Writing AF1.

Next steps
Support: Allow children to write a list of their personification images but in their chosen order. Ask them why they chose that order. Encourage them to read or listen to the poem to see if they want to change anything around.
Extension: Encourage children to perform their poems to other children. Discuss how they would use expression to bring over the effect of the poem.

Key aspects of learning
Reasoning: Children will identify, explore and generate the mental connections represented within various forms of powerful imagery (simile and metaphor) - a vital aspect of thinking, reasoning and understanding.
Self-awareness: Children will discuss and reflect on their personal responses to the texts.

Phase ② Aunts and uncles

Learning outcome
Children understand how poets can use powerful images to communicate with their readers.

Success criteria
- I can identify how a poet can use powerful imagery to change a person into something else.
- I can evaluate the imagery in a poem.

Setting the context
Work with one group at a time in a guided reading session. Remind each group how personification gives objects human characteristics. Explain to the children that they are going to hear a poem where a group of humans are described as animals or objects using powerful imagery. Give them copies of the photocopiable page 'Some Aunts and Uncles', which shows the poem by Mervyn Peake, and read it to them.

Assessment opportunity
Ask guided questions, such as: *What are your first reactions to the poem? How does the poet use the aunts' and uncles' names to decide on what they will be? Where does Aunty Mig float? Which image do you like best? Why? Which image don't you like? Why? Are there any images you don't understand?* Take notes of children's responses to your questions about the poem and use of language. At the end of the session, encourage children working at levels 2-3 to draw an image of their favourite aunt or uncle with the verse written out underneath and a completed sentence of 'I like this verse because...' Ask those at levels 4-5 to write a short review of the poem using quotes from the poem to support their views.

Assessment evidence
At levels 2-3, children should understand how the humans in the poem have been turned into animals or objects. Through guided questions they should explain which images they like and which they don't, giving simple but clear reasons. At levels 4-5, children should be able to look more deeply at the images, such as 'I think Aunty Mig might be a jealous person'. They should also be able to evaluate the poem giving quotes to back up their reasons. Use the notes of the children's responses and their written reviews and pictures as evidence against Reading AF5.

Next steps
Support: For children who struggled with the imagery, suggest they think of an object or animal that rhymes with the name 'Uncle Pat', such as 'cat' or 'hat'. Ask them to imagine he has suddenly turned into a cat or a hat. Ask: *What does he do? What does he feel like? What happens to him?*
Extension: As homework or in an extra session, encourage children to think of more aunts' and uncles' names that rhyme with an animal or object and write two more verses about what happened to them and how they felt. Encourage them to share and read out the results.

Key aspects of learning
Enquiry: The children will seek the answers to their own and others' questions in their reading.
Information processing: Children will explore and tease out the information communicated through the language and forms of poetry.
Reasoning: Children will identify, explore and generate the mental connections represented within various forms of powerful imagery (simile and metaphor) - a vital aspect of thinking, reasoning and understanding.
Empathy: In discussing and writing about the poems and their images, children will need to imagine themselves in another person's position. They will explore techniques that facilitate this process.
Self-awareness: Children will discuss and reflect on their personal responses to the texts of ICT.

POETRY

Phase ② Animal images

Learning outcome
Children understand how poets can use powerful images to communicate with their readers.

Success criteria
● I can identify and explain how metaphors are used to create powerful images.
● I can identify and explain how similes are used to create powerful images.

Setting the context
Work with children in their guided reading groups. Remind them how similes and metaphors can be used in poems to create powerful images. Display and read the poems 'Orang-utan' and 'The Magnificent Bull' (a traditional Dinka praise poem) from the photocopiable page 'Animal images'. Ask guided questions to encourage the children to discuss how metaphors and similes are used to create powerful images of the two animals. Use the version 1 of the photocopiable page 'Guided questions checklist' for groups working at levels 2-3 and version 2 of the photocopiable page for those at level 4-5.

Assessment opportunity
Using the guided questions, encourage the children to respond, analyse and evaluate the poems. Work with the children at levels 2-3 to help them find words or quotes from the text using reading and spelling cues. Encourage children at levels 4-5 to locate and read out words or phrases to back up their thoughts and ideas. Jot down all the children's comments on the sheet with their initials for later reference. Encourage discussion and list other questions/comments the children may raise about the poems. Have a class discussion about the two poems. Identify whether any particular child has difficulty understanding the use of a metaphor or a simile for possible extended activities. At the end of the session, encourage the children to look at their success criteria to decide whether they feel they need more support.

Assessment evidence
Use the comments on the checklists as a record of the children's oral responses and discussion of the two poems. At levels 2-3, children should be able to evaluate the poems and identify similes and metaphors. At levels 4-5, children should be able to analyse the poems more deeply and support their ideas with words and phrases from the poems. Use the comments on the checklists as evidence against Reading AF5.

Next steps
Support: For children who find it hard to understand metaphors and similes, ask them to describe fire and to explain what fire is to them? For example, 'Fire is warmth'. Write down their ideas and explain that they have created metaphors. Now ask the children to compare each description with something to create a simile, such as 'Fire is warm like a snug, cosy bed'.
Extension: Show images of an orang-utan and a bull to the children. Ask half to individually write a poem describing the orang-utan using only similes and the other half to individually write a metaphor poem of the bull. How do the poems change in their effects?

Key aspects of learning
Enquiry: Children will seek the answers to their own and others' questions in their reading.
Information processing: Children will explore and tease out the information communicated through the language and forms of poetry.
Reasoning: Children will identify, explore and generate the mental connections represented within various forms of powerful imagery (simile and metaphor) - a vital aspect of thinking, reasoning and understanding.
Self-awareness: Children will discuss and reflect on their personal responses to the texts.

Phase ② Stag poem

Learning outcome
Children can write a poem that begins to use powerful imagery effectively.

Success criteria
- I can write a poem using metaphors effectively to describe a stag.
- I can create a poem which uses powerful imagery effectively.

Setting the context
Remind the children how metaphors can be used to create powerful images within poems. Display the image 'Stag' from the CD-ROM. Explain that they are going to create a poem about the stag using metaphors. Ask: *What is it thinking? What is it doing? What does it like? What doesn't it like? How does it move? What does it look and sound like?* Use children's responses to develop ideas for their poem. Children at levels 2–3 can work in pairs or small groups, with adult support, on the interactive activity 'Stag poem'. Children at levels 4–5 can study the 'Stag' image closely then write their ideas for words and phrases on the photocopiable page 'My stag poem'. Display the success criteria in the classroom.

Assessment opportunity
Children at levels 2–3 should read the stag poem frame and select words to create metaphorical descriptions. Discuss their word choices and their effects on the completed poem. Encourage them to evaluate how the poem could be more effective. Can they think of other metaphors to describe the stag? Record their comments and choices. As the children at levels 4–5 create words and phrases for their poem, ask each one about the images they want to convey. Identify good examples of metaphors. Assess which children find it difficult not to use similes to describe the stag and take notes. Ask the children to evaluate their completed poems with a partner. Would they know it was a stag from the imagery used? Encourage all the children to self-assess their work against the success criteria.

Assessment evidence
At levels 2–3, children should be able to choose and explore the correct metaphor to complete the stag poem and discuss each one's effect. At levels 4–5, children should create their own metaphors using the stag as a stimulus. Use the photocopiable notes and written poems along with notes of children's responses from the interactive activity as evidence against Writing AF1.

Next steps
Support: For children who found it hard to think of metaphors to describe the stag, create a word game. Create five word cards for the antlers, eyes, mouth, main body and nose, and five descriptions – the crown, amber marbles, bottomless pit, golden cloak, shiny black pebble. Ask the children to match the two sets.
Extension: Encourage children to find a picture of a deer and write down words and ideas that could be used to create a metaphorical poem about it. Compare it with the stag poems. Ask: *How are they different?*

Key aspects of learning
Reasoning: Children will identify, explore and generate the mental connections represented within various forms of powerful imagery (simile and metaphor) – a vital aspect of thinking, reasoning and understanding.
Empathy: In discussing and writing about the poems and their images, children will need to imagine themselves in another person's position. They will explore techniques that facilitate this process.

POETRY

Phase ③ The Painting Lesson

Learning outcome
Children understand how poets can use surreal, surprising and amusing images to communicate with their readers.

Success criteria
- I can identify and explain surprising and amusing images within poems.
- I can respond to and analyse a poem that uses surprising and amusing images.

Setting the context
Remind the children how poets can create fun, nonsense poems by using imagery that can surprise and amuse a reader or listener. Explain to the children that they are going to look closely at an amusing poem. Display the photocopiable page 'The Painting Lesson'. Read the poem to the children. Ask for their reactions: *Who was surprised by the ending? Was it something you expected?*

Assessment opportunity
Within levelled groups, discuss what makes the poem a surprise and amusing, for example, a familiar situation with an unexpected end. Ask: *Who has painted something which has been misunderstood or changed by an adult? Could you empathise with the child in the poem? Do you think it happened once to the poet?* Ask the children what the text tells them about the teacher, for example, reference to being new, use of dialogue and capital letters for emphasis. Ask the children what sentence sets up the amusing image at the end of the poem. Ask: *Why does the simple ending make such an impact? What do you think happens to the teacher?* Take notes of individual children's responses as they discuss the poem.

Assessment evidence
At levels 2-3, children should be able to note how the poet has used punctuation and structured the poem to create an amusing scene, for example, 'The capital letters show how the teacher talks to the child'. They may also notice the choice of language. At levels 4-5, children should be able to discuss the overall structure of the poem, such as the connection between the beginning of the poem and the surprise ending and the use of language. Use the children's responses and discussion about the poem as evidence against Reading AF4 and AF5.

Next steps
Support: If children have difficulties commenting on or quoting from the text, create a one-to-one situation and ask more guided questions such as: *Where do you think the poem is set? Do you want to laugh at the teacher? Why?*
Extension: Put children in groups and encourage them to put together a performance of the poem. Highlight the use of language, the clues for pauses and the need for expression. Discuss how they could create the maximum impact on their audience for the last part of the poem. Invite the children to perform to each other.

Key aspects of learning
Enquiry: Children will seek the answers to their own and others' questions in their reading.
Information processing: Children will explore and tease out the information communicated through the language and forms of poetry.
Reasoning: Children will identify, explore and generate the mental connections represented within various forms of powerful imagery (simile and metaphor) - a vital aspect of thinking, reasoning and understanding.
Empathy: In discussing and writing about the poems and their images, children will need to imagine themselves in another person's position. They will explore techniques that facilitate this process.

POETRY

Phase ③ An amusing day poem

Learning outcome
Children can write a poem that begins to use surreal, surprising and amusing imagery effectively.

Success criteria
● I can create amusing and surprising images.
● I can write a poem that uses surprising and amusing imagery.

Setting the context
Remind the children how poets can use different techniques to create an amusing poem, for example, use of dialogue, a punchline, and so on. Re-read the poem, 'The Painting Lesson', from the photocopiable page. With the children, briefly look at the poem's layout and style. Using 'The Painting Lesson' as a model, ask the children to write a poem about an everyday situation, such as going to the library, or a shop and create an amusing and surprising ending.

Assessment opportunity
Children at levels 2-3 will have version 1 of the photocopiable page 'An amusing day' which provides suggested ideas and scenarios. With support, the children can use some of the ideas or choose their own ideas to write their poem. Children at levels 4-5 will have version 2 of the photocopiable page on which to record their ideas, then write out their poem. As they work, walk round the class and discuss and take notes of individual children's ideas and techniques used to create amusing images. Encourage the children to perform their completed poems to the class. Encourage the children to look at their own success criteria. Ask them: *What have you achieved? What can you improve?*

Assessment evidence
At levels 2-3, children should be able to use the given ideas to create an amusing and surprising poem with some effective words within a structured frame. At levels 4-5, children should be able to create an amusing poem that includes a clearly developed idea. Use the children's explanation of their ideas, selection of words and how they created the poem as evidence towards Writing AF7. Use their photocopiable pages and written poems as further understanding and evidence against Writing AF1.

Next steps
Support: For children who struggled to turn everyday situations into amusing and surprising experiences, talk through what would normally happen in those situations. Suggest a surreal idea, such as a dragon and princess looking for fantasy books in the library, and encourage the children to develop it.
Extension: Encourage children to collect and read nonsense poems. Ask: *Are metaphors and similes used to create the images? How effective are the poems?*

Key aspects of learning
Reasoning: Children will identify, explore and generate the mental connections represented within various forms of powerful imagery (simile and metaphor) - a vital aspect of thinking, reasoning and understanding.
Empathy: In discussing and writing about the poems and their images, children will need to imagine themselves in another person's position. They will explore techniques that facilitate this process.
Self-awareness: Children will discuss and reflect on their personal responses to the texts.

Phase ③ My Dad is Amazing!

Learning outcome
Children understand how poets can use surreal, surprising and amusing images to communicate with their readers.

Success criteria
● I can identify surreal images within a poem.
● I can explain the meaning behind surreal images.
● I can understand the surreal images' effect on the reader.

Setting the context
Remind the children how some poets use surreal images to encourage readers or listeners to look at familiar things in a surprising way. Give examples such as 'The Owl and the Pussycat' or 'Jabberwocky'. Read the poem 'My Dad is Amazing!' from the photocopiable page. Show how the poet has set out all the things the dad does in a list, which gets more surreal as the poem progresses. Ask the children if they know where the poet got his ideas from (they are all well-known sayings). Explain that by boasting that the dad can actually do the actions, the poet creates surreal images. If possible, have a copy of a sayings book and look up one of the sayings from the poem. Discuss the real saying compared to the surreal saying. Display the success criteria in the classroom.

Assessment opportunity
Ask the children to complete the photocopiable page 'My Dad is Amazing! - analysis sheet'. Children at levels 2-3 should be in a supported group with an adult acting as a scribe to record their findings. Children at levels 4-5 can work independently. Ensure there is a sayings dictionary in the class for reference. The children have to identify the 11 sayings in the poem to complete the photocopiable. When they have finished, ask the children at levels 2-3 to discuss their findings as a group and the children at levels 4-5 to pair-share their work with a partner. Walk round the pairs and groups and observe and take notes of their discussions. Ask the children to choose a partner to pair and share their findings. Ask: *What do you like and dislike about the poem? How effective is it?*

Assessment evidence
At levels 2-3, children should be able to locate and, with support, record the 11 sayings. They should discuss and record simple explanations of the real and surreal meanings and their effect in the poem. At levels 4-5, children should be able to record longer explanations. Use the children's responses and their analysis sheets as evidence against Reading AF5.

Next steps
Support: Show examples of surreal work by Salvador Dali, and read more examples of surreal poetry. Examine how familiar objects or situations are turned upside down and observed in an unusual way.
Extension: Encourage children to collect and read other poems with surreal images. Ask them to collect their favourite phrases and words and record them in their reading journals. Encourage them to create their own.

Key aspects of learning
Information processing: Children will explore and tease out the information communicated through the language and forms of poetry.
Reasoning: Children will identify, explore and generate the mental connections represented within various forms of powerful imagery (simile and metaphor) - a vital aspect of thinking, reasoning and understanding.
Self-awareness: Children will discuss and reflect on their personal responses to the texts.

Phase ③ Who is amazing?

Learning outcome
Children can write a poem that begins to use surreal, surprising and amusing imagery effectively.

Success criteria
- I can create surreal images.
- I can write a poem using surreal imagery for effect.

Setting the context
Re-read and display the poem 'My Dad is Amazing!' by Ian Souter to the children. Remind them how he uses popular sayings and gives them a surreal twist to create a totally different meaning. Explain to the children that they are going to find ten more sayings which they are going to give a surreal twist and then write a poem in a similar style to 'My Dad is Amazing!' The poems could be about another member of the family, friends, themselves or anyone else.

Assessment opportunity
Give the children copies of the photocopiable page 'Well-known sayings'. Ask them to identify ten sayings they would like to use in their poem. Children at levels 2-3 may need some support. Walk round the class and discuss with the children how the sayings could be twisted into fun, surreal images. Once they have chosen their ten sayings, they can write their poem. Children at levels 2-3 can write it on the photocopiable 'Who is amazing?' poem frame. Children at levels 4-5 can write their poem on paper or the computer. Encourage the children to read out their completed poems. Ask them to think what imagery works well and what needs improvement.

Assessment evidence
At levels 2-3, children may choose sayings with easy-to-understand meanings, such as 'barking mad' or 'cat's whiskers'. They should be able to discuss a surreal fun idea for an image and draw images around the side of the frame. At levels 4-5, children should choose more complex sayings and use them to good effect. Use the children's explanation of their ideas, selection of sayings and how they created their poems as well as their written poems as evidence against Writing AF1.

Next steps
Support: For children who find it hard to create a surreal image from a saying, choose simple actions, such as cooking, and ask them to think of a surreal twist to those actions, for example, cheesy toes instead of cheese on toast. Encourage them to think of more kitchen-based surreal images and write a poem using those ideas.
Extension: Encourage the children to perform their poems to the class. Ask them to think of how they are going to present it and what kind of expression they would use to emphasise unusual, surreal images. Discuss the performances and the poems with rest of the class. Praise the children for imaginative and original ideas. Encourage positive suggestions from the audience.

Key aspects of learning
Reasoning: Children will identify, explore and generate the mental connections represented within various forms of powerful imagery (simile and metaphor) - a vital aspect of thinking, reasoning and understanding.
Empathy: In discussing and writing about the poems and their images, children will need to imagine themselves in another person's position. They will explore techniques that facilitate this process.
Self-awareness: Children will discuss and reflect on their personal responses to the texts.

POETRY

Phase ④ Poem reviews

Learning outcome
Children value their own poems and those of others and enjoy sharing them.

Success criteria
● I can create a list of qualities that make up a good poem.
● I can work with others to create agreed criteria to review and evaluate poems.

Setting the context
Put the children in pairs. Match those in need of support with a more confident learner or an adult. Give the children copies of one of their completed poems and some paper. Explain that they are going to assess and evaluate their own poems and those of others. Ask the children for all the qualities found in a good poem and write them on the board, for example, an interesting subject, good use of imagery, a clear structure, and so on. Display the success criteria in the classroom.

Assessment opportunity
Ask the children to work in pairs to write out their list of all the qualities needed in a poem. Invite some children to write their list on the computer. Discuss their lists with them. Identify any areas that haven't been covered. Once they have made their lists, ask the children to share their findings with another pair and to revise their lists. Ask the pairs to create a poetry review sheet which they can use to assess poems, allowing space to write examples of words, phrases and comments. Ask the children to use their completed sheets to review their own poem and their partner's. Have a class discussion on their findings. Which poems matched the criteria?

Assessment evidence
At levels 2–3, children should be able to identify the need for strong imagery and use of descriptive words. They should give examples, such as similes, metaphors and personification. They should also be able to examine the effect of the poem on the reader and where it could be improved. At levels 4–5, children be able to should identify areas of structure, organisation and devices, such as punctuation, to create an effect. Use the children's discussion and oral responses along with their list, planning sheets and the poetry review sheets as evidence against Reading AF5.

Next steps
Support: Give one-to-one support to children who find it hard to create criteria to assess their poem. Draw a grid with three columns. With the children decide what questions could be asked about the poem and put them in the first column. In the second scribe their comments and in the third ask them to give a score out of ten.
Extension: Copy children's review sheets and ask them to use them on other poems they have written. Encourage them to compare the reviews with their other poems. Ask: *Which poem is the most successful in matching the criteria? Why? Which poem needs more work? How could this be achieved?*

Key aspects of learning
Enquiry: Children will seek the answers to their own and others' questions in their reading.
Reasoning: Children will identify, explore and generate the mental connections represented within various forms of powerful imagery (simile and metaphor) - a vital aspect of thinking, reasoning and understanding.
Self-awareness: Children will discuss and reflect on their personal responses to the texts.

Periodic assessment

Reading

Learning outcome
Children understand how poets can use powerful images to communicate with their readers.

Success criteria
I can explain the use of metaphors as powerful images within a poem.

Setting the context
Remind the children that poets can use powerful images to convey ideas. Read the poem 'What's my name?' from the photocopiable page 'Poetry 1 Reading assessment text'. Explain that the poem uses metaphors in the form of a riddle. The children work in groups to record their discussion on the metaphorical using the photocopiable page 'Poetry 1 Reading assessment'.

Assessment opportunity
Circulate among the groups and ask questions about their thoughts on the different metaphors used in the poem. Record their responses. Ask: *Who or what do you think the poem is describing?* (School) *What image is the poet trying to convey when he says 'I'm the pure, blue sky and leafy green'? What verbs describe what happens when a teacher tells a joke? How do these verbs help convey an image? Which are your favourite metaphors? Why? Do any of the images remind you of anything you have seen or felt?*

Assessment evidence
Children at levels 2-3 may discuss what the poet is trying to describe: 'I think the images are about parts of school'. They may notice the use of verbs and adjectives, such as 'dribbling', 'laughing'. Children at levels 4-5 will describe in detail the images conveyed by the metaphors and the effective use of verbs and adjectives, 'The verb "startling" is good. It describes the poem and matches with the metaphor at the start of the line, "I'm a star"'. Use your notes and the children's sheets as evidence for Reading AF2, AF5 and AF6.

Writing

Learning outcomes
● Children can write a poem that begins to use powerful imagery effectively.
● Children value their own poems and those of others and enjoy sharing them.

Success criteria
I can create metaphors as clues within my poem.

Setting the context
Re-read the poem from the photocopiable page 'Poetry 1 Reading assessment text'. Explain that, as well as metaphors, the poet includes interesting verbs and adjectives to complete the images in the poem. Tell the class that they will create a riddle poem about a person, a place or an animal. The children will use the photocopiable page 'Poetry 1 Writing assessment'.

Assessment opportunity
Give children the photocopiable page 'Poetry 1 Writing assessment'. Before writing, let them note ideas of metaphors for each of the five senses, and to think of verbs and adjectives to describe each sense. Ask: *That's a good metaphor but would an interesting adjective make it a more powerful image?*

Assessment evidence
Children at levels 2-3 may create metaphors, such as 'My kitchen is baked beans.' Children at levels 4-5 may use metaphors to create powerful images, 'I am a shiny bell, struck by strong and weak to impress their loved ones.' Use children's responses and poems as evidence against Writing AF1 and AF7.

POETRY
UNIT 2 Finding a voice

Literacy objectives

Speak and listen for a wide range of purposes in different contexts
Strand 1 Speaking
- Use a range of oral techniques to present persuasive arguments and engaging narratives.
- Participate in whole-class debate using the conventions and language of debate, including standard English.
- Use the techniques of dialogic talk to explore ideas, topics or issues.

Strand 2 Listening and responding
- Analyse and evaluate how speakers present points effectively through use of language and gesture.

Strand 3 Group discussion and interaction
- Understand and use a variety of ways to criticise constructively and respond to criticism.

Strand 4 Drama
- Improvise using a range of drama strategies and conventions to explore themes such as hopes, fears and desires.
- Consider the overall impact of a live or recorded performance, identifying dramatic ways of conveying characters' ideas and building tension.

Read and write for a range of purposes on paper and on screen
Strand 6 Word structure and spelling
- Use a range of appropriate strategies to edit, proofread and correct spelling in their own work, on paper and on screen.

Strand 7 Understanding and interpreting texts
- Understand underlying themes, causes and points of view.
- Understand how writers use different structures to create coherence and impact.

Strand 8 Engaging with and responding to texts
- Read extensively and discuss personal reading with others, including in reading groups.
- Compare how writers from different times and places present experiences and use language.

Strand 9 Creating and shaping texts
- Select words and language drawing on their knowledge of literary features and formal and informal writing.

Strand 10 Text structure and organisation
- Use varied structures to shape and organise text coherently.

Key aspects of learning

Enquiry
- Children will seek the answers to their own and others' questions in their reading.

Information processing
- Children will explore and tease out the information communicated through the language and forms of poetry.

Evaluation
- Children will share their own writing outcomes, as well as those of others. They will discuss success criteria, give feedback to others and judge the effectiveness of their own work.

Key aspects of learning (contd)

Reasoning
- Children will identify, explore and generate the mental connections represented within various forms of powerful imagery (simile and metaphor) – a vital aspect of thinking, reasoning and understanding.

Empathy
- In discussing and writing about the poems and their images, children will need to imagine themselves in another person's position. They will explore techniques that facilitate this process.

Self-awareness
- Children will discuss and reflect on their personal responses to the texts.

Communication
- Children will develop their ability to discuss effective communication in respect of both the language and content of poetry they are reading and writing. They will sometimes work collaboratively in pairs and in groups. They will communicate outcomes orally, and in writing (possibly including the use of ICT).

Assessment focuses

Reading
AF5 *(explain and comment on writers' uses of language, including grammatical and literary features at word and sentence level).*
AF6 *(identify and comment on writers' purposes and viewpoints, and the overall effect of the text on the reader).*

Writing
AF1 *(write imaginative, interesting and thoughtful texts).*
AF7 *(select appropriate and effective vocabulary).*

Speaking and listening
Speaking (adaptation to audience; use of standard English).
Listening and responding (understand the main points; respond appropriately).
Group discussion and interaction (support others and take turns).
Drama (plan, perform and evaluate performances).

Resources

Phase 1 activities
Photocopiable page, 'Names'
Photocopiable page, 'What's in a name?' (versions 1 and 2)
Photocopiable page, 'Give and Take'
Phase 2 activities
Photocopiable page, 'Give and Take'
Interactive activity, 'Give and Take – extended poem'
Photocopiable page, 'Give and Take – extended poem'
Phase 3 activities
Photocopiable page, 'Poetry evaluation checklist'
Photocopiable page, 'Poetry report sheet' (versions 1 and 2)
Periodic assessment
Photocopiable page, 'Poetry 2 Reading assessment'
Photocopiable page, 'Poetry 2 Writing assessment'

Unit 2 Finding a voice

Learning outcomes	Assessment opportunity and evidence	Assessment focuses (AFs)		Success criteria
		Level 2	Level 3	
Phase ① activities pages 168–169				
What's in a name? Children understand how writers can use poetry as a powerful way of communicating their thoughts and feelings about a particular issue.	● Supported group activity where children identify the use of names as a way of highlighting issues and think of more negative and positive names related to eco-issues. ● Children's oral responses. ● Teacher's notes.	**Reading AF6** ● Some awareness that writers have viewpoints and purposes. ● Simple statements about likes and dislikes in reading, sometimes with reasons.	**Reading AF6** ● Comments identify main purpose. ● Express personal response but with little awareness of writer's viewpoint or effect on reader.	● I can explore a meaningful issue. ● I can understand how poetry can be used to highlight an issue.
Comparing eco-poems Children understand how writers can use poetry as a powerful way of communicating their thoughts and feelings about a particular issue.	● Group activity where children discuss the comparisons of the structure, language and effects of two poems about eco-issues. ● Children's oral responses and discussions.	**Reading AF5** ● Some effective language choices noted. ● Some familiar patterns of language identified.	**Reading AF5** ● A few basic features of writer's use of language identified, but with little or no comment.	● I can compare and contrast the impact of two poems about the same issue. ● I can compare and contrast the styles and language of two poets about the same issue.
Phase ② activity page 170				
Give and take ● Children can write a poem that begins to use language and form effectively and powerfully to communicate to a reader their thoughts and feelings about a particular issue. ● Children can discuss the choice of words and their impact.	● Independent activity where children listen to and discuss the use of contrasting images in a poem and then read and place eight contrasting images within a poem template. ● Children's oral responses and discussions. ● Completed interactives.	**Writing AF1** ● Mostly relevant ideas and content, sometimes repetitive or sparse. ● Some apt word choices create interest. ● Brief comments, questions about events or actions suggest viewpoint. **Writing AF7** ● Simple, often speech-like vocabulary conveys relevant meanings. ● Some adventurous word choices.	**Writing AF1** ● Some appropriate ideas and content included. ● Some attempt to elaborate on basic information or events. ● Attempt to adopt viewpoint, though often not maintained or inconsistent. **Writing AF7** ● Simple, generally appropriate vocabulary used, limited in range. ● Some words selected for effect or occasion.	● I can write extra verses for a poem about a particular issue. ● I can create powerfully contrasting images to highlight an issue.
Phase ③ activity page 171				
Evaluating poems Children value their own poems and those of others and enjoy sharing them.	● Supported paired activity where children read their own poems and comment on them as they complete evaluation sheets and then evaluate their partner's poem. ● Children's oral and written responses and evaluations.	**Reading AF6** ● Some awareness that writers have viewpoints and purposes. ● Simple statements about likes and dislikes in reading, sometimes with reasons.	**Reading AF6** ● Comments identify main purpose. ● Express personal response but with little awareness of writer's viewpoint or effect on reader.	● I can evaluate my own poem and a partner's poem. ● I can give feedback in a constructive way. ● I can use examples from a poem to make constructive comments.

Unit 2 Finding a voice

Learning outcomes	Assessment opportunity and evidence	Assessment focuses (AFs)		Success criteria
		Level 4	Level 5	
Phase ① activities pages 168–169				
What's in a name? Children understand how writers can use poetry as a powerful way of communicating their thoughts and feelings about a particular issue.	• Independent activity where children read a poem and create more names that represent negative and positive eco-issues. • Children's oral responses. • Teacher's notes.	**Reading AF6** • Main purpose identified. • Simple comments show some awareness of writer's viewpoint. • Simple comment on overall effect on reader.	**Reading AF6** • Main purpose clearly identified, often through general overview. • Viewpoints in texts clearly identified, with some, often limited, explanation. • General awareness of effect on the reader, with some, often limited, explanation.	• I can explore a meaningful issue. • I can understand how poetry can be used to highlight an issue.
Comparing eco-poems Children understand how writers can use poetry as a powerful way of communicating their thoughts and feelings about a particular issue.	• Group activity where children discuss the comparisons of the structure, language and effects of two poems about eco-issues. • Children's oral responses and discussions.	**Reading AF5** • Some basic features of writer's use of language identified. • Simple comments on writer's choices.	**Reading AF5** • Various features of writer's use of language identified, with some explanation. • Comments show some awareness of the effect of writer's language choices.	• I can compare and contrast the impact of two poems about the same issue. • I can compare and contrast the styles and language of two poets about the same issue.
Phase ② activity page 170				
Give and take • Children can write a poem that begins to use language and form effectively and powerfully to communicate to a reader their thoughts and feelings about a particular issue. • Children can discuss the choice of words and their impact.	• Independent activity where children read a poem, highlight the use of contrasting images to highlight eco-issues and then write four more pairs of contrasting images to create two new verses. • Children's oral responses and discussions. • Children's written poems.	**Writing AF1** • Relevant ideas and content chosen. • Some ideas and material developed in detail. • Straightforward viewpoint generally established and maintained. **Writing AF7** • Some evidence of deliberate vocabulary choices. • Some expansion of general vocabulary to match topic.	**Writing AF1** • Relevant ideas and material developed with some imaginative detail. • Development of ideas and material appropriately shaped for selected form. • Clear viewpoint established, generally consistent, with some elaboration. **Writing AF7** • Vocabulary chosen for effect. • Reasonably wide vocabulary used, though not always appropriately.	• I can write extra verses for a poem about a particular issue. • I can create powerfully contrasting images to highlight an issue.
Phase ③ activity page 171				
Evaluating poems Children value their own poems and those of others and enjoy sharing them.	• Paired activity where children read their own poems and comment on them as they complete evaluation sheets and then evaluate their partner's poem. • Children's oral and written responses and evaluations.	**Reading AF6** • Main purpose identified. • Simple comments show some awareness of writer's viewpoint. • Simple comment on overall effect on reader.	**Reading AF6** • Main purpose clearly identified, often through general overview. • Viewpoints in texts clearly identified, with some, often limited, explanation. • General awareness of effect on the reader, with some-often limited explanation.	• I can evaluate my own poem and a partner's poem. • I can give feedback in a constructive way. • I can use examples from a poem to make constructive comments.

POETRY

Phase ① What's in a name?

Learning outcome
Children understand how writers can use poetry as a powerful way of communicating their thoughts and feelings about a particular issue.

Success criteria
● I can explore a meaningful issue.
● I can understand how poetry can be used to highlight an issue.

Setting the context
Discuss with the children what they think are the main eco-problems facing the world. Discuss different ways in which people could help look after the world, such as recycling and saving energy. Remind the children how writers can use poetry writing to raise awareness about an issue. Read the poem 'Names' from the photocopiable page to the class. Ask: *What eco-issues are highlighted in the poem? How do the names and their comments indicate what the poet thinks are the main problems with eco-issues?* Explain that they are going to create new 'not-caring' and 'caring' names like those used in the poem.

Assessment opportunity
Children at levels 2–3 can work in a discussion group with adult support as scribe. Read a verse from the poem and check that the children understand that the names are comments that people who don't care about eco-issues might say. Encourage the children to think of other examples and record them on version 1 of the photocopiable page 'What's in a name?'. Children at levels 4–5 can work independently on the version 2 of the photocopiable page. Take observation notes as they work. Encourage the children to share their finished images and names with the class and give positive feedback.

Assessment evidence
At levels 2–3, children should be able to understand why the poet uses the names within the poem. At levels 4–5, children should be able to deduce the main issue of the poem. They should also understand how the poet manages to criticise those who don't care about the Earth and identify eco-issues at the same time. They should all use the information from the photocopiable page and the children's responses during the activity as evidence towards Reading AF6.

Next steps
Support: Identify children who struggled to understand how the poet used names as a tool to highlight the poem's issues. Individually give each child one of the names in the poem and discuss their characters and how they might look. Invite the children to draw their ideas and label them for a display with the poem.
Extension: Encourage children to use their name ideas from the photocopiable page and write a couple more verses using the 'Names' poem as a model. They could also follow it up with a poem using the positive names. Display these poems or put them in a class anthology.

Key aspects of learning
Information processing: Children will explore and tease out the information communicated through the language and forms of poetry.
Reasoning: Children will identify, explore and generate the mental connections represented within various forms of powerful imagery (simile and metaphor) – a vital aspect of thinking, reasoning and understanding.
Self-awareness: Children will discuss and reflect on their personal responses to the texts.
Communication: Children will develop their ability to discuss effective communication in respect of both the language and content of poetry they are reading and writing. They will sometimes work collaboratively in pairs and in groups. They will communicate outcomes orally, and in writing (possibly including the use of ICT).

Phase ① Comparing eco-poems

Learning outcome
Children understand how writers can use poetry as a powerful way of communicating their thoughts and feelings about a particular issue.

Success criteria
● I can compare and contrast the impact of two poems about the same issue.
● I can compare and contrast the styles and language of two poets about the same issue.

Setting the context
Work with the children within their guided reading groups. Discuss with the children why caring for the world is such an important issue. Ask: *Why would writers use poetry to highlight issues such as eco-problems?* Explain to the children that they are going to listen to and then evaluate two poems written by different poets about the eco-issues of the world. Display and read the photocopiable pages 'Names' and 'Give and Take'. Ask: *What are the poems' similarities?* Discuss the attitude or mood of each poem, such as exasperation or anger.

Assessment opportunity
On the board, draw a table, labelling one side 'Names' and the other 'Give and Take'. Ask: *Has the writer made you think about eco-issues?* Encourage all the children to give you examples of style, content, powerful language and the impact from each poem and write them out in the appropriate columns. With children working at levels 2-3, use guided questions to help the children discuss examples: *'Poisonous' is one of the adjectives used in 'Give and Take' to describe the state of the Earth. Can you find me a few more?* Assess and record all the children's responses as they discuss the two poems. At the end of the session, ask all the children: *Which poem do you think is more powerful in bringing over the message about eco-problems? Why? Which line or verse do you think stands out? Why?*

Assessment evidence
At levels 2-3, children should be able to discuss straightforward examples, such as the patterns in each poem. At levels 4-5, children should be able to discuss in depth the style, language and impact of the two poems and explain their reasons. Use the evidence collected and spoken during the group discussion as evidence against Reading AF5.

Next steps
Support: Identify children who found it difficult to compare the two poems. Choose one area, such as comparing the impact of the poems, and use a highlighter to show the different parts that illustrate this.
Extension: Challenge children to find more poems about caring for the world. Encourage them to create poetry review sheets for each poem looking at the style, language and impact of each poem. With the children's help, create a display of eco-poems with labels, highlighting features and the issues raised.

Key aspects of learning
Information processing: Children will explore and tease out the information communicated through the language and forms of poetry.
Reasoning: Children will identify, explore and generate the mental connections represented within various forms of powerful imagery (simile and metaphor) - a vital aspect of thinking, reasoning and understanding.
Empathy: In discussing and writing about the poems and their images, children will need to imagine themselves in another person's position. They will explore techniques that facilitate this process.
Self-awareness: Children will discuss and reflect on their personal responses to the texts.
Communication: Children will develop their ability to discuss effective communication in respect of both the language and content of poetry they are reading and writing. They will sometimes work collaboratively in pairs and in groups. They will communicate outcomes orally, and in writing (possibly including the use of ICT).

Phase ② Give and take

Learning outcomes
● Children can write a poem that begins to use language and form effectively and powerfully to communicate to a reader their thoughts and feelings about a particular issue.
● Children can discuss the choice of words and their impact.

Success criteria
● I can write extra verses for a poem about a particular issue.
● I can create powerfully contrasting images to highlight an issue.

Setting the context
Display the success criteria in the classroom. Read the poem 'Give and Take' from the photocopiable page to the class. Ask: *What is the meaning and purpose of the poem? Why has the poet called the poem* 'Give and Take'? Identify how the poet has written pairs of contrasting powerful images to illustrate his feelings and thoughts about eco-issues. Show by example how to create more contrasting images. Discuss the killing of an endangered species, such as a tiger. *What adjective would you use to describe tigers? How would you describe an outcome of killing the tiger?* Read out the result and discuss its impact. Children working at levels 2-3 are given eight examples on the interactive activity 'Give and Take – extended poem' to put into contrasting pairs in order to create two more verses for the poem. Invite children at levels 4-5 to write two more verses by creating four new pairs of contrasting images, using the photocopiable page 'Give and Take – extended poem'.

Assessment opportunity
Children at levels 2-3 can work individually on the interactive activity. As they work, ask them to read out the adjectives. Invite the children to discuss their final choices and why they think they are so effective. Encourage them to think of two more contrasting images using effective adjectives and record their ideas. Children at levels 4-5 can work individually using the photocopiable 'Give and Take – extended poem' to plan and write their verses. Ask them to find a partner and carry out pair-share assessments of each other's completed poems. Move round the pairs and take notes by encouraging them to discuss which contrasting images they think are most effective for communicating their feelings, and how they came up with their images.

Assessment evidence
At levels 2-3, children should be able to choose appropriate words to complete the poem. At levels 4-5, children should be able to create powerful contrasting images using effective adjectives, for example, 'I give you glittering oceans, You give me suffocating oil slicks.' Use the notes and observations of children's responses and the completed photocopiable pages as evidence against Writing AF1 and AF7.

Next steps
Support: Encourage children who had problems visualising the contrasting images to draw and label the two images side by side, such as the 'blackbird' and 'stealth bomber'. Discuss the differences and what message the poet was trying to give.
Extension: Encourage children to research eco-issues, such as rainforest deforestation or global warming. Ask them to write a poem about the issue using powerful verbs, adjectives and a simple repetitive structure.

Key aspects of learning
Evaluation: Children will share their own writing outcomes, as well as those of others. They will discuss success criteria, give feedback to others and judge the effectiveness of their own work.
Reasoning: Children will identify, explore and generate the mental connections represented within various forms of powerful imagery (simile and metaphor) – a vital aspect of thinking, reasoning and understanding.
Self-awareness: Children will discuss and reflect on their personal responses to the texts.
Communication: children will develop their ability to discuss effective communication in respect of both the language and content of poetry they are reading and writing. They will sometimes work collaboratively in pairs and in groups. They will communicate outcomes orally, and in writing (possibly including the use of ICT).

POETRY

Phase ③ Evaluating poems

Success criteria
- I can evaluate my own poem and a partner's poem.
- I can give feedback in a constructive way.
- I can use examples from a poem to make constructive comments.

Setting the context
Display the success criteria in the classroom. Explain to the children that they are going to evaluate their own and a response partner's poems, which have been written about a particular issue. Remind the children that evaluation helps them appreciate the strengths of their work and highlights the weaknesses, allowing them to improve their poem and writing skills. Ask the children for examples of criteria that make up a good poem, such as vivid images, strong and interesting language and an effective structure. Write their suggestions on the board.

Assessment opportunity
Children at levels 2-3 should work in pairs with adult support for their comments on photocopiable pages 'Poetry evaluation checklist' and version 1 of the photocopiable page 'Poetry report sheet'. Put children working at levels 4-5 into pairs and ask them to complete the 'Poetry evaluation checklist' and then version 2 of the photocopiable page 'Poetry report sheet' for their own poem. When they have finished, ask the children to pass their poem to their partner and fill in new copies of the same sheets for their partner's poem. Encourage all the children to read their poems and share their findings with each other. Follow up with a group or class discussion on the feedback.

Assessment evidence
At levels 2-3, children should be able to discuss and give simple reasons why a poem may need work, such as 'I think the poem is too long because I lost interest'. At levels 4-5, children should be able to read and evaluate their poems and explain the effect the poem has on the reader. When discussing their evaluations with a response partner they should identify the good points and areas that need improvement, such as vocabulary techniques to bring over the issue more effectively. Use the children's responses as evidence against Reading AF6.

Next steps
Support: For children, who struggle to evaluate their work to set criteria, suggest they look at one particular area, such as the use of adjectives or verbs. Copy the poems and using highlighter pens, allow the children to highlight examples of adjectives or verbs. Use one colour for examples that they like and another colour for ones that need more work. Discuss their reasons.
Extension: Invite the children to write out their poems in an eye-catching style.

Key aspects of learning
Enquiry: Children will seek the answers to their own and others' questions in their reading.
Evaluation: Children will share their own writing outcomes, as well as those of others. They will discuss success criteria, give feedback to others and judge the effectiveness of their own work.
Reasoning: Children will identify, explore and generate the mental connections represented within various forms of powerful imagery (simile and metaphor) – a vital aspect of thinking, reasoning and understanding.
Self-awareness: Children will discuss and reflect on their personal responses to the texts.
Communication: Children will develop their ability to discuss effective communication in respect of both the language and content of poetry they are reading and writing. They will sometimes work collaboratively in pairs and in groups. They will communicate outcomes orally, and in writing (possibly including the use of ICT).

Periodic assessment

Reading

Learning outcome
Children understand how writers can use poetry as a powerful way of communicating their thoughts and feelings about a particular issue.

Success criteria
● I can identify the use of repetition in a poem to communicate an issue.
● I can identify the use of powerful verbs in a poem about an issue.
● I can identify the use of adjectives in a poem about an issue.
● I can evaluate how the poem communicates well the poet's thoughts and feelings.

Setting the context
Put less confident learners in a group with adult support and more confident learners into pairs. Explain that they are going to read a poem by Clare Bevan called 'What will you do?' (from the photocopiable page 'Poetry 2 Reading assessment') which tackles the issue about caring for the world. Remind the children how poets use imagery, language and form to communicate their thoughts and feelings about an issue that is important to them. Display and discuss the success criteria and explain that they are going to read the poem individually and use highlighter pens to show the different ways Clare Bevan has constructed her poem to convey her feelings.

Assessment opportunity
Allow time for the children to read and highlight the poem on the photocopiable page 'Poetry 2 Reading assessment'. Children at levels 2–3 can discuss their findings within their guided group led by an adult who records their responses. Children at levels 4–5 should compare their findings with their partner and discuss the effect of the poem, quoting words and text as evidence. Take observation notes of the children's discussion. Once all the children have completed their discussions, ask each pair or group to report back to the class with their responses. Make a record of children's responses in the class discussion. Encourage the children to look at the success criteria so that they can assess their progress and future learning needs. Use the children's photocopiable pages to assess whether they can identify the use of verbs, adjectives, rhyming words and repetitive text within the poem. In the class or group discussion record each child's responses and feedback to assess whether they can identify and use evidence to back up their understanding on how the poem's form and language effectively convey the poet's thoughts and feelings about eco-issues.

Assessment evidence
At levels 2–3, children should be able to recognise some language features within the poem. They should understand the main points of the poem and have some awareness of what the poet is trying to convey. At levels 4–5, children should be able to identify the use of verbs, adjectives, rhyming words and repetitive text within the poem. They should also understand how the poem's form and language effectively convey the poet's thoughts and feelings about eco-issues. Use the children's completed photocopiable pages and your records of class discussions to make level judgements against Reading AF2, AF5 and AF6.

Periodic assessment

Writing

Learning outcome
Children can write a poem that begins to use language and form effectively and powerfully to communicate to a reader their thoughts and feelings about a particular issue.

Success criteria
- I can plan and write an issue-based poem.
- I can use suitable vocabulary to create a poem that conveys a message about an issue.
- I can use suitable imagery to create a poem that conveys a message about an issue.
- I can successfully communicate my feelings and thoughts about the issue in a poem.

Setting the context
Explain to the class that they are going to plan and write an issue-based poem. Working with adult support, if appropriate, children will use the photocopiable page 'Poetry 2 Writing assessment' to plan a poem about an issue that is important to them. (An example issue is suggested if necessary – the effects of dropping litter.) Children can use the photocopiable to record and plan out their ideas for the poem's form and language. On a separate sheet of paper they can then write out their poem using the photocopiable page for guidance. Display the success criteria in the classroom.

Assessment opportunity
With the children at levels 2–3, discuss and record their responses to the vocabulary they have used and why for their poem. Praise them for aspects of their poem and ask them what they would like to improve and how. With children at levels 4–5, discuss and record the process of their planning, the imagery and vocabulary they have chosen and how they have structured their poem to convey their message. Ask the children to look at the success criteria to help them see what they have achieved and what needs more work. Invite the children to perform their finished poems to the class. Encourage them to use intonation and expression to bring over the poem's message. Discuss with the class which poems successfully conveyed the message the writers wanted to bring across.

Assessment evidence
Children at levels 2–3 should show their understanding of how vocabulary can be used to convey powerful images and a message. The poems written by children at levels 4–5 should show clear reference to the issue they have chosen. Record their choice of style such as limericks, fun rhymes, acrostics and the use of vocabulary to create powerful images, such as metaphors, personification, similes, powerful verbs, adjectives, adverbs and the ways these successfully convey the poem's message. Use the photocopiables, poems and children's discussion to make level judgements against Writing AF1 and AF7.

Transitional assessment

Activity	Type	Level	Description
2.1	Reading comprehension	2	30-minute two-part test based on a narrative extract from *The Snow Lambs* by Debbie Gliori and the poem 'Weather at Work' by Jenny Morris
2.1	Shorter writing task	2	15 minutes; writing a report about different kinds of weather
2.1	Longer writing task	2	30 minutes; writing a recount based on personal experience of problem weather
3.1	Reading comprehension	3	30-minute two-part test based on narrative extracts from *The Sheep Pig* by Dick King-Smith and a non-fiction leaflet for a farm visitors' centre
3.1	Shorter writing task	3	15 minutes; writing an imaginative description of a special pet
3.1	Longer writing task	3	30 minutes; writing letter to persuade the teacher to take the class on a trip to a farm
4.1	Reading comprehension	4	40-minute two-part test based on extracts from *Street Child* by Berlie Doherty and an historical account about Dr Barnardo
4.1	Shorter writing task	4	20 minutes; writing a report on how a typical day in the classroom has changed since the 19th century
4.1	Longer writing task	4	40 minutes; writing imaginative recounts for Dr Barnardo's diary
5.1	Reading comprehension	5	40-minute two-part test based on non-fiction articles on healthy eating and two poems, 'My brother is making a protest about bread' by Michael Rosen and 'Oh, I wish I'd looked after me teeth' by Pam Ayres
5.1	Shorter writing task	5	20 minutes; writing a leaflet to explain 'Good Health Day'
5.1	Longer writing task	5	40 minutes; writing a cautionary tale about healthy eating

NB There are two transitional assessments provided for each level. Transitional tests and tasks 2.2, 3.2, 4.2 and 5.2 are not shown here. All tests and tasks are available on the CD-ROM.

Reading tests: instructions

There are two reading comprehension tests provided at each level (levels 2–5) on the CD-ROM. Each reading test is divided into two parts.

Administering the test
- Allow 30 minutes for both parts of the test at levels 2 and 3, and 40 minutes at levels 4 and 5.
- Children should work unaided.
- Do not read questions or words to them.

Equipment for each child:
- Pencil, eraser (or children may cross out mistakes).

Marking and levelling the children
- Mark the test using the Reading Mark Scheme provided on CD-ROM.
- Add together the marks from both parts of the reading tests (possible total of 30 marks).
- Use the levelling grid at the end of the Mark Scheme to level the test.
- When awarding an end-of-year Teacher Assessment Level, you will also need to consider a child's performance during Periodic and Day-to-Day Assessments. If a child has achieved a low level 3 or above in the transitional tests, it can be assumed that they have achieved AF1 at that level.

Writing tasks: instructions

There are two writing tasks provided at each level (levels 2–5) on the CD-ROM. Each writing task is divided into two parts: shorter and longer writing tasks.

Administering the tasks
Shorter writing task
Allow 15 minutes for each task at levels 2 and 3, and 20 minutes for each task at levels 4 and 5.
Longer writing task
Allow 30 minutes for each task, which could include 5 minutes' planning time at levels 2 and 3. Allow 40 minutes for each task, which could include 10 minutes' planning time at levels 4 and 5.
- Children should sit so that they cannot see each other's work.
- You may read the task to the children; do not explain the task or help them.
- The task may be administered to groups of children or to the whole class.
- Do not allow children to use dictionaries or word books.

Equipment for each child:
- Pencil, eraser (or children may cross out mistakes) and sheets of plain paper.

Introducing the writing tasks
Say to the children:
I am going to ask you to do some writing.
I will read the task to you, but I cannot help you with your ideas.
If you make a mistake, you should cross it out (or rub it out neatly) and write your word clearly.
Spell the words as best you can, building them up as you usually do.

Marking and levelling the children
- Mark each piece of writing separately using the Writing Mark Scheme, Table 1, provided on the CD-ROM.
- Double the marks gained for the longer Writing task and add this total to the mark gained for the shorter Writing task.
- Assess spelling and handwriting across both pieces of writing using Table 2, provided on the CD-ROM.
- Add the total gained from Table 1 to the total from Table 2.
- Use the grid at the end of the Mark Scheme to find a level for each child.